AUTOBIOGRAPHY AND I

Theatre and Performance Practices

General Editors: Graham Ley and Jane Milling

Published

Christopher Baugh   *Theatre, Performance and Technology*
Greg Giesekam   *Staging the Screen*
Deirdre Heddon and Jane Milling   *Devising Performance*
Deirdre Heddon   *Autobiography and Performance*
Helen Nicholson   *Applied Drama*
Michael Wilson   *Storytelling and Theatre*
Cathy Turner and Synne K. Behrndt   *Dramaturgy and Performance*

Forthcoming

Philip B. Zarrilli, Jerri Daboo and Rebecca Loukes   *From Stanislavski to Physical Theatre*

Autobiography and Performance

DEIRDRE HEDDON

palgrave
macmillan

First published 2008 by
PALGRAVE MACMILLAN
Houndmills, Basingstoke, Hampshire RG21 6XS and
175 Fifth Avenue, New York, N.Y. 10010
Companies and representatives throughout the world

PALGRAVE MACMILLAN is the global academic imprint of the Palgrave Macmillan division of St. Martin's Press, LLC and of Palgrave Macmillan Ltd. Macmillan® is a registered trademark in the United States, United Kingdom and other countries. Palgrave is a registered trademark in the European Union and other countries.

ISBN-13: 978–0–230–53752–1 hardback
ISBN-10: 0–230–53752–9 hardback
ISBN-13: 978–0–230–53753–8 paperback
ISBN-10: 0–230–53753–7 paperback

This book is printed on paper suitable for recycling and made from fully managed and sustained forest sources. Logging, pulping and manufacturing processes are expected to conform to the environmental regulations of the country of origin.

A catalogue record for this book is available from the British Library.

A catalog record for this book is available from the Library of Congress.

10   9   8   7   6   5   4   3   2   1
17   16   15   14   13   12   11   10   09   08

Printed and bound in Great Britain by
Antony Rowe Ltd, Chippenham and Eastbourne

For my mum, June: always my role-model, and therefore always still here.

Contents

List of Illustrations

General Editors' Preface

This series sets out to explore key performance practices encountered in modern and contemporary theatre. Talking to students and scholars in seminar rooms and studios, and to practitioners in rehearsal, it became clear that there were widely used modes of practice that had received very little critical and analytical attention. In response, we offer these critical, research-based studies that draw on international fieldwork to produce fresh insight into a range of performance processes. Authors who are specialists in their fields have set each mode of practice in its social, political and aesthetic context. The series charts both a history of the development of modes of performance process and an assessment of their significance in contemporary culture.

Each volume is accessibly written and gives a clear and pithy analysis of the historical and cultural development of a mode of practice. As well as offering readers a sense of the breadth of the field, the authors have also given key examples and performance illustrations. In different ways each book in the series asks readers to look again at processes and practices of theatre-making that seem obvious and self-evident, and to examine why and how they have developed as they have, and what their ideological content is. Ultimately the series aims to ask: What are the choices and responsibilities facing performance-makers today?

Graham Ley and Jane Milling

Acknowledgements

This book has been a long time in the writing and like all creative endeavours it has involved a great deal of collaboration. There are many people I want to thank. First, to all those who have opted to study performance and autobiography, since I first offered a course in 1998. You each taught me so much about teaching, and particularly about teaching autobiography and performance. Without your probing questions, keen insights, creative spirits and moments of resistance, this book would never have been started. It would not have been finished without the ongoing support provided by my many friends, but most particularly Jane Milling and Stephen Hodge. I am also grateful to the many colleagues who took up the slack when I was on research leave, and this includes my new colleagues in Theatre Studies at Glasgow University who were all gracious enough to allow me to see this project through to its completion during my first semester as a member of their team. Thanks also to the University of Exeter who granted me a Semester's research leave in 2005 and to the AHRC who provided funding for me to extend it.

Many artists and programmers have generously given of their time, allowing me to interview them, to view their documentation materials and archives. Thanks in particular, but in no particular order, to Lois, Lisa, Tim, Mike, Joshua, Leslie, Helen, Joey, Martha, Peggy, Lenora, Fiona, Martina, Alex, Denise, Phil, Natalie, Chris, Annie, Penny and Bobby. Many more artists than I have been able to write about in *Autobiography and Performance* have inspired me, moved me and occasionally enraged me. Without their work, there would be no book.

On the long journey taken in the writing of *Autobiography and Performance* I have been fortunate to have been accompanied by others who have offered feedback at various stages and would like to thank Elaine Aston, Lenora Champagne, Jill Dolan, Gerry Harris, Maggie Gale, Viv Gardner, Jo Gill, Roberta Mock and Peter Thomson.

Any shortcomings remain my own. I am also particularly grateful to Graham Ley for his astute editorial comments, to Adrienne Scullion for her ability to spot split infinitives and misplaced commas and to Kate Wallis and Paula Kennedy at Palgrave who have shown unstinting commitment to this project. Finally, although I thank her everyday of my life for everyday she is in my life, my deepest thanks to Rachel.

Earlier versions of this work have been published: (2003) *Glory Box*: Tim Miller's Autobiography of the Future, *New Theatre Quarterly*, 19 (3), 243–56; (2004) Performing Lesbians: Constructing the Self, Constructing the Community. In M. B. Gale & V. Gardner, eds., *Auto/Biography and Identity: Women, Theatre and Performance*. Manchester: Manchester University Press, pp. 217–38; (2006) Personal Performance: The Resistant Confessions of Bobby Baker. In J. Gill, ed., *Modern Confessional Writing: New Critical Essays*. London: Routledge, pp. 137–53; and (2006) The Politics of the Personal: Autobiography in Performance. In E. Aston & G. Harris, eds., *Feminist Futures? Theatre, Performance, Theory*. Basingstoke: Palgrave Macmillan, pp. 130–48. I am grateful to the publishers for their permission to use this work. I am also grateful to the various artists and photographers who have kindly given me permission to reproduce their images here.

Deirdre Heddon is supported by

**Arts & Humanities
Research Council**

The AHRC funds postgraduate training and research in the arts and humanities, from archaeology and English literature to design and dance. The quality and range of research supported not only provides social and cultural benefits but also contributes to the economic success of the UK. For further information on the AHRC, please see our website www.ahrc.ac.uk.

Introduction

John Humphries: You've exploited being Tracey Emin.
Tracey Emin: But I *am* Tracey Emin.
(*On the Ropes*, BBC R4, 24 July 2001)

The Attraction of Autobiographical Performance

I think it was 1988 when I saw Bobby Baker's *Drawing on a Mother's Experience*. Then, I was a second year undergraduate student at the University of Glasgow, studying Theatre, Sociology and English. Though uneasy about constructing a linear narrative which looks back from the present and arranges the past into a series of stepping stones that comfortably leads me to here, to this Introduction, I do consider Bobby Baker's performance a 'beginning' of some sort. *Drawing on a Mother's Experience* was my first experience of explicitly autobiographical performance, and it is an experience that I have drawn on ever since.[1] Another beginning might be feminism, to which I was also introduced during my second year at university. Feminism brought home to me that politics was not something 'out there', but rather that the political was always close, that the macropolitical and micropolitical were intimately connected. Yet another beginning might be Bertolt Brecht, whom I encountered around the same time – particularly his *verfremdungseffekt*, making the familiar strange so that we can understand it as neither natural nor inevitable, and therefore something that can be challenged and changed. The final beginning, though chronologically a bit later, might be my becoming a lesbian. Stepping into that location in the early 1990s the idea of marginal was felt rather than conceptualised.

Since that first encounter with Bobby Baker's work in 1988 I have actively sought autobiographical performances, and I admit from the outset that I am something of an advocate. I am attracted to them

1

as 'performance[s] of possibility', where, in the words of D. Soyini Madison, the possible suggests 'a movement culminating in creation and change' (1998, p. 277). This takes for granted that change is necessary, desirable and within reach. Change is also, of course, inevitable, and its effects always uncertain. But such continuous movement and prevailing absence of guarantee should make a personal commitment to change even greater. It would, though, be sensible to add a small rider here: autobiographical performances are *possible* performances of possibility; even that possibility cannot be taken for granted.

If pressed to think of the best-known performers in the USA who consistently use autobiographical material in their performances, names most likely to spring to mind might include Rachel Rosenthal, Laurie Anderson, Deb Margolin, Annie Sprinkle, Holly Hughes, Lisa Kron, Robbie McCauley, Alina Troyano, Kate Bornstein, Tim Miller, Ron Athey, Lenora Champagne, Peggy Shaw, Lois Weaver, Luis Alfaro, Marga Gomez and Spalding Gray. Gray, as the white, straight male here proves to be the exception.[2] From this list we might deduce that the majority of artists who use autobiography in their work are marginalised subjects; other names that we might add include Fred Rochlin, who began performing his personal narrative at the age of 74 – a rare occurrence in the performance world which seems to valorise youth more than experience (see Lathem, 2005). Solo autobiographical performance in the UK is also well-recognised as a mode, and performers here include Bobby Baker, Ursula Martinez, SuAndi, Mem Morrison, Donna Rutherford, Joey Hateley, Adrian Howells, Marisa Carnesky, Leslie Hill and Helen Paris. Mirroring their US counterparts, many of these performers are lesbian, gay and/or black and/or transgender, and their work also addresses explicitly their particular location(s) and the experiences that are inscribed there.

The relationship between marginalised subjects and the appeal of autobiographical performance is not co-incidental. Autobiographical performances can capitalise on theatre's unique temporality, its here and nowness, and on its ability to respond to and engage with the present, while always keeping an eye on the future. In particular, autobiographical performance can engage with the pressing matters of the present which relate to equality, to justice, to citizenship, to human rights. Kim Ima's *The Interlude* (2004), a performance which attempts to tell the story of her father's internment in a camp in the USA during World War II, is a story also of the present and the presence of Guantanamo Bay. Tim Miller's *Glory Box* (1999), a story of the constant threat that hangs over his relationship with his lover, also speaks of contemporary experiences of wider inequality and injustice. I want (and need) to believe that performance can be a transformational act, contributing to a network of political activity.

As Chapter 1 will explore, located within and arising out of the second-wave feminist movement, autobiographical performance was regarded by women as a means to reveal otherwise invisible lives, to resist marginalisation and objectification and to become, instead, speaking subjects with self-agency; performance, then, as a way to bring into being a self. Autobiographical performances provide a way to talk out, talk back, talk otherwise. Here, the marginalised subject can literally take centre stage, and whilst visibility, *per se*, does not mean political power or equal rights (see Phelan, 1993), this potential for agency has been acknowledged by many practitioners and theorists of autobiography.[3] Elizabeth Bell contends that ' "Marginalised subjectivities", the catch-phrase for those denied subjecthood in traditional Western conceptions, move from margin to center (stage) in performance' (2003, p. 315). bell hooks, meanwhile, understands that 'oppressed people resist by identifying themselves as subject, by defining their reality, shaping their new identity, naming their history, telling their story' (1989, p. 43). For Nellie Y. McKay, 'the life story (or portions of it) has been the most effective forum for defining black selfhood in a racially oppressive world' (1998, p. 96). Performer Linda Park-Fuller appreciates her performance of surviving breast cancer as

an attempt to break out of the prescribed, marginalised role of 'patient-victim', and exercise socio-political agency in the world. That exercise of agency, in turn, circles back to transform and constitute me as actor-agent – as *survivor*. (2003, p. 215)

In this, Park-Fuller shares insights with Tami Spry, who similarly claims that performative autobiography is

a site of narrative authority, offering me the power to reclaim and rename my voice and body privately and in rehearsal, and then publicly in performance. The process enables me to speak the personally political in public, which has been liberating and excruciating, but always in some way enabling. (2003, p. 169)

The transformative potential of autobiographical performance refers, then, partly to the performing subject, the 'story-ing' of our lives (Rouverol, 2005, p. 23). Suzette Henke's insistence on the agency afforded by writing one's own story translates well into the performance realm:

> Because the author can instantiate the alienated or marginal self into the pliable body of a protean text, the newly revised subject, emerging as the semifictive protagonist of an enabling counternarrative, is free to rebel against the values and practices of a dominant culture and to assume an empowered position of political agency in the world.   (2000, pp. xv–xvi)

Henke's reference here to the 'revised subject' and their 'semifictive' status should be borne in mind when we turn our attention to the subject of autobiography and the relationship between a lived life and its representation. Whilst the importance of agency in the act of autobiographical performance is marked, nevertheless the connections between self and identity, identity and representation and representation and politics need to be carefully navigated.

The fact that a 'self' appears to lie at the centre of autobiography too easily raises the spectre of self-indulgence for many critics, such as John Howell who, focusing on solo work, proposes that it

> is as often an ego show as a revelation; the virus of the 'I-Did-It-My-Way-/I-Gotta-Be-Me' strain afflicts the larger number of such acts, particularly in the performance art arena which presents amateurish staging techniques and mini-personalities as often as original methods and subjects.   (1979/80, p. 158)

Richard Layzell, however, understands that this dominant conception of autobiographical performance – its supposed self-indulgence – is nothing but a stereotype with which we are stuck until a shift in understanding dislodges it (Ayers and Butler, 1991, p. 49). I very much hope that this book contributes to that shift. Though the charges of egotistical, solipsistic and narcissistic are thrown at the 'self' of autobiographical performance, as we shall see this 'self' is contested terrain.

Given the historical link between women and autobiographical performance, it might not be too cynical to suggest that the predominantly negative responses to the autobiographical form belie deeper prejudices. This is certainly Irene Gammel's view when she considers the specific danger of confessional forms for women, a danger indivisible from wider cultural and historical conceptions of (appropriate) knowledge and its ('disembodied') production. Gammel notes that when personal experiences are expressed via the female voice, they are perceived as being informal and lacking in authority, belonging to the realm of *parole* rather than the more abstract *langue*, and as such are dismissed as being of less concern (1999, p. 4). Leslie Satin and Judith Jerome reach a similar conclusion when they relate that although 'historically, autobiography has been a primarily male province [...] autobiography in its less socially elevated form [...] has long been identified as a woman's genre' (1999, p. 12). Feminised, such autobiographical practices are then trivialised by the description '(merely) autobiographical' (ibid.).

In my experience, the vast majority of autobiographical performances work hard to challenge the notion that there is anything 'mere' to autobiography. The slur of '(merely) autobiographical' resonates with assumptions regarding the narrow reference of 'the personal', or even of 'women'. As I hope to show, although autobiographical performances look, in form, monologic, the public context of their work and the performers' aspirations to communicate with their spectators transform those works into dialogues. Live autobiographical performance takes place not only in shared time, but also in shared space. These performances are made with a spectator in mind. For performer Lisa Kron, 'the goal of autobiographical work should not be to tell stories about yourself but, instead, to use the details of your own life to illuminate or explore something more universal' (2001, p. xi).[4] Tim Miller similarly wants to use his individual experience in order to find 'a window for' the audience (1991/2, p. 140). Most performers create a mode of address that acknowledges the spectator's presence (alongside the theatrical context). If autobiographical performance is a potentially powerful tool of resistance, intervention and/or reinvention, then it must be so for the spectator as much as for the performer. As Della Pollock comments,

performance is a promissory act. Not because it can only promise possible change but because it catches its participants – often by surprise – in a contract with possibility: with imagining what might be, could be, should be. (2005, p. 2)

Integral to the here-and-nowness of autobiographical performance is the visible presence of the performing subject – their here and nowness too. Though the notion of 'presence' or 'aura' that adheres to performance and performers might have been thoroughly challenged following Derrida (the performer is not, cannot be, 'authentic' or unmediated, even if they are 'there'), nevertheless, the fact that the performer is in this space with me might well have an impact on my reception of his/her autobiographical stories. That relationship between performer and spectator does set this mediation of experience apart from other modes. Though it is no less mediated, its different form of mediation enables a potentially different impact that can be capitalised upon strategically.

Many critics have proposed that performance, as a medium, is particularly suited to a political agenda because it is capable of staging a direct and immediate address to the spectator. Peggy Phelan claims, for example, that it 'remove[s] the metaphorical structure of art' (2001, p. 29). The space of live performance is also considered important since, although gathered in this 'space apart', we are nevertheless and inevitably also gathered together (see Dolan, 2001, p. 473, p. 459). Performance might inspire an audience to feel, at least momentarily, part of a community, since to be part of an audience is potentially to be allied with others (see Dolan, 2005). For Tim Miller, 'The real-time heat of live performing is an especially handy crucible for raising awareness and provoking people to action' (2000, p. 89).[5] The fact that Tim Miller himself is standing in front of me sharing stories about Tim Miller makes his fear of the future somehow palpable; I could touch it and am touched by it. Moreover, his appeal that I must 'do something' is spoken directly to me. Though all performances must reckon with the act of communication, the relationship that auto-biographical performances (performances that are ostensibly at least about some 'self') attempt to forge with the spectator (some other 'self') seems to be particularly crucial, and this relationship is one that will occupy much of our attention throughout *Autobiography and Performance*.

Focusing on the 'potential' of autobiographical performance, I recognise its potential to also do harm or to fail in its politically aspirational or transformational objectives. This is precisely the liminal quality heralded by the word 'potential' – it can always go both ways. Some performances might well 'fail' to communicate, or 'fail' to move us, teach us, inspire us, challenge us. Some might prescribe to essentialist notions of self and identity, thereby further repressing or constraining us. Some might speak 'for', rather than 'as', while others might be appropriated in unexpected ways or might appropriate other's stories in inappropriate ways. Some performances might use the politics of the personal in a less sincere way, recognising that 'the personal' functions as a useful marketing tool in today's culture where the personal is a popular and cheaply manufactured commodity. In acknowledging the potential of autobiographical performance, we need also to acknowledge the dangers. Though I am an advocate, I am not a naïve one.

Autobiographical Performance?

In her autobiographical text, 'Count the I's, or, The Autobiographical Nature of Everything', writer and performer Deb Margolin shares with the reader the stark realisation, experienced during her senior year of college, that everything is autobiographical. Her course in psychophysics facilitated an epiphany:

> This was the most dramatic, simple, stupid realization! [...] It meant, firstly and lastly, that what I see is a direct product of my *ability* to see, both physiologically and intellectually, and therefore, every sunset, every tree, everything I see is firstly and lastly about me. (1999, p. 24)

Margolin, with her witty and engaging prose, makes an easy job of refashioning one of the central concerns of contemporary feminist theorists – the inevitability of the 'self' that lies in all acts of production, both creative and theoretical (see Anderson, 2001, pp. 125–7). Against any presumed 'objectivity' in relation to the production of knowledge, feminists have long argued that the self is implicated in all epistemological endeavours, from the concerns that interest us (and similarly those that do not), to the discourses that we choose (or not) to press into service in our research and explorations, to the critical voices that we assume in our rendering of these. Such unavoidable subjectivity of knowledge is now largely accepted.

That all creative production is similarly infused with the personal is not at all contentious. Margolin's conviction that 'we have nothing but ourselves from which to work and about which to speak' is commonplace (1999, p. 25). Jeanette Winterson captures the same idea in her preface to *Oranges Are Not the Only Fruit*: 'Is Oranges an autobiographical novel? No not at all and yes of course' (1985, p. xiv). Creative practices are always informed by who we are, as subjects embodied in time and space, with our own cultures and histories (although it is nevertheless to be noted that some endeavours are unproblematically taken to be more universal – less personal – than others).

Acknowledging the 'autobiographical nature' of everything, I nevertheless practically need to mark some limits. In this text, then, I am using 'autobiographical performance' to refer to work which foregrounds some aspect of a life-story, a *bio*. We might then assume that the *'auto'* signals the sameness of the subject and object of that story: that is, the 'author' and 'performer' collapse into each other as the performing 'I' is also the represented 'I'. This is certainly the 'autobiographical pact' that Philippe Lejeune (1989) identified between the producer and consumer of autobiography. However, one aim of this study is to challenge our assumptions about the 'genre' of autobiography since in practice autobiography typically becomes auto/biography, while the 'I' that performs and is performed is often strategically complex and layered.[6] Given the collaborative nature of performance, this is perhaps unavoidable. The Wooster Group's early work, directed by Liz LeCompte, offers useful illustration. In the trilogy *Three Places in Rhode Island,* company members drew upon, interacted with and responded to autobiographical material relating to Spalding Gray's life, and the performance was collectively devised and performed. Whilst the source material for the pieces was Gray's *bio*, and Gray himself performed this, Theodore Shank notes in relation to *Rumstick Road* (1977) that 'the play is a collective work resulting from "group associations around facts in my life" ' (Gray cited in Shank, 1982, p. 174). In addition to the collaboration of the actors, LeCompte also played an important part in structuring these 'autobiographical' pieces, and Gray's own performance within them. She reflects that

> Spalding sits for a portrait that I paint. [...] There is a dialog between the sitter and the painter. The portrait, the persona that emerges is an amalgam of the sitter's image of himself and the vision of him [...] that the painter sees and constructs. When the painter and the one painted *both* recognize themselves in the final portrait, it is a perfect kind of collaboration. The persona named Spalding Gray is made from this kind of collaboration.   (Bierman, 1979, pp. 13–14)[7]

LeCompte recognises the different Spalding Grays in operation here, with the performed Gray being understood as a 'persona'. However, she also raises the possibility that existing inside Gray's performance is the autobiography of LeCompte – alongside LeCompte's biographical rendering of Gray.

Although *Three Places in Rhode Island* was a group effort, in fact most theatrical events, including solo performances, involve some form of collaboration. The vast majority of performers work with producers, directors, designers and production managers. Many also show their work to spectators (invited or public) during the process of its making, using feedback to revise and develop it. The performance of autobiographical material, then, is typically a collective affair which will have an impact on the representation of that autobiography or the re-presentation of the 'self'. The 'self' in performance is plural in many ways then, beyond the psychoanalytic understanding of the divided self.

Admitting that autobiography is also often biography, or auto/biography, insisting even on the explicit presence of the *bio* in auto/biographical performance is not without its problems. The referential status of that *bio* is open to question and one task of this study is to theorise the relation between 'a life' and its performed representation. I do not want to assume any easy or transparent relationship between a lived life and its portrayal. All autobiographical productions involve processes of selection, scripting, editing, revising, etc. However, neither do I want to erase completely the *bio*, for in all of the performances that I explore here that *bio* is politically significant and is the reason for the performance. Autobiographical performances strategically work with life experiences, but rather than rendering them self-evident the political task is to discern the subtext (Madison, 2005, p. 150).

Ultimately, of course, one can never be totally sure that the material in a performance *is* auto/biographical. For some years I have cited Claire Dowie's insightful *Why Is John Lennon Wearing a Skirt?* (1996) as a good example of an autobiographical work. Dowie employs certain strategies which prompt this reading, including performing solo, speaking in an intimate mode of address while using 'I' throughout, dealing with what appears to be congruent content and portraying a character who could very easily be the performer. Indeed, Gabriele Griffin has written of Dowie's work in a collection entitled *Auto/Biography and Identity: Women, Theatre and Performance* (2004) and, like me, acknowledges that Dowie uses devices that propose the work as being '(auto)biographical' (2004, p. 154). However, Griffin also warns us of the complexity of self-representation:

> Performance is, of course, always citation, and as such instantly troubles the I-dentity of character and performer. If I perform me performing me, we are in the world of deconstructionist traces where there is no self-sameness, only the infinity of the split, endlessly (re)enacted in a Sisyphian attempt to approximate the self.   (ibid., p. 155)

Dowie, when explicitly asked, evades the question of the autobiographical status of her work, insisting instead on the power of fiction.[8] Her strategic evasion of categories does not mean that her work is *not* autobiographical though; in fact, given that Dowie's work is precisely about refusing the application of labels her skirting here is entirely appropriate to the politics inscribed within her performances. What is also revealed, though, is that the binary between fictional/real is notoriously unstable in all autobiographical performance. Autobiographical *productions* are always that. Moreover, stories that are ostensibly 'fictional' nevertheless have an impact on the 'real' sense of self. Applied theatre practitioner Helen Nicholson captures this interrelationship well: 'fictionalised narratives found in myth and legend are integral to narratives of selfhood and community' (2005, p. 66). In the last instance, of course, the decision of whether a work is considered autobiographical must lie with the spectator. This, perhaps, begs the question of whether the autobiographical 'status' of a work matters. That I believe something *has* happened (or *will* happen or *will happen again*) does place my experience of the theatrical event into a different emotional register. The 'real', even if intellectually understood as contingent, nevertheless retains its pull – and so it should, given that its impacts are often painfully tangible.

Retaining the real as a reference point, many performers nevertheless also strategically create ambivalence about the status of their autobiographical work in order to prompt questions about the supposedly given, as well as the mode of autobiography and its potential power. In many instances, as we shall see, engagements with autobiography are doubled: both knowingly playful with and challenging of the form, whilst still utilising its rhetorical function for political effect.

The Performance of Autobiography

As the various chapters of this book reveal, there are a multiplicity of ways in which the auto/bio of the 'self' is represented in performance. I have deliberately chosen to keep my frame of reference open, rather than drawing neat boundaries around different practices. Conversations are usefully staged across different 'genres' allowing us to learn from different applications, and anyway the boundaries are porous. 'Autobiographical performance', then, is adopted in this text as a broad term which encompasses examples of solo autobiographical work, community and applied drama, oral narrative and oral history performance, verbatim drama, documentary drama, testimonial performance, performance art and instances of site-specific and time-based practice. The risk is that the field is deemed too large to be useful; however, the limits are set by a strict focus on the *auto* and *bio*.

Since the 1980s, spurred on first by feminist studies, but also by black, queer, postcolonial and more generally poststructuralist and postmodern discourses, the practice of autobiography has received mounting interest from across disciplines.[9] Primarily, such critiques have tended to take written autobiography (the graphed auto) as their ground but, in the past decade, the study of autobiography has extended beyond the literary sphere and into other disciplines, including psychology, geography, criminology, history, philosophy and sports science. In the field of performance, a number of early writings engaged with autobiographical practice including Moira Roth's 'Autobiography, Theater, Mysticism and Politics: Women's Performance Art in Southern California' (1980) and *The Amazing Decade* (1983), Jeanie Forte's 'Women's Performance Art: Feminism and Postmodernism' (1988) and Lenora Champagne's collection of performance texts, *Out from Under* (1990), which includes a still useful introduction. However, it is really from the late 1990s onwards that there has been a coherent critical engagement with autobiographical performance as a complex 'genre'. Numerous collections of performance scripts began to appear at this time, including Mark Russell's *Out of Character* (1997), Holly Hughes and David Román's *O Solo Homo* (1998) and Jo Bonney's *Extreme Exposure* (2000). Critical analysis has also gathered pace. In October 1997 and January 2000, *Text and Performance Quarterly* published two special editions on autobiography and performance, while in 1999, *Women & Performance: A Journal of Feminist Theory* published a double issue under the title *Performing Autobiography*. A spate of more recent anthologies bears testimony to the endurance of autobiographical performance practice and to the continuing diversity of that. Recent edited collections include Sidonie Smith and Julia Watson's *Interfaces: Women/Autobiography/Image/Performance* (2002), Lynn C. Miller, Jacqueline Taylor and M. Heather Carver's *Voices*

Made Flesh: Performing Women's Autobiography (2003) and Maggie Gale and Viv Gardner's *Auto/Biography and Identity: Women, Theatre and Performance* (2004). Two other texts which share some of my concerns were published just as I was completing *Autobiography and Performance* – Jill Dolan's *Utopia in Performance* (2005) and, *Theatre and AutoBiography* (2006), a collection edited by Sherrill Grace and Jerry Wasserman. There are also publications which intersect with these enquiries, such as Della Pollock's thoughtful anthology, *Remembering: Oral History Performance* (2005). Finally, there are numerous publications by solo autobiographical performers, including Alina Troyano's *I, Carmelita Tropicana* (2000), Rachel Rosenthal's *Rachel's Brain* (2001), Lisa Kron's *2.5 Minute Ride and 101 Humiliating Stories* (2001) and *Well* (2006), Tim Miller's *Body Blows* (2002) and Denise Uyehara's *Maps of City & Body* (2003).

This increased range and diversity of materials is necessary and welcome. However, as a teacher in higher education I nevertheless sense that a consolidated overview of autobiographical performance practice, and the various concerns engaged and raised by it, is missing. Having taught the subject for seven years, I have been prompted to write *Autobiography and Performance*, keeping in my mind's eye my own impassioned, enquiring students. The fact that this is only one book necessarily implies limitations. The archive of autobiographical performance is rich and varied, and I certainly do not propose this as the definitive study of that history and practice; its aims are more modest – simply to introduce the reader to some of what I consider the key concerns implicated in performances that take personal material as their primary source.

My research is also limited to performers located in either the UK or the USA, since these are the works to which I have had access. This is a serious limitation, since the study of other cultural renderings of autobiographical performance might expose the very extent to which the idea of 'identity' and its practice in daily life is a Western rather than universal concept. Other practitioners, teachers, researchers and students (and I variously inhabit each of these locations) might well have chosen different key concerns and different cultures. This text, then, stages only one encounter with a broad practice. It also does not propose to offer any sort of comparative study between the UK and the USA, although I would remind the reader that the specific context of every performance event has an impact on its reception.

This work has been organised into four chapters. My intention has been to provide an introduction to key thematic areas, as these relate to autobiographical performance, namely 'Politics', 'History', 'Place' and 'Ethics'. The devising of such broad categories is partly pragmatic, offering ways to locate the diverse range of autobiographical performances that are available. However, it is also intended to be theoretically useful, since each of these broad categories enables me to introduce various important critical concerns that circulate around autobiographical performance practice, including the status of and relationship between the self, identity, memory, truth and representation in performance.

Given my commitment to uncovering the forward looking – or hopeful gestures – of autobiographical performance, I begin this text by focusing on the political aspirations resident in much of the work. Chapter 1, 'Politics (of Self): The Subject of Autobiography', traces the intersection of the second-wave feminist movement of the 1960s with the practice of autobiographical performance, specifically the politicisation of the personal in the public domain. Arguing that these performances strategically deployed a variety of tactics depending on the context and perceived political needs, I also propose that essentialist gestures were as strategic as others. Like more contemporary performance examples, second-wave feminist performance practitioners walked a consciously fine line between using performance to uncover and forge an identity ('identity' then functions as one of our key focuses in Chapter 1). This dual necessity to work with, but simultaneously to make problematic, experience and identity remains pertinent and is subsequently explored through more recent works including mct's *Fingerlicks* – a 'community autobiography' – and Bobby Baker's and Tim Miller's solo work. In Baker's case she both 'is' and 'is not' Bobby Baker, rendering her subjectivity, and our encounter with it, uncertain. Tim Miller, meanwhile, with his focus on gay rights, blends the auto with the explicitly fictional, using autofiction as a strategy through which to conjure a future that is yet to take place (and which might, then, be avoided). In all of these examples the lived experience that pertains to a certain identity position provides the foundation for the autobiographical act, but at the same time that foundation is strategically (and politically) unsettled *through* the autobiographical act. The term 'politics' in the chapter heading refers, then, not only to the challenges made by performers to their oppressive social environments, but also to how performed practices of the 'self' are related to political praxis.

The context for Chapter 2, 'History: Testimonial Times', is the testimonial culture of the late twentieth and early twenty-first centuries. The autobiographical performances explored in this chapter engage with public, 'cataclysmic' historical events, but read these through personal histories, or local narratives which serve to bring the grand narratives closer to home. Live performance is explored as a response to trauma that not only shares some of the effects of psychoanalysis, but which might also be usefully differentiated from this strategy given that performance is public rather than private. Robbie McCauley's *Sally's Rape* (1989) is exemplary of a performance practice that repeats the narratives of trauma in order that a 'beginning' might be activated, rather than a 'closure' assumed.[10] The rape of McCauley's great-great-grandmother belongs as much to the present as to the past, and her autobiography is one example of auto/biography, where her story is indivisible from her ancestors', but also where my story is indivisible from her story, and her story, then, is also my responsibility that calls forth for some response from me (Oliver, 2001). Kim Ima's *The Interlude* (2004), a performance that structurally performs trauma, also testifies to the impossibility of that performance. Attempting to tell the story of her father, interned in a camp in the USA during World War II, Ima in fact testifies to her father's silence, a symptom of his trauma. However, Ima understands that silence nevertheless speaks and does not then require to be spoken. Refusing to appropriate her father's voice, or coerce him into speaking, the gaps in this family story reflect the gaps in national history. These cannot simply be filled. Chapter 2 closes with Lisa Kron's *2.5 Minute Ride* (1996), a performance that pays testimony to the impossibility of being a 'secondary witness', and of recounting the 'life-story' of another, in this case her father. Acutely aware of the cultural context in which the 'Holocaust' is the signifier *par excellence* for 'trauma', Kron's challenge is to find a way to pay homage to her father, a survivor of the Holocaust, without reducing him to a cliché.

Chapter 3 moves from history to place, specifically 'the place of self'. A 'self' is inseparable from a 'place'. As philosopher Edward S. Casey puts it: 'just as we are always with a body, so, being bodily, we are always within a place as well. Thanks to our body, we are in that place and part of it' (1997, p. 214). Bodies are, though, raced and gendered (and differently abled, and variously aged ...) and some bodies will find that they are out of place. However, place is as conditional as self and they are intimately related. In Chapter 3 I explore this interrelation between place and autobiography, specifically the mechanisms through which place performs self and self performs place (sometimes differently), understanding both as mutual sites that are equally open to contingent and shifting narratives. Again to quote Casey,

> The body, or more exactly *my own body*, is unique in bringing together here and there in a manner that resists the allure of simple location, according to which the 'here' is merely the pinpointed position of my body regarded as an indifferent thing and the 'there' the equally pinpointed spot of the contemporary object opposite me. Instead, the 'there' *ingresses* into the 'here,' and vice versa.   (ibid., pp. 214–15)

As feminists have taught us, there is nothing 'indifferent' to the body. The body is also a place.

My deployment of the term 'autotopography' renders the self of place, and the place of self, transparent. In *Bubbling Tom* (2000), Mike Pearson devises a tour for his childhood locale, the village of Hibaldstow, Lincolnshire. Staged to mark his fiftieth birthday, which happened to coincide also with the millennium, the self and place that Pearson performs for us are multifaceted and literally open to rewriting since Pearson's walking tour leaves space for other walkers to tell the tale differently. Phil Smith's *The Crab Walks* (2004), again a walking performance, similarly returns to the place of childhood, this time the seascape of Devon. Like the crab, Smith's perambulatory methodology is the sideways scuttle which avoids the obvious connections seeking instead the unexpected and the unusual. In place of a nostalgic search for a lost self, Smith's performance enables an extroverted, outward-lookingness, where the local is rendered global and the potential networks in space are infinite; walking like a feminist, Smith renders place as a meeting-place of potentiality (Massey, 2005).

The experience of place is variable. Some people are out of place and some places are out of bounds to some people. Boundaries are usually built around particular bodies. Providing a contrast to the outside, perambulatory performances of Pearson and Smith, Chapter 3 closes by introducing two 'domestic', contained performances where private space is nevertheless publicised. Though 'home' might most often be considered a safe environment, Bobby Baker's *Kitchen Show* (1991) and Curious' *On the Scent* (2003) show this site as being as layered, significant and political as that of the outside world. Indeed, the 'inside' is always also the 'outside'. Performing in her kitchen,

Baker reveals it as a place of both frustration and aesthetic possibility. Curious, meanwhile, conjures smells that transport us home. Resisting the pull of 'homesickness', and putting a different spin on that term, they propose that the home is often a place of sickness.

If Chapters 1, 2 and 3 have focused on the political potential of autobiographical performance, the final chapter of *Autobiography and Performance* shifts attention to the politics of process. Starting from the premise that every 'self' is relational (since no person is an island), Chapter 4 raises questions about the responsibility that performers bear to the 'others' that both wittingly and unwittingly appear in their work. Taking seriously Paul John Eakin's insistence that 'Because our own lives never stand free of the lives of others, we are faced with our responsibility to those others whenever we write [perform] about ourselves' (1999, p. 159), I ask what such a responsibility might mean in the field of autobiographical performance and how it might be deployed. This enquiry into ethical practice begins with a survey of 'verbatim drama', where the experiences of others are appropriated in what might be considered an act of ventriloquism. The dangers of verbatim drama, a form explicit in its biographical gestures, usefully illuminate some of the general problematics of auto/biographical performance. These 'impersonal' performances are then contrasted with two which perform the biographies of significant or intimate others, Spalding Gray's *Rumstick Road* (1977) and Lisa Kron's *Well* (2004). *Rumstick Road* takes as its primary event Spalding Gray's mother's mental illness and her suicide, while *Well* ostensibly focuses on Lisa Kron's mother's physical health. G. Thomas Couser has proposed that, in intimate life writing, the degree of vulnerability is greater as is the degree of potential betrayal (2004, p. xii). Whilst Gray's performance might be read as a betrayal of his family, it could also be considered as a means of using performance to gain some agency over the past, a way of structuring his mother's death even if not of understanding it. Finally, though, *Rumstick Road* exposes theatre as an unavoidable act of betrayal to life and people, an insight that resonates with *Well* which confronts the process by which an other becomes 'storied'. Whilst *Well* asks whether one has the right to perform the 'other', it also suggests that Kron, in her negotiation with her mother, was acutely aware of her responsibility to her and her mother's past and future, a future being written/performed in the very process of that collaboration.

Though arranged in four chapters, each of these inevitably overlaps. There is, for example, a politics implicit in the practice of testimony, place is always acutely political, while politics and ethics are never far apart. Questions pertaining to ethics, then, might as easily have been addressed in Chapters 1 and 2, whilst questions relating to politics might have easily been addressed in Chapters 3 and 4. These connections are, I think, self-evident.

The Conclusion seeks to locate autobiographical performance within the context of its production and reception, including the wider context of the contemporary glut of mass-mediated confessional opportunities – 'reality tv' shows, chat shows, internet chat rooms, blogs, etc. In spite (or because) of this mass-mediation of 'autobiography', autobiographical performance remains a popular mode. This begs the questions of whether, and how, it can remain politically urgent and useful. When and where is the personal political?

The continuing appeal of autobiographical performances in the professional world is matched by the devising of autobiographical, often solo, performances by students in university and college departments of Drama, Theatre, Performance and Communications Studies. The reasons for this 'turn' to, or embrace of, the autobiographical in higher education are multiple. First, as this book will map out, autobiographical performance necessarily intersects with many of the critical concerns currently engaged in many university curricula, including issues relating to identity and subjectivity (via postmodern, postcolonial and poststructuralist theory), historiography, feminist and queer theory, the status of memory, truth/fiction, ethnography and rights and ethics, to name just a few. The study and practice of autobiographical performance enables an engagement with the various discourses with which such performances are in dialogue. Second, the practice of autobiographical performance facilitates the inhabiting of a critical stance in relation to some of the dominant or commonsense assumptions students might hold about their immediate worlds. The self-reflection required in the making of autobiographical performances demands the taking of a certain distance from what seems all too obvious. Refracting one's experiences through discourses that might include feminist and queer theory often undoes the fixed, stable and 'given' (Heddon, 2001; see also Aston, 1999, 2000b). Devising autobiographical performances, then, provides a means for the critical analysis and questioning of our immediate social environments and their impact on everyday practices. Third, and matching one reason for the initial 'turn' to autobiography in the 1960s, given that the only essential resource for such performances is the performer, autobiographical performance is, potentially at least, extremely economical, a feature which makes it attractive to cash-strapped and often resource limited educational institutions. The fact that women predominantly fill drama and performance courses in the HE sector is also pertinent, particularly given the continuing shortage of roles for women in more traditional theatre. Creating a solo autobiographical show means literally creating a part for yourself. Finally, drawing on and engaging with the matter of everyday life, autobiographical performance potentially matters. I would suspect that I am not alone in sharing Jill Dolan's pedagogic aspirations:

> I want to train my students to use performance as a tool for making the world better, to use performance to incite people to profound responses that shake their consciousness of themselves in the world.   (2001, p. 456)

My hope for this book is that it helps with that training, contributing to the informed practice of practice by foregrounding questions and issues that pertain to autobiographical performance.

Whilst I do not want to curtail creative exploration by proposing tried and tested models of 'good' autobiographical practice (such models, in their familiarity, might rather be considered 'bad'), I do want to explore various performances as a way to impress some of the key issues that attach to this mode of performance. If the works discussed here are 'exemplary', it is because they render visible the various possibilities, alongside the associated and always present dangers, afforded by autobiographical performance practices. My selections have, therefore, been motivated by a number of considerations; first, each of the performances considered in any depth are performances which I feel engage with or illuminate the particular issues being explored. In this sense, I would consider them to be exemplary within the specific context of this book. Second, I have deliberately attempted to embrace a range of practices, taken from across time, and from the well-known to the little-known. Though performances such as Robbie McCauley's *Sally's Rape* and Bobby Baker's *Drawing on a Mother's Experience* have already received extensive coverage, it is precisely this ubiquity and their considerable influence that recommend they take their place in *Autobiography and Performance*. To leave them out would seem to be an oversight. I am also sensitive to the fact that most people will not be able to access the autobiographical performances that I discuss (either because they are no longer toured or because they only tour to large, urban centres). Whilst there is no substitute for the live performance experience, and liveness is a property I often stress here, I nevertheless do think that access to a published script of a performance, or to a documentational recording of it, remains useful. It allows certain engagements and analyses to be undertaken or significant questions to be posed – at least about the experiences offered by those other texts, if not by the live experience. Some of the more well-known performances can be read as performance scripts, whilst others can be viewed as video or DVD recordings, and this may at least allow and encourage some debate and dialogue.[11] I also hope that this book extends the knowledge and understanding that readers might already have about certain performers and performances, whilst introducing them to significant works that are little known outside of the local communities in which they were performed, particularly those that are community- and site-specific and which therefore do not easily tour. The questions and concerns raised, in relation to all of the performances, can be applied to, further develop or be challenged by the vast numbers of performances that are not included here, but which you, the reader, will want to address. Finally, and perhaps most importantly, all of the work discussed in *Autobiography and Performance* is work that has personally mattered to me because it has engaged me, bothered me and motivated me. Is *Autobiography and Performance* an autobiographical text? No not at all and yes of course.

1 Politics (of Self): The Subject of Autobiography

The autobiographical and the political are interconnected. Who speaks? What is spoken? What sorts of lives are represented, contested, imagined? The vast majority of autobiographical performances have been concerned with using the public arena of performance in order to 'speak out', attempting to make visible denied or marginalised subjects, or to 'talk back', aiming to challenge, contest and problematise dominant representations and assumptions about those subjects. Within the realm of performance, where performer and spectator share space and time, the political potential is manifest as performance enables the staged life to 'resonate in the broader realm of public consequence' (Miller *et al.*, 2003, p. 4). These are autobiographical voices that defiantly speak 'with an agenda' (Festa, 2000, p. 3), embracing the autobiographical form as a useful tool in the struggle for emancipation, equal rights, recognition, debate or simply the means to take (a) place. In many examples, autobiographical performances represent the already lived in order to beckon us towards, urge us to imagine or compel us to create the yet to be lived. Sidonie Smith's insights have resonance here: 'Autobiographical practices become occasions for restaging subjectivity and autobiographical strategies become occasions for the staging of resistance' (1998 [1993], p. 434). Smith's recognition of subjectivities being 'restaged' and her linking of 'strategy' with 'resistance' are worth underlining since both signal the complexity of the politically motivated autobiographical act, a complexity to be uncovered throughout this chapter.

Beginnings: Autobiography and Feminism

Though the use of autobiography in performance pre-dates the second-wave feminist movement,[1] it was in the early 1970s that the political potential of autobiographical performance was harnessed for the first time. While the aim of this book is not to provide a historical overview, it is nevertheless important to acknowledge the significance of the second-wave feminist movement for autobiographical performance practice. It is with the intersection between feminism, autobiography and performance that I want to begin this study, not least because of what that early intersection can teach us about the 'politics' or problematics of making autobiographical work.

The translation of personal – or autobiographical – material into live performance was inarguably tied to consciousness-raising activities which focused analysis specifically on women's experiences (under the banner of 'the personal is political'). Collective consciousness-raising activities intended to enable women 'to realise that their problems [were] not individual but [were] part of a collective oppression of the whole sex' (Whelehan, 1995, p. 66).[2] Areas explored included work and pay, relationships with men, relationships with women, love, couples, jealousy, anger and children (Bruley, 1981, p. 62).[3] Feminist activists from the period reflected that most of 'these [areas] were not normally the subject of politics. Yet these are the problems of everyday life, the problems about which women talk most to other women' (Rowbotham et al., 1979, p. 13).

If the subjects of the 'everyday' were not normally the matter of politics, neither were they the typical matter of contemporary art or theatre, and the entry of the explicitly personal into the aesthetic should itself be considered a political gesture. Admittedly the predominantly minimalist or formalist art produced in the USA had already come under challenge from various earlier counter-cultural and avant-garde experiments (see Sandford, 1995).[4] Allan Kaprow, for example, had insisted that 'the line between art and life should be kept as fluid, and perhaps as indistinct, as possible' (1966, p. 189). Feminist artists, however, took this mantra in a different direction. Consciousness-raising generated self-consciousness on the part of women which allowed an articulation of specifically female (everyday) experiences in art (see Broude and Garrard, 1994, p. 21).[5]

The experiences of women artists on the West Coast of the USA during the late 1960s and early 1970s are well documented and provide indisputable evidence of the way in which consciousness-raising fed into feminist art making, and in particular the placing of the autobiographical within the work.[6] Faith Wilding, a participant in Judy Chicago's women's programme at Fresno and CalArts, offers the following recollection of the process:

> During the first six weeks we met in each other's houses for consciousness-raising, reading, discussion, and sharing our first art pieces. Once, after an emotional consciousness-raising session about street harassment, Chicago suggested we make a piece in response. (1994, p. 34)

As Wilding states, 'by fortuitous accident, it seemed, we had stumbled on a way of working: using consciousness-raising to elicit content [...] to reveal our hidden histories' (ibid.).

Though experimental performance was increasingly recognised as an art practice by the late 1960s (see Goldberg, 1988), the entry of explicitly autobiographical material into performances was also prompted by the intersection of live art and feminism as 'personal history was being ransacked, analyzed, displayed and reinvented by one woman performer after another' (Roth, 1983, p. 18).[7] The *Womanhouse* project of 1972 is usefully illustrative in terms of its content, but it was also radical and influential in its scale and in its publicisation of the seemingly 'private', with 23 women transforming an abandoned house in LA into a public gallery. Each space of the house became an opportunity for an appropriately feminist-themed installation or environment, such as Chicago's *Menstruation Bathroom*, Kathy Huberland's *Bridal Staircase* and Sandra Orgel's *Linen Closet*. The living room was designated a theatre space, with performance workshops led by Chicago where pieces were developed from 'informal working sessions in which the women "acted out" aspects of their lives' (Chicago and Schapiro, 1972).

Throughout the 1970s performers continued to 'ransack' and 'reinvent' their personal history for and through performance. In 1975, for example, Rachel Rosenthal presented her first autobiographical performance, *Replays*, connecting her diseased and painful knees with her painful childhood. In the same year, Carolee Schneemann performed *Interior Scroll*, pulling a scroll of text from her vagina and sharing with the audience her experiences of being a female artist, marginalised in an art world that notably dismissed 'personal clutter' and read the 'diaristic' as an 'indulgence'. In 1977 Suzanne Lacy devised *Three Weeks in May*, a public work that, drawing directly on women's experiences, exposed the extent of sexual violence that women in Los Angeles were subjected to on a daily basis (see Chapter 3). Between 1969 and 1977, Mierle Laderman Ukeles undertook her Maintenance Art Works, bringing attention to the art of everyday work, a focus prompted by her experiences of being a new mother and responsive to the feminist rhetoric of the time, as shown in her 'Manifesto for Maintenance Art':

> I am an artist. I am a woman. I am a wife. I am a mother. (Random order.) I do a hell of a lot of washing, cleaning, cooking, renewing, supporting, preserving, etc. Also, (up to now separately) I 'do' Art. Now I will simply do these maintenance everyday things, and flush them up to consciousness, exhibit them, as Art.   (cited in Phillips, 1995, p. 171)

Lucy Lippard comments that Ukeles' turn to the 'everyday' was motivated by her realisation that 'as a mother of small children she was not going to have time to make art' (1984 [1983], p. 144).[8] In 1978 Nancy Buchanan performed *Deer/Dear*, juxtaposing her dreams of violence with actual violence she had experienced, while The Waitresses used their experiences of being waitresses in their collective performances (ibid., p. 142). In 1979, Terry Wolverton directed the devised show, *An Oral History of Lesbianism* (see Wolverton, 2002), and in the same year Catherine Elwes performed *Menstruation*, inside a glass box, wearing white in order that her menstrual blood would be visible. Elwes admits to having 'inherited a set of values that were challenged in the 1970s by a growing awareness of the women's movement' (cited in Reckitt, 2001, p. 130). With the glass a direct reference to the act of making the invisible visible (the private public), Elwes wrote on the glass walls in response to questions from spectators.

As is evident in these few examples, the binary between art and life, just as between public and private, collapsed as feminists consciously incorporated their lives into their art making. So too did the binary between the aesthetic and the social, or art and politics, as many artists strategically understood their art as feminist praxis. As Rachel Rosenthal reflected, performance 'was a perfect vehicle, an art way of making personal and political statements. This was more effective than going on a soapbox, writing an article, or giving a lecture for women, this was a fabulous way to get out of the closet and be who we are' (cited in Meola, 1997 [1992], p. 57). The public form of performance offered an ideal medium to publicise feminist issues, making it the 'theatricalized extension of feminist consciousness raising' (Withers, 1997, p. 160). Art historian Lucy Lippard similarly observed at the time that 'there are an increasing number of artists [...] who are devoting themselves to an ongoing, high structured art conceived not as an aesthetic amenity but as a consciousness-raising or organizing tool' (1984 [1983], p. 318). Lippard's statement stresses that the political aims of the work were served by careful attention to the art's composition (rather than an abandonment of such aesthetic concerns).

The potential intersections between performance and consciousness-raising and performance and community-building were also well recognised by feminist theatre collectives, such as those working in the UK during the 1970s, although the cultural context here was different. Initially aligned with the vibrant Left of the time and committed to a broadly Marxist politics, the Women's Liberation Movement (WLM) sought to identify and fill a gap in Marxist theory – namely, the unaccounted-for position of women. Particular focus was placed on the role women played in the reproduction of both the next generation of the workforce and the maintenance of the present one. Such work was recognised by feminists as being invisible, unpaid and yet crucial to the overall mechanisms of a capitalist economy. Whilst the WLM had many links to other Left organisations, with many of its members also members of other groups, it was considered an autonomous movement that rejected the notion of *stageism* – the idea that women's liberation could wait until the liberation of the working-class (Segal, 1979, p. 164). Many feminists also increasingly felt that women were subordinated within groups which were supposedly sensitive to women's equality, leading to the formation of women-only or women-focused groups, including theatre companies. A feminist praxis was applied not only to the structural organisation of companies (typically collectives), but also to the work produced – the majority of it necessarily new work since the existing repertoire was felt to be unrepresentative of women's lives.

Consciousness-raising, already used as an internal tool of education by socialist theatre groups such as Red Ladder, was also considered by feminist companies a practice useful to the creation of new work and a means of identifying and addressing issues that mattered to women. For example, the devising of the Women's Theatre Group's first performance, *My Mother Says I Never Should* (1975), began with group debate, and then subsequent discussion with girls, parents and teachers. These encounters provided the material for group improvisations and the production of a script. The women's section of Gay Sweatshop utilised a similar model with *Care and Control* (1977), using interviews with women as primary material that was subsequently developed in workshops and ultimately transformed into a script with the assistance of Michelene Wandor (see Goodman, 1993).[9]

Gay Sweatshop had already realised the importance of the auto-biographical gesture within a society in which gay men felt almost entirely invisible or misrepresented.[10] Its first play, *Mister X* (1975), was addressed specifically to a gay constituency, embracing gay life experiences. Created for a conference of the Campaign for Homosexual Equality, the production reflected the experiences of the writers/performers, showing that they had 'travelled from being scared and closeted to being self-confident and proud to be gay' (Osment, 1989, p. xx). Significantly and radically the play concluded with the main actor abandoning his fictional role and declaring his own name and address: 'My name is Mister ... My name is Alan Pope and I live at 10 Marius Mansions, Marius Road, London SW17 and I'm gay.' Such a declaration was an explicitly public claiming of a gay identity and as such, in this historical context, it was important that it was the actor, not a fictional character, who made it.

Consciousness-raising as feminist praxis was also extended to spectators. Many groups held post-show discussions with the audiences and considered these as wholly part of the theatre event. Evidence again of the desire to close the distance between life and art, the post-show discussion served to bridge any perceived gap between the 'stage' and the 'real world' (perhaps an equivalent to the unmasking of Mister X). Such discussions prompted the spectator to reflect on his/her own personal experiences, but to do so publicly, allowing links to be drawn between these and the theatre show, but also, and as importantly, between each other.

Tensions: Experience and Its Representation

One frequent criticism of feminist work produced throughout the 1970s was that it served to promote an idea of an essential (female) subject, denying differences between women. Griselda Pollock, for example, reads Judy Chicago's labour as an attempt to reclaim 'women's essential identity and integrity' (2003 [1988], p. 221). A risk particularly attending autobiographical performance is that the sign 'autobiography' serves as an authenticating symbol which underwrites an appeal to an unproblematised truth. In the context of the feminist movement 'the "personal" is not just the political but "the truthful" ' (Smith, 1999, p. 38). Whilst feminist challenges to supposedly 'objective' knowledge are to be embraced, a move towards the subjective also needs to be handled carefully. The assumed authenticity that attaches to experience serves to equate it with 'authority' and personal experience can easily become an unwitting but persuasive guarantor of 'truth': because I saw and felt, then it must necessarily be so. In this scenario, 'I' become the evidence. Where the supposedly objective location guaranteed 'truth' precisely because it was considered distanced, paradoxically the openly subjective location guarantees 'truth' because it is admittedly close.

Any assumed equation between 'I' and 'truth' might be considered less problematic if there are enough 'I's telling their experiences since this would allow the production of a multiplicity of 'truths'. However, as many critics of the second-wave feminist movement pointed out at the time, the 'I' that was most frequently represented spoke in a white and middle-class voice. The experiences that were drawn upon and circulated were inevitably similar rather than diverse. This reproduction and recirculation of the same images and messages, in place of a diversity and multiplicity of experiences, might well have proposed that female artists were subscribing to a concept of innate femininity, a consensus that would have made it difficult for other women to perform different stories. Ironically, many women felt marginalised by or invisible within the feminist movement. Indeed, it was this general lack of awareness of multiplicity residing within the category 'woman' that led to the fragmentation of that movement in the 1980s, enabling women to claim their racial, ethnic, sexual and/or class-based differences under the banner of identity politics. While this did allow for greater diversity of representation, in fact it did not address the concomitant problem of performing potentially essentialising gestures. 'Identity politics' simply made the reach of those gestures wider. Here too, to speak 'as' can still easily become to speak 'for'.

Assuming an equation between 'experience' and 'truth' is to forget that experience is always already implicated in the structure of language since it is at the level of language that experience is interpreted, determining what, specifically, any event is able to mean. Each experience is made sense of, and given meaning, within the cultural references available. Every 'experience', then, rather than being individual, is a cultural phenomenon and already culturally approved.

Feminist critic Joan W. Scott (1992) advises that experience is always an interpretation and always in need of interpretation. Mediated in and by language, experience cannot then be taken as some 'pure' knowledge or 'truth' about any subject, including the self. The 'self' is as much a discursive construct as anything else, constructed in particular times and places. For Stuart Hall,

> Identity is always in part a narrative, always in part a kind of representation. It is always within representation. Identity is not something which is formed outside and then we tell stories about it. It is that which is narrated in one's own self.   (1991a, p. 49)

There is no 'true' self at the core that can be unmasked because the 'self' is 'a hypothetical place or space of storytelling' (Smith, 1993, p. 56).

The activity of representing the 'self' adds a further problematic layer to notions of 'truth' because, in the act of representing the self, there is always more than one self to contend with; the self is unavoidably split. There is the self who was and the self who is. There is the self who is performed, and the performing self. Which 'self', then, is being presented? Every autobiographical act requires taking some distance from the self, and therefore 'imports alterity into the self by the act of objectification which engenders it' (Marcus, 1994, p. 203). Paul de Man explains that in the realm of the written autobiography the process of figuring the self, of writing the self, inevitably writes over, writes out, erases the writing 'self' since language is always metaphorical and cannot hope to represent the 'real'. In the production of autobiography, then, a self is not recorded but is rather made up (see de Man, 1979), because 'in the end there is only writing' (Anderson, 2001, p. 13).

In the field of performance, the act of representing the self perhaps resonates somewhat differently, since in place of the absent self which all self-referential writing unavoidably figures, the spectator is confronted rather by the physically present self. Indeed, this makes performance all the more tempting (and dangerous) a medium through which to make claims for the 'real' or 'truthful' self, and is part of the immediacy of performance that we have already noted.[11] We need to remember that the presentation of self (in performance particularly) is a re-presentation, and often a strategic one. The performer's task, then, might be to harness the potential of the felt immediacy of form (Tim Miller's 'real-time heat', 2001) for political purposes, whilst simultaneously challenging assumptions of unmediated presence. Further, we should not forget that performance, where it is read as such, unavoidably foregrounds its status *as performance*. Performance is *not* the real world (though it might very well prompt us to consider whether and how the 'real world' is performance, or at least performative).

Revisiting the feminist work made in the 1970s, art historians Broude and Garrard in fact claim that assertions of 'biological essentialism' are misplaced since some of the work might be better considered examples of *'cultural essentialism* and *political essentialism'* (1994, p. 25; emphasis in original); or perhaps we might conceive of it as representative of strategic essentialism. Whilst it is necessary to re-emphasise that any strategic essentialism might not be quite so enabling for all women, the cultural and historical contexts in which the wide variety of work was made *does* need to be recognised because those contexts inspired or required certain responses. These autobiographical performances were made for particular, political purposes that in turn determined choices of form and content. Rita Felski sensibly advises us that 'feminist confession is not a self-generating discourse to be judged in abstraction from existing social conditions' (1989, p. 120). A pragmatic response to the performances would be to ask what they each enabled, in particular places and at particular times (see Plummer, 1995, p. 172). As is clear from the accounts by many women at the time, they felt invisible or marginalised in a cultural sphere largely dominated by men. The appeal of essentialism, in this time and place (and indeed in more contemporary times and certain places), was its potential to perform as an 'enabling myth' (Broude and Garrard, 1994, p. 28). Nicole Ward Jouve's challenge to post-structuralism resonates strongly here: 'you must have a self before you can afford to deconstruct it' (1991, p. 7). These performances performed 'selves' into existence – selves that demanded all sorts of rights, including the right to speak.

Dominant perspectives that were taken to be universal were recognised by women as being, in fact, particular, thereby opening up the possibility for the representation of alternative, counterhegemonic perspectives (Personal Narratives Group, 1989). Counter-narratives not only provide feminist revisions of knowledge, they also propose other potential life-models for the viewer or reader, and in this sense they 'offer new cultural possibilities' (ibid., p. 65). Having been the objects of art and theatre, but rarely the subjects, autobiographical performances proffered the opportunity for women to tell their own stories from their own, different perspectives. Feminist performers, reviewing their work of the 1970s, have insisted that their approach was always tactical and that the intention was never an uncritical appeal to any essentialised, ahistorical 'woman'. For Faith Wilding, the work 'attempted to deconstruct the myths of femininity and the traditional representations of women' (1994, p. 46). Such representation by women, of their own experiences, created, in critic Jeanie Forte's opinion, a 'dissonance with their representation, Woman, throwing that fictional category into relief and question' (1988, p. 225). Whilst this may have led to an assumption by some that the 'fictional' category was being replaced with a 'non-fictional' one, surely the very act of unmasking so-called truth places the alternative truth under equal epistemological pressure, with perspectivalism beckoning from the horizon – particularly when the applied methodology is performance. Further, while acknowledging the essentialising dangers that attended to autobiographical performance practices in the 1970s, that the *bios* of women's lives were represented *at all* seems politically significant, particularly given that to this point all women had been so markedly *in*visible. We would also do well to remember that this work explicitly signified, through its very presence and particular feminist content, a defiantly political *act* and in that sense might be considered performative before anything else.

The great variety of autobiographical performances produced within different contexts and for different aims should also warn against making generalisations about the work of this period. Some performances mixed the seemingly factual with the explicitly fictional. Eleanor Antin, for example, devised four different 'mythical' selves – a king, a ballerina, a nurse and a black movie star. Critic Moira Roth records that the different attributes of each of these personae were identified by Antin as being 'significant within her own personality and are played out by her in an attempt to answer the psychological, social and political demands of life' (Roth, 1983, p. 76). Lynn Hershman's construction of Roberta Breitmore (1975–8), though an entirely invented character, nevertheless blurred the boundaries between autobiography and fiction. Her invention of Breitmore included – or relied upon – the construction of convincing auto/biographical paraphernalia: résumés, bank statements, social security number, psychiatric reports and other personal data. Although there was no 'real' Roberta Breitmore, enough real auto/biographical fragments were generated for this character to engender the appearance of reality, of having really been there, of having really existed. Already, then, performers like Antin and Hershman were challenging the boundaries between the real and the performed, the autobiographical and the fictional.

Politically, too, the work made by feminists was diverse. For example, some performances might be considered exemplary of a radical or cultural feminist practice, such as Donna Henes' *Cocoon Ceremony* (1978), in which she aligned her female body with the rhythms of nature; whilst others might utilise a more materialist feminist strategy, such as Suzanne Lacy's *Three Weeks in May* which revealed that societal attitudes towards sexual violence against women are ideologically embedded. Moreover, performances may propose multiple readings. Felski warns that 'the dividing line between a repressive stereotype and an empowering symbol of cultural identity is often a very narrow one' (1989, p. 119). It might also be a question of spectatorial perspective, since we need to remember that the 'meaning' of any performance is ultimately created in the interaction between performance and spectator. Carolee Schneemann's *Interior Scroll* (1975) could be taken as an early example of Hélène Cixous's *écriture féminine*, with Schneemann 'writing' woman's body and desires. However, it could also be read as a deconstructive performance that enacts 'binary terror' through troubling linguistic and cultural structures, including artist/woman, artist/model, culture/nature, inside/outside, mind/body, subject/object, nude/naked.[12]

Reading performances from the 1970s as simply essentialist might in itself be something of an essentialising gesture that fails to do justice to the complexity of many autobiographically inflected performances, to their specific historical location, to their tactical and strategic devices and to their relationships with their spectators. This is not to deny that some performances may be recognised with the benefit of hindsight as being in part politically problematic, or politically naïve, but it is also to insist on the importance of that feminist work in its own time – and on its enduring influence in these times. Indebtedness to those feminist pioneers (for both their successes and their failures) remains tangible. Tim Miller is one artist who pays tribute to his heritage. Growing up in California he was able to witness first hand the work of feminist artists: 'When I was in high school I was going to the Women's building in downtown L.A., in '76, '77...L.A. was sort of the centre for feminist performance art as that version of feminist art practice and it had a huge impact' (2001c). The act of turning the personal into the publicly political is one that has endured across time.

In-Between: Experience and Its Representation

Recognising that all identities are discursive constructions and therefore historically and culturally located does not make the various
experiences that adhere to any 'identity' less real or felt (see Bordo,
1995). This is as true today as it was in the 1970s. Contemporary
autobiographical work demonstrates that many bodies remain subjected to oppression and repression. Learning from and building on
the work of their feminist predecessors (who in some cases might
well be younger examples of themselves) the challenge that continues
to face practitioners is that of navigating a path between dislodging
dominant cultural representations by showing other representations
drawn from experience, whilst understanding that these experiences
are themselves culturally and historically contingent. The imperative
is to appreciate that one lives variably 'as', for example, a white lesbian Scottish woman whilst still recognising the discursive and shifting
nature of this multiple location.

The task of autobiographical performances that engage with explicitly political remits is threefold: (i) to use personal experience in order
to render visible oppression and inequality; (ii) to render simultaneously such experiences historically contingent (and therefore possible
to change); (iii) to deny any simple referentiality between a life and
its representation while acknowledging that representation is itself
a discursive technology. The multiplicity of this challenge makes it
hugely complex and in the following we will explore recent performances by mct, Bobby Baker and Tim Miller in order to realise further
the potentials and dangers attached to autobiographical performances
that work *between* identity and its construction. In *Fingerlicks*, mct
negotiates the relationship between self and community, and between
'becoming' and 'being' a lesbian; Bobby Baker (whoever she is) plays
in-between herself and a persona; while Tim Miller works on that
in-between space that blurs fact and fiction, moving between past and
future.

mct: The Autobiography of Community

Throughout the 1990s numerous performances devised in Glasgow
aspired to make visible the details of gay and lesbian lives. *Talking Bollocks* (1995), *Talking Bollocks II* (1998), *Fingerlicks* (1998),
Fingerlicks 2 (1999) and *Just Pretending* (2000) all drew on the life-
stories of the participants – gay men and lesbians with little or no

previous experience of theatre – and might be considered examples of 'community autobiography'.[13] 'Community', though, is a problematic concept and practice. As we have seen, one criticism of the second-wave feminist movement was that political efficacy and power were felt to be dependent on the formation of a community conceptualised as being singular and coherent. This 'community of women' was based on sameness (we are all united under the banner 'woman'), with any differences between women ignored, denied or erased. Even more problematically, the experiences of some women (middle class, heterosexual, white) were taken to be representative of all women. Ironically, the feminist movement unwittingly repeated the mistake of humanism, with many women ignorant of the fact that their (universally) 'female' outlook was actually an embodied, subjective and specific perspective. Judith Butler's critique of any so-called feminist community is astute: 'Through what exclusions has the feminist subject been constructed, and how do those excluded domains return to haunt the "integrity" and "unity" of the feminist "we"' (1992, p. 14).

Butler's insights apply equally well to the formation of a lesbian community and though we would do well to keep her reservations in mind, in order to appreciate the political importance of mct's work its specific cultural context needs to be addressed. In 2000, the research-survey company MORI Scotland interviewed a sample of adults in Scotland for the *Sunday Herald* newspaper, to determine public attitudes towards homosexuality. Thirty-three per cent of those polled agreed with Scotland's senior Catholic Cardinal Winning's description of homosexual relationships as 'a perversion'. Fourteen per cent indicated that if schools were to be allowed to discuss homosexuality, they should 'teach children that homosexuality is wrong, and should not be tolerated as a way of life', while twenty-four per cent responded that schools should 'teach children that homosexuality is wrong, but should be tolerated as a way of life'.[14] According to these figures, more than one in three people, in Scotland, at the start of the twenty-first century, continued to believe that 'homosexuality is wrong'.

Within this atmosphere of general and widespread intolerance the need for community, and the insistence upon the gay or lesbian self's right to be, became imperative rather than academic or theoretical. Reminiscent of the historical context prompting particular agendas of the second-wave feminist movement, it was this particular culture and context of homophobia that prompted so many shows to take as their foundation the 'real stories' – the lived lives – of actual gay men and lesbians. Using their own voices, the performers had the means publicly to be seen and heard, insisting on their right to be, and specifically to be lesbian and gay. Importantly, the voices here were the voices of gay men and lesbians living (and talking out) in Scotland.

Fingerlicks: Coming to Voice

mct, a Glasgow-based company with a specifically gay and lesbian agenda, was aware of the lack of representations of lesbians in theatre in general, and in Scottish theatre in particular.[15] In 1998 it aimed to devise a production that would 'reach out' to lesbians. Over a period of six months, voluntary participants, none of whom had previous theatre experience, met on a weekly basis. Employing a historically feminist mode of theatre practice, the group collectively devised the performance that would eventually become *Fingerlicks*. The primary material used was the participants' experiences of being lesbians, with the performance structured around each woman telling her own story. For director Natalie Wilson,

the uniqueness of the group is the diversity of the lesbians involved. The common denominator is that they all have little or no experience of drama and have come together to create a theatre piece. The women come from all walks of life and by being together on stage they create a microcosm of the spectrum of lesbian sexuality.   (2001)

In an enduringly heteronormative society, the performance of a lesbian 'life' implicitly challenges the assumption that a heterosexual identity is the only, or only legitimate, identity, proposing instead other lives and other life-paths. On a very simple level, the stories performed extend the range of stories available. Being part of discourse they also extend the range of lives available to be lived. Such stories are preoccupied with a 'literary and political re-shaping of language and thus consciousness' (Stanley, 1992, p. 116). The fact that the stories are performed by self-identified lesbians is also politically crucial. These 'lay' stories potentially challenge the historical 'expert's story' of the dysfunctional, immature, under-developed, inverted lesbian, or the alternative 'clergy's story' of sinful and unnatural behaviour, the latter particularly significant in a Scottish context. In Ken Plummer's words, the 'sexual stories of authority – given to us from on high by the men in black frocks and white coats – are fracturing in the face of *participant stories*' (1995, p. 138). The author-performer of the lesbian autobiographical narrative is a subject in her own story, rather than the medical or psychiatric object of interest.

Not only do such performance narratives debunk 'expert knowledge', these performances and the performers also provide possible role models, perhaps prompting further coming to voice. Stories have an inspirational, educational and consciousness-raising potential and might then have real effects on the future lives or life-courses of their witnesses. This potential effect of the story is its 'social role':

> These stories work their way into changing lives, communities and cultures. Through and through, sexual story telling is a political process. (ibid., 1995, p. 144)

The autobiographical performances also serve to strengthen the idea of the lesbian community since 'stories gather people around them' (ibid., p. 177), and are 'instrumental in creating networks' (Zimmerman, 1985, p. 261). Plummer also identifies a dialectical movement between communities, politics, identities and stories, as communities and stories feed 'upon and into the other' (1995, p. 87).

The majority of the stories performed in *Fingerlicks* represent that moment of coming-into 'being a lesbian'; they are 'coming-out' stories in which the tellers use 'some kind of causal language, sense of linear progression, talk with unproblematic language and feel they are "discovering a truth"' (ibid., p. 82). Biddy Martin similarly recognises coming-out stories as being

> tautological insofar as they describe a process of coming to know something that has always been true, a truth to which the author has returned. They also describe a linear progression from a past shrouded in confusion or lies to a present or future that represents a liberation from the past. Coming out is conceived, then, as both a return to one's true self and a desire and a movement beyond distortion and constraint, grounding identity and political unity in moral right and truth. (1988, p. 88)

Many of the performances in *Fingerlicks* match the template identified by Martin. Alba's story is illustrative, beginning as it does with a quote from William Shakespeare's *Hamlet*: 'To thine own self be true.' The narrative figures a journey in which Alba, supposedly on the path towards her self, endures much pain, including rape by her former husband. By the end, however, Alba declares with confidence that she knows who she is, repeating the refrain, 'And to thine own self be true' (*Fingerlicks*, 1998).

Alba's journey, narrated directly to the audience, is one that travels from despair to freedom, although the route taken is less linear than circular, as Alba *returns* to what she believes she always was, a return literally remarked in her text through the repetition of the first and last line. Correlating with Martin's insights, Alba's story is less one of development than of *rediscovery*. This narrative trajectory is equally evident in Caroline's story. In spite of her early awareness of her attraction to women, Caroline nevertheless gets married, has a child and endures an unhappy and abusive marriage. She then meets a woman and her story ends with the declaration:

> We've been in love for seven years now. My son and I live with Brenda. Same village, same avenue, same neighbours. Just a different life. And I know I never had a choice – I'm a lesbian. I always have been. I no longer feel any guilt or shame. I'm good. I'm happy. I'm happy about who I am.
> (*Fingerlicks*, 1998)

In both these examples Martin's tautology – *coming to know something that has always been true* – is explicit. Caroline 'had no choice' while Alba has returned to her 'true' lesbian (core) self. This return to a 'truth' simultaneously suggests that the life previously lived was an untruth, an inauthentic life. Charles Guignon's observations on 'authenticity' are helpful here: 'the ideal of authenticity is becoming the person you are' (2004, p. 3). In both Alba's and Caroline's performances we witness Martin's 'movement beyond distortion' and towards 'liberation', in which is inscribed 'moral right'.

Constricting the Self

The telling of stories about oneself is part of the construction of an identity for that self. Moreover, the stories one tells are already, to some extent, written or performed; the story of what it 'is' to be a lesbian exists as a 'biographic norm of the community' (see Ponse, 1978, p. 125). The frame in and through which the supposedly 'unique' self is constituted is already there. This gay and lesbian 'auto/biographical norm' is itself not immune to or divorced from wider narrative imperatives. Plummer recognises that coming-out stories

> fit so well into the widely-held narratives of taking a journey, suffering and finding a home, [that] it is easy to see why they have become so pervasive. There is a fit; they sit well with what we already know.   (1995, p. 60)

For Plummer, then, the coming-out story is not specific in its formula, since it contains *generic* elements of modern stories structured around the key points of suffering, epiphany and transformation (ibid., p. 54). The ways in which lesbians make sense of their experiences, and of whom they are, are influenced by the existence of such dominant patterns of story telling.

In addition to such general dominant narrative models, within *autobiographical* storytelling there are also dominant models, themselves patterned on the novel form, with its linear progression and its narrative drive to resolution. Though autobiography emerged independently of the novel, 'its development from the late eighteenth century onwards involved a borrowing of novelistic techniques' (Marcus, 1994, p. 237). While written autobiography has a different history to the performance of autobiography, there are nevertheless moments of influence. Cultural imperatives and conventions also adhere to what a 'self' is, and how it might be represented (Stanley, 1992, p. 62).[16] Lesbian autobiographical narratives, such as those represented by Alba and Caroline, work between various models: the dominant models of autobiography (both written and performed), the dominant model of lesbian auto/biography, which may be oral in form, and the dominant model of narratives, *per se*. The dominant narrative of sexuality in the contemporary Western world is that one *has* a sexuality – and specifically a singular sexuality. It is precisely this dominant narrative that many of the stories performed in *Fingerlicks* seek to represent. We might, then, read these representations of lesbian sexuality as liberalist appeals for inclusion within this dominant narrative ('we are really all just the same'), rather than radical challenges to it.

Though I am empathetic to the political necessity to claim an identity in a cultural context where such an identity is met with hatred, fear, denial or derision, what appears to be neglected in Alba's and Caroline's performances is any recognition of the discourses used to construct these identities that they claim – including the 'scientific', 'medical' or 'genetic' discourses of 'innate sexuality'. In Betty Bergland's words, 'to claim an essentialist self is to deny the way in which conditions, material forces, and cultural discourses shape articulations of the self' (1994, p. 162). In Alba's and Caroline's performances, experiences and *interpretations* are figured as essences and incontrovertible evidence. The confusing, lived experience of sex and sexuality, the contradictions, the contingencies and the contexts, seem to have been erased or ignored in the urgency to proclaim the 'truth' of sexual

identity. 'Generic' stories, conforming to and performing the dominant and/or lesbian 'auto/biographical norm', might well limit what
stories can be told about 'being' lesbian, or anything else. Ken Plummer puts it simply when he stresses that stories 'have conservative,
policing control tasks – as well as transgressive, critical, challenging
tasks' (1995, p. 176). Bergland also warns us that 'as autobiographies
naturalize certain subject positions they serve to prescribe these positions' (1994, p. 160). Each time the 'homo-normative' narrative of
what it is to be lesbian is recited, the more difficult it becomes to
imagine, propose, recite or live other lives. Moreover, since stories
and communities are so intertwined, communities established on the
grounds of an assumed sameness will discourage deviations from the
dominant narrative. To perform otherwise is to risk isolation.

Performing Lesbians

Set within a local context of intolerance, the political character and
intentions of *Fingerlicks* are of course primary. These tales of homophobia and its effects are not imagined since homophobia is really
felt and lived with daily. However, the performance does also play
ambiguously, though strategically, with the referent. In tension with
the appeal to 'truth' inscribed both in the direct address and in the
'low' production values of the performance is the unavoidable fact
that what we see before us is a performance, performed in a well-
known theatre venue in Glasgow city centre (The Arches).[17] Though
the scenography is minimal, the women are nevertheless separated
from the audience, performing at some distance, and stage lighting
and music are used. The medium – and mediation – is here always
apparent. We see it. Even without a lavish set, or costumes, the theatrical 'frame' which separates us from the performers is always present
and what take place within this frame are 'enactments'. This is not a
fly-on-the-wall documentary, situated in supposedly real time.[18] This
is Caroline re-enacting her story and these are women playing other
characters, including men. Finally, the very constructed nature of the
stories, the explicit presence of the narratives: the neat resolutions,
the recurring motifs and repetition of key phrases; and the carefully
managed comic timing make the status of these *stories* apparent. It is
difficult, sitting in a theatre, to mistake a representation for the real.
  Though it is possible to criticise *Fingerlicks* for its inscription of
sexual essences, it is difficult to ignore the fact that there are eight
different performers, with eight different lives, each performed in a

different way. While individual stories might contain moments of resolution, the presence of eight individual tales strategically told in different theatrical modes (including narrative, dramatic and musical) results in an overall production that is neither seamless nor coherent. This is a deliberate dramaturgical choice. Similarly, while Alba's and Caroline's stories follow the predictable narrative trajectory, from silence to speech/from guilt to celebration, Lynne's story refuses to fulfil the demands of this convention. Like Alba and Caroline, Lynne does share her 'coming out' experience, but inscribes a difference within this. Having come out to her parents, Lynne is left alone, her mother's words reverberating around the space:

Mother: What have you done to us?

The scene ends with Lynne sitting alone in an armchair. The lights fade on her down-turned head, leaving her in darkness. Greenday's track 'She Screams in Silence' plays the scene out. Lynne's performed story does *not* end happily. However, what is important about this story is that there *is* no narrative ending. Instead, there is a pause. Lynne is the youngest participant in *Fingerlicks*. Unlike the other women, she does not yet have a secure lesbian present from where she can look back and reinterpret or rewrite her past. In life, her sexual story has not been resolved, so she cannot provide a neat resolution. Lynne's story appears to capture the uncertainty of the present, before it becomes a narratable past event. Moreover, this present is *here*, in front of us – this *is* the teenage Lynne that we are witnessing. This is also, I would argue, the privileged moment of live theatre, and its aptness as an autobiographical medium.

Of course, the fact that Lynne *is* here, in front of us, *telling* this story now, actually suggests a different story, a sub-text. What she says and where she says it from do not quite correlate. This is, again, the unique potential of theatre (and a reminder that we should never take the theatrical 'given' at face value). Whilst her performance shows a young woman screaming alone in silence, that same performance is the scream made loud; and Lynne, here and now in this theatre space, is far from alone. Her involvement in this project is itself some sort of outcome. The ultimate sign of a shift from guilt, self-loathing and con-fusion to acceptance and affirmation is performing in this very public production. Further, who knows what real effect Lynne's participa-tion in *Fingerlicks* will have on the actual paths her life now takes? The future life becomes implicated by the reporting of the life already lived and an involvement in *Fingerlicks* necessarily becomes a part of the life-story, rather than merely commenting upon it. Although the lights come down on an isolated, rejected and abjected Lynne, her very presence here bears witness to the fact that this is *not* where this story actually ends.

At the end of the piece, the eight women line up, side by side, each one reciting a single phrase from her story. The words do not add up to any cohesive statement but instead are reminders of the diverse stories and experiences that have been shared. The very last phrase of *Fingerlicks*, however, is spoken by all of the women simultaneously:

Together. Fingerlicks.

This final line figures a community arrived at without imposing a sense of closure and resolution onto the production – or onto the community. Instead, what we are left with is an image of a group of women who have come together, for *this* project. This project, and in turn our witnessing of their stories, has only been possible through their shared participation and collaborative efforts. What is brought into focus at the end, then, is the project, *Fingerlicks*, and the collaborative experience of this, rather than a single, shared experience of 'being' a lesbian. Perhaps this ending of *Fingerlicks* suggests, by example, the possibility of navigating a path between the powerful but potentially dangerous authority of individual experience and the active creation of communities in particular times and places, for particular ends. Here, and for this moment only, *Fingerlicks* is the community.

Bobby Baker: The Indeterminate Subject

As we have seen with mct's *Fingerlicks*, the performance of autobiography enables the construction of self, through both the production of narratives that constitute that self and through the staging of the self. Autobiographical performance brings to the fore the 'self' as a performed role, rather than an essentialised or naturalised identity. This is one of autobiographical performance's formal strengths, and it is a property much capitalised on by many performers as a means to reveal not only the multiplicity of the performing subject, but also the multiplicity of discourses that work to forge subjects (and the contradictions within discourses that enable some degree of agency). Vivian Patraka proposes that 'if the autobiographical is still present in feminist performance, it has mostly become a space of indeterminacy and shifting personae' (1992, p. 171). The playing of multiple selves is a political act that resists the authority accruing to the 'I', since this I is unknowable. It is also an act that refuses to let the 'I' be fixed by the spectator, as the work of British performer Bobby Baker reveals.

Bobby Baker has been creating and touring performance and installation works internationally for over twenty-five years. Across that span of time, her focus on aspects of the quotidian has been consistent and unremitting, epitomised by the performances gathered together under the title 'Daily Life Series'. In this respect, her work shares some of the aims of earlier feminist performances, seeking to disclose the hidden aspects (both physical and emotional) of her everyday experiences as a woman, wife and mother, and often the tensions (again, social and personal) between these locations and her positioning as an artist. Her first explicitly autobiographical piece, *Drawing on a Mother's Experience* (1988), also the first in the 'Daily Life Series', draws, as suggested by its title, on Baker's own experience of becoming a mother: from preparing to give birth, to giving birth, to post-natal depression, to her subsequent recovery from that and her attempt to become a working mother. The drawing is also playfully literal as Baker 'draws' onto a white household sheet, performing her own Jackson Pollockesque action painting using various food and drink as her material. Swirls of black treacle signify her depression, frozen fish pies the nurturance provided by her own mother, dribbles of Guinness referencing her preferred nourishment when pregnant.

The second in the series, *Kitchen Show* (1991; see also Chapter 3), which premiered in Baker's own London kitchen, explores Baker's mechanisms for coping with daily life, devising thirteen 'actions' or daily activities (a Baker's dozen) that she regularly carries out whilst in her own kitchen, including making tea, 'grazing' and tidying drawers. As in *Drawing*, where Baker found in the everyday matter of life instances of beauty – for example, a bowl of stewed red berries and Greek yoghurt becomes extolled for its contrast of colours – so, in *Kitchen Show*, the kitchen becomes an artist's palette: a tub of margarine contains a moment of pure delight underneath its unopened lid, in the shape of a margarine nipple (perfect form); cool water running from a tap onto wrists is hugely sensuous. All of Baker's works are appeals to the senses, where memory resides. If the bed sheet was the canvas in *Drawing*, Baker's body is her canvas in *Kitchen Show*, with each action inscribed directly onto her body so that her body bears the weight of her daily activities and mixed emotions, making both visible. At the end of *Drawing*, Baker wears her sheet, taking her past into her future; in *Kitchen Show*, the body bears testimony to the weight of the present.

The third in the series, *How to Shop* (1993), a lecture-based performance that again draws on Baker's own experiences, is a comical and sometimes painful shopping 'pilgrimage', 'formulated as a quest, "shopping for life" or "shopping for enlightenment"' (Harris, 1999, p. 113). Structurally resembling her earlier works, *How to Shop* draws on John Bunyan's *The Pilgrim's Progress* and is based around the search for seven items, each signifying one of the seven virtues.

Box Story (2001), the last in the 'Daily Life Series', premiered in Baker's own church, and is a confession of key moments from her life where she accepts (like Pandora) the blame and guilt for the events that transpire, finally claiming that everything is all her fault. As with the earlier pieces, each story that is performed is made tangibly visible through the use of everyday materials, specifically 'domestic products'. During the performance, Baker creates a 'world' in ten actions, using the contents from various boxes including cornflakes, mustard, matches and Black Magic chocolates. Tipping the contents from each box directly onto the floor, Baker builds a graphic image of a world beset by disasters of global proportion. In a final act of agency, however, she then sweeps this world away, depositing it into a large freezer packaging box.

In each of her performances, Baker is supremely skilful at forging a path between using experience and simultaneously problematising experience's affinity to 'truth' and it is this 'slippage' that I want to focus on here.[19] Baker's performances all explicitly draw on the life of Bobby Baker, but at the same time 'Bobby Baker' veers between being absent and present; real and not real. The various stories that Baker shares in *Drawing on a Mother's Experience*, for example, are all drawn from the life of Bobby Baker, and the person who performs these stories is Bobby Baker, so in classic autobiographical form, the 'writing' subject is also the subject of the story – subject and object are one. There is, however, a layer of complexity missing from my rendering of this subject–object equation, which pertains throughout all of her performances. Between the Baker who performs and the stories being performed, there are at least two other Bakers: the Baker who is performed and the non-performing Baker.[20]

In each performance there is what is best described as a *persona*, and it is this persona that Bobby Baker, the performer, performs. The visible 'signs' of Baker's persona include her trademark 'uniform' – her overall (Persil-white in all of her shows other than *Box Story*, where it became Virgin-Mary blue), which she has worn in every performance since 1988. She also persistently performs exaggerated middle-class mannerisms, erring dangerously towards stereotypical allusions to feminine 'neurosis' and 'hysteria', including the compulsion to look after, to 'clear up' as she goes along.[21] In *Drawing*, before placing the Persil-white sheet onto the floor, Baker covers the floor with a plastic sheet, saying as she does so,

> This is to avoid mess. Extra mess. Because one discovers quite early on, as an intelligent mother, that if you think ahead, you can save yourself a lot of work.   (1988)

Appropriate to this image, Baker then also repeatedly references and uses a 'damp J-cloth.' In a similar vein, there is the repetitive trope of the resourceful housewife, caring about the environment, avoiding unnecessary waste and saving money. Another repetitive gesture which signals the constructed nature of 'Bobby Baker', a British, middle-aged, middle-class woman, is that of avoiding embarrassing subjects, such as giving birth, 'women's problems' and breast feeding. These topics, through their avoidance, are positioned as 'unsuitable subjects': 'I don't want to embarrass you too much with sort of nasty details about childbirth'; 'I had – women's trouble –'; 'We'll move on quickly'. Anger, an 'inappropriate' emotion for the good housewife/mother, erupts only to be summarily washed or swept away, as in *Kitchen Show* when we learn that 'action 3' involves hurling a ripe pear at a kitchen cupboard. Baker then informs us that the good thing about using a pear is that you can simply wipe the mess off the cupboard door afterwards. Anger is acknowledged and admitted, then, but only momentarily.

In the construction of her performed 'self', Baker self-consciously observes herself. Her very process admits to the gap between who she is outside of performance, and who she plays: 'I step on stage, I start performing, I become something else' (2001b). Of course, the moment anyone is on stage, they arguably become something else. However, Baker also admits to 'sort of develop[ing] that persona' (ibid), or developing a style of presentation. Baker's performance, then, might resemble what Sidonie Smith has termed, ' "I"-lying', a strategic practice which 'gestures towards the fictiveness of the "I" that seems to speak in autobiography', thereby disrupting 'the surface of the unified, authoritative, essential "self", a fiction of a regime of truth that would specify identity, contain it, capture it, universalize it, essentialize it' (1999, p. 47). This is a strategic – or doubled – use of the 'I'.

While seemingly adhering to Philippe Lejeune's (1989) autobiographical pact, where subject and author are one and the same, the obvious presence of the persona troubles the pact; whose stories are these that are being shared with us – Bobby Baker the performing subject's or Bobby Baker the performed subject's? And if the Bobby Baker who offers up these stories is a persona, how referential or stable or truthful can these autobiographical renderings be presumed to be? Reading the signs of Baker's persona, it is evident that in her performance of herself (and she *is* a middle-class mother of two), Baker performs an exaggerated, cultural (rather than strictly personal) version. The Bobby Baker that we see performed is one who, through repeated cultural circulation, we 'know', but who in all probability does not actually exist.

The representation of Bobby Baker is also complex because whilst she might portray 'herself' as being in one moment a subjected housewife/mother, passive and apologetic, other 'identities' and attitudes puncture that representation (not least that at the same time she is evidently a skilled, professional artist). Within her performances, Baker can be self-deprecating and authoritative, controlled and unpredictable, respectable and outrageous, revelatory and secretive, logical and intuitive. In effect, one culturally inscribed image of the 'housewife', 'mother', even 'woman', is simultaneously undermined by that same character, as Bobby Baker not only makes a cake but splatters the contents over a bed sheet; not only admits to a sense of guilt, but also spits jelly and pours wine over her head; not only wears a Persil-white overall, but also rolls herself in the sheet imprinted with Guinness, tea and Greek yoghurt; not only gives the audience refreshments, but also shoves a tin of anchovies into her mouth. In all of her work, one prescribed image of 'Bobby Baker' – neat, tidy, clean, calm, organised, resourceful and self-effacing – clashes with other, more challenging images (see Baldwyn, 1996).

It could of course be argued that the Baker who resists the cultural position of the passive housewife/mother is the performer, Baker, and not the housewife/mother, Baker. However, it is difficult to tell where the persona begins and ends. Confronted by Bobby Baker playing Bobby Baker, I have no idea who Bobby Baker is. It would be more accurate, then, to refer to the identi*ties* constructed in her work, since there is no single, cohesive subject being represented. The contradictions and ambiguities are crucially important devices in undercutting the inhabited stereotypical representations and suggesting the inherent complexity of subjectivity, of 'being' a person. If autobiography enables the production of subjectivity, then Baker uses this strategically to construct a 'self' that is multiple, complex and perhaps ultimately unknowable. As Gerry Harris writes, in relation to *How to Shop*,

> Baker performs a subjectivity which is at the same time not Bobby Baker and not not Bobby Baker, both a hyperbolic, theatrical character and the 'real thing,' an ideological construct and a situated historical object, both entirely socially constructed and unique. (1999, p. 137)

For Harris, this 'doubled' positioning results in a 'hiatus in iterability' – a moment of unintelligibility or unreadability (of both the performance and the performer), producing a moment and space of agency for Baker.

Importantly, whilst we may not be certain who the subject of Baker's autobiography is, the subject of her performances seems clear. What is revealed is not a 'self', but the discursive forces that bring about certain experiences – experiences which include depression, guilt, sadness, repressed anger and the aestheticisation of the quotidian. Sidonie Smith's insight into female autobiographers fits Baker's work well:

> writing her experiential history of the body, the autobiographical subject engages in a process of critical self-consciousness through which she comes to an awareness of the relationship of her specific body to the cultural 'body' and to the body politic. (1993, p. 131)

Baker's supposed acts of self-revelation become, in actuality, acts of social revelation and what is actually presented for analysis is precisely the relation of her 'life' to the culture that inscribes it.

Tim Miller: Rewriting the Future

Like Baker, American performance artist Tim Miller is a seasoned performer, having toured performances internationally for nearly thirty years, developing what has become his trademark autobiographical storytelling mode. In all of his numerous works, Miller has explored the events of his own life, marking their connection with wider social and political factors. Miller's use of 'personal experience' is a deliberately self-conscious, politically expedient use. Working *with* performance and theatricality, like Baker, Miller both explicitly plays his 'self' and plays with his 'self', rendering as problematic any assumed referential status of autobiography. However, Miller continues to place value on the personal experiences that accrue to identity as a means to lay bare, prompt dialogue about, make sense of and hopefully, ultimately, change our contemporary worlds and the lives that can be lived (and told) in them (1991/2, p. 134). His performance storytelling, about the life he has lived and has yet to live, is one means of bringing about that change.

The stories that Miller tells, 'which . . . bring in, in as pointed and direct a way as possible, the experiences I am going through' (ibid., p. 131), focus very much on his location as a gay American, and although Miller does perform his pieces to mixed audiences in various venues (from professional city theatres to college campuses), his address is often primarily to a gay and lesbian 'constituency'. *Glory Box* (1999), for example, is a love story charting a love that refuses to be beaten by homophobic legislation. Focusing on the fact that bi-national couples of the same-sex are denied immigration rights in the USA, Miller uses his own life as the grounds upon which to stage an exploration of the issues. In the process, he exposes the systemic inequality and the attitudes embedded in such inequality – as well as the very real effects that such legislation has on the lives of thousands of gay men and lesbians.[22] Though Miller and his partner have been together since 1994, Alistair, an Australian, faces deportation. If they were heterosexual, their relationship would be recognised and Alistair could legally stay in the country.

Glory Box, like all of Miller's performances, constructs a non-linear narrative as he weaves together various stories, from different periods in his life, in a combination of fact and fantasy, past, present and future. As with all autobiographical productions (literary and performance), Miller is concerned here with a process of creation, in which the self that tells the life-story is as much a product of creative construction as is the life-story itself. Whilst this is a solo show, Miller uses various modes of address, plays multiple roles and *shows* his stories using his dramatic skills. There are moments of enacting events, there are moments of narrating events, there are moments of acting out other characters and staging dialogues. Stories are played with humour, poignancy, urgency, anger, despair, hope, compassion and love. Tensions and emotions mount and are alleviated as the pace shifts. Although difficult – impossible – to

Tim Miller, *Glory Box*. Photo Darrell Taylor

place Miller's live body into this written text, what I am attempting to get across here is the *theatrical* nature of this event, in which Miller works his own body into a sweat as he stages his political appeal.

As in many of Miller's performances, the theatrical devices implicit to performing are shown. Early in the performance Miller metaphorically places all the negative things he has received from his culture into his hope chest, amongst them 'the hundreds of times I was called a sissy or faggot as a kid growing up..., the thousands of signals I received...that told me my relationships with other men aren't worth shit...'. Miller then pulls himself up short, and in a moment of self-irony (as well as self-consciousness), foregrounds the act of construction:

> Oops, I'm getting ahead of myself. I have found, over many years of performing, that you should never put the overbearing political rant in the first 45 seconds of the show. It's much better to wait for at least one good joke and perhaps some cheerful nudity.

Whilst Miller explicitly draws on autobiographical material, he also explicitly marks the gap between the self that is being narrated and the self that is performing, in contrast to Baker who leaves it unremarked, even if self-evident. As Miller enacts his five-year-old self stripping naked and getting into a chest, he draws attention to the unrecoverability of this past and the fact that it 'is actually peopled by a succession of selves as the [performer] grows, develops and changes' (Stanley, 1992, p. 62). Comically he informs us that, 'In case you're wondering, at the age of five my body was much smaller then and I had no pubic hair'. It is in such moments that Miller makes clear that the act of remembering is precisely that, *an act*, which involves considering past events from the location of the present, such that the present provides a perspective from which to give past events particular meanings. In Mark Freeman's words, whilst we tend to think of autobiographical narratives as unfolding so that the beginning leads to the end, in actual fact, 'there is also a sense in which the end leads to the beginning, the outcome in question serving as the organizing principle around which the story is told' (1993, p. 20). For Freeman, the idea that the life-story is starting at the beginning of a life is a 'trick' of autobiography, since the story has actually begun at the end, at the point of writing – or in this case, devising. It is from this 'end' point that one then returns to the so-called beginning. Such 'stories thus move in the opposite direction from linear time' (ibid., p. 96).

In *Glory Box*, however, as in Lynne's story in *Fingerlicks*, there *is* no end, or at least no autobiographical end. Instead, what Miller presents us with is an imagined, fictional end, a theatrical 'what if', where his lover, Alistair, is refused re-entry into the USA. At the end of this fictional story, which has been interwoven throughout the autobiographical material (although in places Miller strategically confuses the status of each), Alistair is *'next in line'* at the airport immigration desk. It has taken him the entire show to get here. The immigration officer asks him whether his visit to the USA is for business or pleasure. Alistair replies that he is a student:

'I'm here for study. I'm here to do an MFA in Creative Writing at Antioch University in Los Angeles.'

The immigration officer suddenly looks down at her computer screen.

It's not a big look, but it's enough for me to know that something bad is about to happen.

And indeed something bad does happen, as the immigration officer informs Alistair that, as they have reason to believe he has 'developed significant ties to certain persons in the US and that you will have no intention of leaving the US', he is being denied entry and will be returned to Australia on the next plane. Miller attempts to intervene, but to no avail. As he holds Alistair close, declaring his love for him, an officious cop tears them apart, dragging Alistair off in a chokehold. Alistair, looking over his shoulder, begs that Miller 'do something! Don't let them send me back!' Miller, in turn, is being dragged out the exit:

> You assholes, he's my lover, my partner, my husband. You can't do this. I'm a fucking American citizen. I have rights! You can't do this.

As Miller and Alistair have just found out, this is precisely what they can – and do – do. The door is shut on Alistair. The immigration officer simply shouts, 'Next'.

It is of vital importance that this narrative thread is placed in the performance as fictional because the actual story has not yet been written. It is yet to be written; and in that sense, this scene can in fact be rewritten. The outcome of this 'real' story – Miller's and Alistair's autobiography – depends on the bringing about of real changes in the legislature. Miller, then, through constructing a 'future-oriented' dimension to his autobiography (Marcus, 1994, p. 293), is willing the audience to provide the ending for the 'real' story. Alistair's plea to Miller, recited by Miller here and now, rings loudly in the auditorium: '*Do something*'. It is the spectators' activity that will determine how Miller's and Alistair's life-stories turn out (in relation to the issue of immigration, at least). This surely puts a different spin on the 'spectator as author' (see Barthes, 1977), for, in this instance, the spectator, through his or her actions (which include non-actions, simply doing nothing) will actually author Miller's autobiographical story.

Miller (1999) has admitted to an enduring belief in the act of writing about a life being a transformation of that life. As in Lynne's story, here past, present and future become complexly intertwined. In Miller's words,

> Writing about my life has always carried the potential for liberation. [...] I have a completely unsubstantiated faith that if I write this story, I may be able to affect how the story will end. I have always used the memories of things passed to rewrite the ending of what is to come.   (Miller, 1999, n.p.)

In giving us this story, Miller hopes that collectively we might be able to rewrite 'the ending of what is to come'. Whilst Miller claims his own agency through writing and performing, in *Glory Box* he also demands an agency from the spectator. If we want a different future to happen (for Miller, Alistair, ourselves and others), then it is up to us to contribute our energies to enabling that transformation. Whilst Miller *could* choose to rewrite the story here and now, providing his own happy theatrical ending, such a rewriting would be literally textual rather than material, and what Miller and Alistair urgently need is a material transformation. For Miller, this is 'the future we're haunted by' (2001c). If so, then an exorcism is called for. Miller's political appeal is not simply to the active spectator. Just as Miller locates himself, through his practice, as an activist or social citizen, his use of multiple theatrical devices, and autobiographical storytelling that draws on the 'real', attempts to *activate* the spectator, transforming them through this process into *activist* spectators. Miller himself acknowledges that it is these activated spectators who are the 'absolutely crucial agents for change' (2000, p. 90).

Joey Hateley: The Endurance of the Personal

Measuring the 'efficacy' of performances that intend a political effect is notoriously difficult, if not impossible. Would success, in Miller's performance, be the number of signatures he collects on his petition at the end? This would be a relatively easy way to 'gauge' the impact of his work. But is this the only possible political outcome? Other responses might be less immediately tangible, such as the decision by spectators to implement Miller's appeal for a 'boycott' of heterosexual marriages until same-sex partners also have the right to marry; or the writing of letters to government officials; or simply refusing to be a complicit agent in or witness to acts of homophobia. How can we possibly predict or track the after-life of a performance, given the multiplicity of possible relations between the event and the spectator? Della Pollock offers us a useful reminder when she writes that 'As much as we may want to determine its effects – whether as a matter of intention or retrospection, it would [...] be counter-productive to do so. Whatever effects performance may have live beyond scientific controls and measures, in the ongoing reckonings of human understanding' (2005, p. 2). Equally, we might be asking too much of performance to equate it with direct political action. Whilst some aspects of autobiographical performance can be considered political gestures (the act of talking out, for example), more often performances are part of wider social movements aiming to influence change, not least through transforming the consciousness of its spectators. Miller's work, for example, contributes to the work carried out by organisations, such as Stonewall, that lobby government for equal rights for gay men and lesbians. As social attitudes change, so legislative changes often follow; equally, sometimes legislative shifts are ahead of cultural ideological shifts, leaving a gap that needs to be closed. Challenging the assumptions or ideological positions of spectators, asking them to reconsider, to think or to think again and think differently – or at the very least to enter into debate and dialogue – is a shared aim of much of the work explored in this book, and a common starting point remains personal experience. A younger generation of performers continues to press the personal into political service, using performance as a consciousness-raising tool. One such performer is Manchester-based Joey Hateley.

Like many of her predecessors, Hateley mixes the factual with the fictional in her one-person show, *A:Gender* (2003), which explores female masculinity (thereby drawing on 'identity' while troubling the very idea of 'identity' from the start). Taking on various personae, juxtaposing the live with the recorded and spoken text with movement text, Hateley's performance makes explicit the impact of discourse on the bodies and lives (the identities) we inhabit. As Professor L. Gooner, Hateley introduces us to the medical discourses that variously construct the 'transgendered' body, including the 'developmental model', 'the psychodynamic model' and the 'biological model', each one proffering to 'explain' the 'transgender case study' and presenting their perspectives as 'facts' or 'truths'. Hateley's revelation of abstract discourse is set beside the material experience of performing a different script to that of 'hetero-normativity'. On video, we see Hateley subjected to scrutiny and abuse in the ladies toilet because she appears to be 'out of place' (see Chapter 3). However, even in these scenes Hateley is presented as a curiosity, an object of study as a documentary voice-over introduces the action:

> And here we have our deviant bathroom user once again entering the female public toilets, making their way swiftly towards a cubical...

A:Gender functions explicitly as a consciousness-raising or educational model; in the guise of 'Gender Joker' Hateley attempts to challenge any preconceptions or cultural assumptions that we might have about gender and sexuality (and their alignment) by instructing us that 'there are over 70 recognised intersex conditions'. I am reminded here of queer theorist Eve Kosofsky Sedgwick's long list of 'identity characteristics' which reveals that, while sexual identity may be assumed to be unitary, it is actually constituted from various and diverse elements, including:

Joey Hateley, *A: Gender*. Photo Jason Lees

your biological (e.g. chromosomal) sex, male or female;

your self-perceived gender assignment, male or female (supposed to be the same as your biological sex);

the preponderance of your traits of personality and appearance, masculine or feminine (supposed to correspond to your sex and gender);

the biological sex of your preferred partner;

the gender assignment of your preferred partner (supposed to be the same as his/her biological sex) [...]

Sedgwick acknowledges that 'what's striking is the number and *differ-ence* of the dimensions that "sexual identity" is supposed to organise into a seamless and univocal whole' (1993, pp. 6–8). It is precisely this assumption of 'unity' that Hateley contests:

> As soon as they see you, even before they begin to talk to you, people need to know. 'WOW! Are you male or female?' [...] It's not as simple as that anyway. I'm not ... people aren't as simple as that.

Having seen *A:Gender* as part of Manchester's *Queer Up North* festival, a question that might be posed (and might well be posed by a lot of the work explored here) is whether it merely preaches to the converted. However, such a question assumes or presumes a unified 'we' in the first place, which is simply not the case (see Román, 1992).[23] The issue/choice of 'transgendered' and 'transsexual' identities remains hotly debated in the lesbian and gay 'community' (as does the issue of 'marriage'). Hateley's performance speaks to a diverse spectatorial constituency as she attempts to find the 'same' in 'difference' (or, more radically, to 'queer' the normative), by inviting audience members who may think they are 'other' to Hateley to recognise moments of identification. On the other hand, spectators who easily identify with Hateley may very well also find themselves 'othered' as the 'normative'.[24] For example, Hateley is careful to draw attention to the differences that race and class make to transgendered experiences/interpretations. The political aim of *A:Gender* is to create a place to be something other than 'other' by insisting on the prevalence of differences across gender, sex, race and class; we are all variously 'others'. Drawing on her own experiences, but using these to stage an exploration of cultural technologies and their relationship to those 'personal' experiences, Hateley continues the work – the agenda – begun nearly forty years earlier. What she and other politically focused young practitioners expose is that we are far from being in a post-feminist era.[25]

2 History: Testimonial Times

Placing autobiographical performance and the performance of history in dialogue, the focus in this chapter is on performances that engage with public 'cataclysmic' historical events. The opening questions of Chapter 1 can be translated here with the same political urgency and framed by feminist and postcolonial discourses. What history is spoken? Who speaks it? With what effect? Equally, which and whose histories are not told – and why not?

Many commentators have proposed the end of the twentieth century and into the beginning of the next as an 'age of testimony' (Felman and Laub, 1992), an age of bearing witness or testifying. This is perhaps best epitomised by the recent spate of Truth and Reconciliation Commissions, such as those staged in South Africa and Australia. Testimonial culture is part of, and arguably related to, a more general 'memory boom' (Winter, 2001) or 'decade of life narratives' (Schaffer and Smith, 2004, p. 2), itself indebted to the transformation of the personal into the political, as discussed in Chapter 1.[1] However, as suggested by the proliferation of testimonies that perform witness to 'cataclysmic public history' (Walker, 2003, p. 110), another context for our testimonial culture is also that of geopolitical upheavals which include wars and genocide and have their related human costs such as displacement, mass-migration and the need for asylum. The persistent presence of crimes against humanity, when set beside the Universal Declaration of Human Rights as adopted by the General Assembly of the United Nations in 1948, arguably positions each of us as 'witnesses', compelling 'an ethical responsibility to testify' (Marcus, 1994, p. 213).[2] Our 'time of testimony' might also be considered inseparable from our 'age of trauma' (Miller and Tougaw, 2002, p. 1), and indeed testimony and trauma are frequently positioned as opposite sides of the same coin, the one being held as the mechanism of 'recovery' – individual and/or cultural – from the other.

Whilst our focus here is on the local stories of more historical grand narratives, there are, of course, many instances of autobiographical performances that we might consider to be less public, but which also might be read from within the frame of 'trauma', where 'performance' equates with 'personal healing'.[3] Bobby Baker, for example, regards art making as a way 'to *respond to life*' and in this vein, she makes 'stories up to *make* sense of the world' (2001b; emphasis mine). Baker's autobiographical performances, then, are a pragmatic response to the actual lived, messy experiences of life: experiences that include, as she tells us in *Box Story*, such non-rationalisable tragedies as a parent drowning when swept out to sea during a family holiday.

Spalding Gray's early performance trilogy, undertaken with The Wooster Group (see Chapter 4), while bearing witness to his mother's mental health and her eventual suicide, is simultaneously a vehicle by which Gray attempts to be reconciled to this traumatic event. Linda Montano's performance and video recording, *Mitchell's Death* (1978), made following her ex-lover's death by a supposedly accidental gunshot, similarly offers itself as a model of reconciliation in the face of loss, 'a powerful instance of the act of mourning' (Phelan, 2001, p. 29). With acupuncture needles inserted into her face, Montano chants an hypnotic autobiographical litany, or mourning ritual, that records her experience of learning of Mitchell's death and her responses to that (see Shank, 1979). Reflecting on the work, Montano acknowledges that it was 'an attempt to make sense of the death, to repeat the death over and over, to concentrate on it using my work . . . . I immediately ran to my art for comfort' (cited in Festa, 2000, p. 11; original in Blumenthal, 1984, p. 20). Repetition, here, carries a double meaning, for there is the repetition of the performance, if it is performed more than once (and many of the works explored in this text are). There is also the repetition that is bound up in planning, devising, rehearsing and making any performance. Suzette Henke suggests that 'It is through the very process of rehearsing and reenacting a drama of mental survival that the trauma narrative effects psychological catharsis' (2000, p. xix). Whilst Henke is here referring to the act of writing, in performance that process of rehearsing and reenacting is of course literal. In Baker's, Gray's and Montano's work, performance might be understood as an act of 'recovery', achieved through the empowering affect of constructing a narrative around the traumatic experience. Indeed, this dominant 'narrative' surrounding narrative recovery is itself made explicit in Montano's comments:

Somehow along the way I heard that, if you verbally repeat things over and over, they diffuse. I knew that the internal combustion would begin to lessen if I talked about it. (op. cit.)

Tami Spry's *Skins: A Daughter's (Re)construction of Cancer* (1994) (Spry, 2003) similarly uses performance as a means to work through the traumatic experience of loss, in this case of her mother, while Linda Park-Fuller's *A Clean Breast of It* (1993) confronts her own experience of having breast cancer, a confrontation that provides 'therapy' through allowing Park-Fuller to take up the position of speaking subject rather than passive object of medical discourse (2003, p. 215). Lynn Miller and Jacqueline Taylor further observe that although Park-Fuller's piece is personally transformative, its public form enables it also to bear witness to others affected by breast cancer and to offer itself as a strategy 'for recovery and reintegration' (Miller *et al.*, 2003, p. 11). Performance as a public act is perhaps its greatest potential in the realm of testimony and witnessing.

Psychoanalysis and Trauma

The West's understanding of trauma has most often been theorised from within a psychoanalytic frame of reference. The primary effect of trauma is understood to be a 'wound' to the sense of self. Trauma 'refers to the self-altering, even self-shattering experience of violence, injury and harm' (Gilmore, 2001, p. 6). During traumatic events, subjectivity becomes annihilated; the subject disappears or becomes transformed into an object – powerless, lacking agency and, in the most brutal of examples, less than human. The status, or more accurately the lack of status, of the 'self' lies at the centre of trauma. Even if we understand the 'self' as a fictional construct (in Lacanian terms, an 'imaginary subject'), most also recognise that it is a fiction necessary to our participation in society. The 'self' is an 'enabling myth' (Henke, 2000, p. xvi).[4] Thus, it is the recovery of this self that enables recovery from trauma. In psychoanalytic therapy, this recovery is linked to speaking about the traumatic experience, an impossible task, in fact, because trauma is precisely an event that cannot be made sense of, and, therefore, cannot be represented (see Van Alphen, 1999). Psychoanalyst Dori Laub summarises that

> [trauma is] an event that has no beginning, no ending, no during and no after. This absence of categories that define it lends it a quality of 'otherness', a salience, a timelessness and a ubiquity that puts it outside the range of associatively linked experiences, outside the range of comprehension and mastery.   (Felman and Laub, 1992, p. 69)

The work of psychoanalysis, then, is precisely to enable comprehension, achieved through the means of narrativisation, a 'therapeutic process' by which history (and the story) will be reconstructed and transmitted, thereby enabling the event to be externalised. Further, the process of narrativisation itself enables a sense of subjective agency, inserting it retrospectively into the event where that very agency was destroyed (Oliver, 2001, p. 93). It is also through constructing a narrative from the fragmented memory of trauma that the traumatic event is given a place within the life-story, and to that extent the trauma becomes 'mastered'. Words provide a 'therapeutic balm' as the 'unconscious language of repetition', manifested in such symptoms as flashbacks, memory loss and re-enactments, is rather 'replaced by a conscious language that can be repeated in structured settings' (Gilmore, 2001, p. 7). In this sense, narrative memory is a performative act that enables the recreation of a 'self' (Brison, 1999, p. 40) and narrative memory needs to be understood as an act of creativity, what Henke (2000) tellingly calls 'scriptotherapy'. The work that narrativising performs is the transformation of the seemingly unrepresentable into the symbolic, thereby giving it a name and a place.[5]

Integral to psychoanalytic practice is the necessity of a 'confirming witness' (Bal *et al.*, 1999, p. x). Laub stresses that 'the testimony to the trauma . . . includes its hearer, who is, so to speak, the blank screen on which the event comes to be inscribed for the first time' (Felman and Laub, 1992, p. 57). Within the psychoanalytic frame the essential second witness is of course the psychoanalyst who must commit to the transferential process, but in a wider context this 'other' witness can be anyone who willingly and fully listens. The testimony, to be testimony, must be addressed to someone, and it is in that address and its hearing that 'the "knowing" of the event is given birth to' (ibid., p. 58). Being witness to the testimony creates a structure of exchange or intersubjectivity that enables the narrative to be constructed. The 'second witness', then, bears something of a 'joint responsibility' to this necessary process of narrativisation (ibid., p. 85). The very presence of the second witness, to whom the testimony is made, confirms for the primary witness their status as subject. Kelly Oliver explains the process: 'To conceive of oneself as a subject is to have the ability to address oneself to another, real or imaginary, actual or potential' (2001, p. 17). As a witness, one has a 'responsibility to response-ability', an ethical duty to 'respond in a way that opens up rather than closes off the possibility of response by others' (ibid.). Central to Oliver's argument is the understanding that, as mutually constituting subjects, we are all equally invested in the dialogic relationship between address-ability and response-ability; the very process of subjectivity itself engenders each of us as necessary witnesses.

The Limits of the Talking-Cure

Whilst I have no desire to underestimate the therapeutic potential and affect of narrativising painful events, psychoanalysis is only one frame of reference and might not always be the most appropriate.[6] Some critics have recently critiqued psychoanalysis' pathologisation and medicalisation of trauma, recognising also that 'one of the hazards of the recovery movement has been a shift from movement politics toward therapeutic culture as the means to a transformation that has become personal rather than social' (Cvetkovich, 2003, p. 31). In this scenario, the personal remains privatised rather than operating within the realm of a public politics.

The palliative attributes of 'talking' about traumatic experience, as promoted within psychoanalytic practice, have extended to other realms including the various Truth and Reconciliation Commissions (TRCs).[7] Though focusing on South Africa, Kay Schaffer and Sidonie Smith's identification of the progressive aspirations of this TRC are more widely applicable:

> Healing and restorative truth emerges out of the production of a collective, consensual narrative of nation through which the new South Africa can remember its past and find its future, a narrative of nation that listens for the voices of the formerly voiceless and disenfranchised.   (2003, p. 66)

Truth and Reconciliation Commissions might be considered 'historiography-as-therapy' (Colvin, 2003, p. 165). The predominant narrative around TRCs displays a definite, progressive trajectory, whereby the process of recounting or narrativising one's experience leads 'us' from a painful past to an enlightened, peaceful and shared future (ibid., p. 159).[8] However, Yvette Hutchison proposes that the 'path' to recovery is less certain. Though the TRC of South Africa provided the forum for individuals to tell their personal stories (and thereby to be confirmed as subjects), the co-opting of these into a state-driven consensus reconstructed multiple stories and perspectives into a single narrative in order to project a new, unified nation (Hutchison, 2005). Various witnesses to the oppressive apartheid regime in South Africa have also made clear that talking does not in fact cure material social conditions. Stephen Colvin, from his interviews with members of the South African Khulumani Victim Support Group, surmises that the therapeutic model, which relates 'story' to 'cure', 'fails to address or have an impact on the structural and historical problem of what group members often refer to as "real change"' (2003, p. 164). More-over, the appeal to tell your painful story from the past implies that there is no pain or suffering now, in the present, which group members argue is a premature assumption.

Where stories are often solicited in order to put the past behind 'us', and move forwards 'together', the Khulumani group retains the narrative form, but deliberately resists the supposedly therapeutic and reconciliatory function of storytelling, desiring its stories to be used instead to forge connections and solidarity between people who suf-fered and *continue to suffer* in South Africa (ibid., p. 165). Sharing something with the feminist work explored in Chapter 1, its stories are told as a way to forge community, to render visible continued and present suffering, to propose freedom as an illusion and to demand material, social change. Colvin understands that the members of the Khulumani group want to put their memories to use in ways that are not only or primarily ' "therapeutic" or reconciliatory' (ibid.). Ann Cvetkovich would recognise this as a 'depathologising' gesture which, like certain performances, engages with 'traumatic feelings not as a medical problem in search of a cure but as felt experiences that can be mobilised in a range of directions, including the construction of cultures and publics' (2003, p. 47). For Cvetkovich, the experience of trauma does not necessarily have to lead to a psychoanalytically inflected remedy, and trauma might, in fact, render other possible, less individualistic, but nevertheless still broadly therapeutic outcomes. Citing theatre specifically, she recognises that it 'displaces the dyadic and hierarchical relationship between doctor and patient' with a 'pub-lic sphere within which audience members, many of whom, like the participants, are more likely to go to the theater than to therapy, can address collective traumas' (ibid., pp. 286, 282). Here again the shared space and time of theatre is stressed.

Though 'theatrical' testimonial performances might very well have some implicit therapeutic benefit for the performer (enabling agency, talking back, forging self-identity, etc.) performances explicitly call forth a witness. Thinking of Roland Barthes' writing on listening, we might consider that performance, particularly performances of testimony, interpolate us as 'listeners', using 'phatic expression' that compels an intersubjective relationship (1986, p. 251). Such intersubjectivity necessarily extends the performance beyond the performer. Jill Dolan also proposes that the very structure of performance, in which people are gathered together, holds a promise of intersubjectivity between spectators (2005, p. 10). The public testimony to traumatic events aims to have some effect within the public sphere (and this might be simultaneously therapeutic and political and social). Where psychoanalysis works to construct a narrative towards individual healing, public performance might be thought to construct other versions of the narrative for other purposes.

Of course, TRCs *are* public events, and as Hutchison has revealed, they do enable the construction of 'cultures and publics':

> Memory and history are important because they are the means by which we contextualise ourselves, both as individuals and nations, in relation to the past, and thereby define the future.   (2005, p. 354)

However, where the TRC of South Africa chose to organise individual testimonies into a consensual history, projecting a singular future South African identity, Hutchison argues that South African theatre, compelled neither by state nor by law, more properly enabled the presentation of 'plural, complex narratives and perspectives' (ibid., p. 360). Referencing a number of plays, including the Khulumani Support Group's *The Story I'm about to Tell*, Hutchison understands that their lack of consensus prompts an ongoing exploration and negotiation of identity (sharing some of the work done by performance explored in Chapter 1).

In considering the potential effect of testimony it is necessary to pay attention to the context in which the testimony is given in order to avoid assuming any singular outcome. The dominant historical and cultural equation that sets confession in relationship to liberation is too often taken for granted. From diverse realms including law, therapy, medicine and even popular media, to talk is to unburden (or cleanse) oneself (of heavy secrets and/or guilt and/or shame) (see Brooks, 2000). However, James Thompson, an applied theatre practitioner who works in war zones, stresses that 'the exhibition or valorization of a story has no automatic connection to the liberation of the teller' (2005, p. 5). The context of talking also refers to the conditions of telling – whether under duress, for example – and to the location of telling – the potential impact of that telling on the sphere that exists beyond the 'self', the 'telling links' (ibid., p. 37). While stories may unburden, they may also contribute to further oppression, with alternative narratives or counter-discourses appropriated for other (often unforeseen) purposes. Since the stories of selves are bound up with the construction of identities, they are not separate from the material world and might exacerbate tensions between peoples, as much as they might contribute towards constructing a hopeful future.

Performing Testimonial History

The focus in this chapter is on public performances that bear witness to specific historically located traumatic events, but traumas that necessarily transcend their 'histories'. These global histories are domesticated and brought home; history is named and here, again, the personal is transformed into the tangibly political. Robbie McCauley's *Sally's Rape* centres on the slavery of black men and women and the systematic rape of black women by white men as part of that institution – a historical event that is largely ignored or forgotten; Lisa Kron's *2.5 Minute Ride* takes as its subject the Holocaust, but tries to retrieve this from its mythical status by rendering it as a much smaller and more fragile human story; while Kim Ima's *The Interlude* bears testimony to the Japanese-American internment camps in America during Second World War, simultaneously bearing testimony to Guantanamo Bay. Taking seriously McCauley's insistence that 'Art is work' (1996, p. 267), and keeping in mind the deliberately public mode of performance, I want to ask what work these public testimonial performances do and how that is achieved. Are these performances intended to be publicly (or individually) curative or restorative? Do they propose historical revision – the telling of forgotten or marginalised or small stories? Do they provide instances of memorialisation, offering elegies to individuals and historical moments? Are they pedagogical, aiming to educate, advocate or warn?

History is dependent upon memory. For Ludmilla Jordanova, 'the writing of history is about the transmission of memory' and 'the practice of history is [. . .] a highly specialised form of commemoration' (2000, p. 138). *Sally's Rape*, *2.5 Minute Ride* and *The Interlude* all practice or perform their own specialised form of commemoration. Though McCauley's, Kron's and Ima's performances deal with very different historical and cultural events in very different ways and to different potential effect, it is nonetheless notable that the performers bear witness not only or even primarily to their own stories, but to those of previous generations. More accurately, they bear witness to the witnesses: *2.5 Minute Ride* bears witness to Kron's father, a Jew exiled from Germany when he was fifteen as part of the Kindertransport project; *The Interlude* bears witness to Ima's father, a Japanese-American who experienced internment as a four-year-old child; while *Sally's Rape* bears witness to McCauley's great-great-grandmother and her experiences of slavery.[9] McCauley, Kron and Ima could all be considered, then, 'secondary witnesses'. More than this, however, and perhaps more than coincidence, these 'agent[s] of transmission' (Hirsch, 2002, p. 88) are all also daughters (in McCauley's case a great-great-granddaughter). To tell these stories, to insist on their place within and as history, may well be a feminist praxis. Risking essentialism, one could also read these daughters' acts as a gendered cultural imperative, that of a duty to care for family. Here, that duty of care is translated into a duty to care for family history, a 'duty to remember' (Ricoeur, 1999a, p. 9). Each of the performers literally *re*produces such a history, transmitting it through their body art.

Within a context in which 'family history' (interpreted as both immediate and wider) was threatened with complete eradication – of the remembering subject and of the personal documents of history – a 'duty of care' towards 'preservation' is perhaps more keenly felt (Bal *et al.*, 1999, p. x). In such an event, 'memory becomes a valuable historical resource' (Cvetkovich, 2003, p. 8). Here, the borders between 'history' and 'personal memory' become porous as 'the present is perforated by the past in this new form of understanding embodied histories' (Case, 2006, p. 106). The appositeness of feminist theatre critic Sue-Ellen Case's metaphors is hauntingly uncanny here: 'The story telling of the grandmothers and their ghostly performances in the passing flesh, displaced the notion of history with that of cultural memory' (ibid., p. 105). One effect of slavery and transportation to the Americas was that Africans, and therefore their descendents, were forcibly separated from their cultural and ancestral heritage. Acknowledging this explicitly, in one version of *Sally's Rape* McCauley tells us that 'My people didn't jump off the slave ships so now I have to bear witness' (Whyte, 1993, p. 287).[10] Moreover, as first-hand witnesses to certain historical events die, the responsibility of bearing witness to the personal experiences of 'history' passes to the second generation, passing through their bodies. In this respect, McCauley's and Kron's reflections on their role as family historians are strikingly similar:

> People in Mississippi who were in my mother's generation are now old people. And they say, 'the libraries are burning down' – that's what they call themselves – 'so you better get it because the libraries are burning down'. Their line is 'come and talk to us, because we're getting out of here.' And part of my work is performing those libraries. (McCauley, in Patraka, 1996, p. 221)

> Somebody once said that when a person dies, it's as if a whole library burns down. I feel that way about my father. He carries experiences of one of the huge events of the twentieth century, as well as the culture of German Jewry. . . . I've always felt that I have to gather this information, that when he's gone I'm going to be the one who has to hold it. (Kron, in Lester, 1997, n.p.)

For McCauley, 'bearing witness to racism, really, that's what I do' (in Patraka, 1996, p. 226), while Kron reflects that 'sometimes I think I became a performer so I could tell this story' (in Carr, 1999).

The oral histories or personal memories that McCauley, Ima and Kron collect and perform should be considered examples of 'subjugated knowledge', those 'local' or 'popular' knowledges previously considered 'illegitimate' or 'disqualified'. Their representation of history draws from felt experiences, an archive accessible to all (Cvetkovich, 2003, p. 37). Memory, we might propose, is one of genealogy's documents, similar to a parchment 'scratched over and recopied many times', entangled with other memories [parchments] (Foucault, 1977b, p. 139). Within a genealogical practice of history which resists notions of teleology, truth or origins, memory might be considered productive rather than invalid and, in the documents of familial memory, genealogy finds a productively 'unstable assemblage of faults, fissures, and heterogeneous layers'. These serve to disturb 'what was previously considered immobile', 'fragment what was thought unified' and to reveal 'the heterogeneity of what was imagined consistent within itself' (ibid., pp. 146–7).

It is to be noted that McCauley consciously applies the term 'witness' to herself, acknowledging her activity of 'choosing to remember' (McCauley in Patraka, 1996, p. 215). This use of the word 'choosing' is important, suggesting as it does a degree of consciousness and agency in relation to re-membering. Whilst memory is a 'kind of knowledge', 'remembering is a way of *doing* things' and is, therefore, an action (Ricoeur, 1999a, p. 5; emphasis in original). McCauley is making the choice to exercise her memory through remembering a version of a distant past that must necessarily be 'grasped through desire [. . .] grasped through reconstruction' (Hall, 1991b, p. 38). However, Paul Ricoeur also reminds us that the flip side to remembering is forgetting. In some instances 'forgetting' may well be an enforced state. Yet, in other cases it may have more productive effects since it leaves room for the invention of plot, of narrative, and such narratives are 'the place where a certain healing of memory may begin' because 'this exercise of memory is here an exercise in *telling otherwise*' (Ricoeur, 1999a, p. 9; emphasis in original). Memory is consciously put to work within specific contexts, aiming for specific effects, including the offering of different histories which allow different analysis of the past and visions of the future (Pollock, 2005). In testimonial public performances memorising is usefully thought of as potential political action rather than involuntary psychological mechanism. As political action, it is chosen. One can equally choose to ignore the past, forgetting its implications in the present.

Just as the (trauma of the) past has its place in the present, the past of memory is always implicated in, and read through, the present; memory, then, as an active mode of '*recherche* rather than recuperation', existing on the fine line between here and there and, for Andreas Huyssen, 'powerfully alive' (1995, p. 13). Operating within a dialectical relationship, memory arises from and is located within culture (or counter-culture), while memorisation serves to produce and sustain that culture. Memory is 'mortal', and 'needs mortal bodies to take it up and carry it in and through time' (Eisner, 2005, p. 104). Collective memory does not simply exist for all time but must rather be continually performed by each new generation and in each new context (Kurasawa, 2004). This necessity for repetition also suggests that collective memory is perpetually open to flux and revision. Richard Kearney recognises that if one's identity is narrative in nature then 'it is more difficult to make the mistake of taking oneself *literally*, of assuming that one's collective identity *goes without saying*' (1999, p. 26). Whilst this saying might shore up already known or assumed histories and identities, it also enables one to say it differently: 'liberating one's historical consciousness by remembering *oneself-as-another*' (ibid., p. 27). Sympathetic to the political urgency of such other-remembering, and admitting the unavoidable creativity of memory's acts, we might also want to bear in mind Ricoeur's insistence on the ethical difference between memory and imagination, real and unreal, particularly in the field of 'historical event'. For Ricoeur, memory sides with perception, whilst imagination sides with fiction, although there are admittedly often crossovers (1999b, p. 15). The difficulty facing testimonial performances, of course, is that they are, unavoidably, creative endeavours and, therefore, are acts of the imagination. Still, these performances aim to produce/maintain cultural memory; perhaps, then, we might think of them as performances that exist precisely and precariously on the intersection between imagination and memory. As Ricoeur goes on to state, 'testimony would be a way of bringing memory and imagination together', with the work of imagination 'to put memories *before our eyes*' (ibid., pp. 15–16):

> How do we make the past visible, as if it were present, while acknowledging our *debt* to the past as it actually happened?   (ibid.; emphasis in original)

Performing Silence: *The Interlude*

Kim Ima, an actor, director and film producer, premiered her show, *The Interlude*, at La Mamas in the East Village, New York, in 2004. Even though Ima bears witness to an event from World War II, the fact that *The Interlude* was first performed in 2004 provides a contemporary context for the piece that cannot be ignored. *The Interlude* works to display a hidden or forgotten history, but does so in order to link that historical event to more contemporary experiences of injustice, specifically the imprisonment of men without trial in Guantanamo Bay. Performing as a 'second-generation' secondary witness (bearing witness to the longevity of traumatic affect), Ima cannot help but enter into the difficult relationship between memory, testimony and 'historical truth', and of how and to what one might bear witness. Keeping Ricoeur's concerns in mind, Ima seems to navigate a path between imagining and refusing to imagine. *The Interlude* also presses me to ask whether an imaginary investment in the past automatically renders that past untrue and, therefore, worthless. Janet Walker notes in her review of experimental feminist autobiographical documentaries that

Kim Ima, *The Interlude*. Photo Greg Pak

'since one response to trauma is non-veridical memory, the grievances of the traumatized cannot be redressed as long as fantasy is held to mean the absence of truth' (2003, p. 116).[11]

Though Ima employs certain 'authenticating' documents, such as black and white photographs of her father as a young boy, she sets these beside an explicit reconstruction of her father's story, a reconstruction that is made evident through the involvement of six other cast members. *The Interlude* is more theatrical in form than most (solo) autobiographical performances, signalling a deliberate and strategic attempt to move away from the authority so often presumed to inhere in solo autobiographical work (since 'author' and 'subject' are presumed to be self-identical). The use of such an explicit theatricality is recognition of the extent to which a life-story is constructed and, in Ima's case, such a reconstruction becomes a necessary act in the face of silence – both personal silence and cultural silence. Della Pollock's rendering of 'liveness' seems to have resonance here. For Pollock, ' "liveness" means articulating the multiple layers of translations and craft that make up (for) memory' (2005, p. 11). Memory, then, is not proffered as some verifiable or empirical 'truth' but is instead used to propose counter-memories and counter-histories, revealing both memory's and history's politics. The use of an ensemble cast also, importantly, serves to make evident that the story being told here is not Ima's father's alone. He is only one of many.

As noted, testimony requires a secondary witness. The availability of such a witness is far from inevitable, but is, rather, dependent both on historical and cultural context, on political will and willingness, and the 'conditions of possibility for hearing' (Ahmed, 2004, p. 34). These, then, are also the conditions of possibility for speaking. It was only in the 1960s, for example, that testimonies relating the experiences of concentration camps were made publicly available, even though primary witnesses to the Holocaust were always there. Survivors' stories were not yet solicited or heard. Within the immediate post-war context, the desired narratives within countries that had been occupied or had collaborated with Nazis were those of heroic resistance. Only once such narratives had helped create post-war political stability was there a cultural climate receptive to other stories (Winter, 2001). Citing writer and Holocaust survivor Elie Wiesel, Hank Greenspan makes this factor of 'timing' painfully transparent:'

> Through the first quarter-century after liberation, survivors were admonished to put the past behind them and to move on. If they were noticed at all, they were noticed, in Wiesel's phrase, as 'sick and needy relatives' – 'misfits, kill-joys, carriers of disease'.   (1998, p. 27)[12]

America's promoted heroic role in World War II would make it extremely difficult to tell post-war counter-narratives and indeed Ima's father and his family rarely spoke about their experiences of internment in US concentration camps. Such a context makes the central thematics of *The Interlude*, 'silence' and 'secrecy', hugely appropriate. Ima writes in the programme notes to the performance that 'When I went to school, it was barely mentioned. Why the silence? Why isn't it more of a presence in our national consciousness?' (Ima, 2004).

Near the start of the performance Ima, representing herself as a young schoolgirl, addresses the audience: 'Can I tell you a secret? Just between us?' She then discloses that she thinks her father is a secret agent for the American government because he says so little. The relationship between the silence that pervades Ima's life and the silence imposed upon her father (first, literally, and later perhaps through mistrust, shame or the fear of not finding an empathetic – responsible – second witness) is made most visible in a scene in which a letter from the camp is read aloud. The 'letter' is in fact composed of a series of gaping holes cut into a sheet of paper – a physical representation of censorship, of things not allowed to be spoken, of enforced secrets or gaps in family and national history that also serves to expose the relationship between those. Here, again, literal genealogical documents have been destroyed by the machinations of powerful state institutions. And yet the gaps in memories and in documentation nevertheless themselves bear testimony precisely to the state's mechanisms of enforced silence and erasure, of the missing parts. Confronted only with such gaps and silence, Ima's visible recuperation of 'his-story' becomes a conscious and deliberate *act* of re-membering – and of speaking history – in the face of refusals to even acknowledge. Yet Ima does not 'unfold' the history of the internment camps via a neat, linear narrative, nor pretend that gaps in knowledge and memory do not exist or can simply be filled with the 'truth' of the past. The history she tells is a history of silence, of fragments, of projecting. Sequences of abstract, synchronised movement refuse to display the whole story and we, the spectator, are helped to empathise with Ima's experiences as we attempt to decode the deliberately un- and under-stated.

Ima's insistence on presenting an unacknowledged historical event, but refusing to assume she can really ever know or fully represent that story, sidesteps the too easily fixed distinctions between true/false (see Walker, 2003, p. 110). Like Rea Tajiri's autobiographical documentary film, *History and Memory* (1991), *The Interlude* 'calls attention to the "unspeakable", here both spoken and shied away from by the elliptical style employed' (ibid., p. 111). Using different types of documents – old and contemporary film and television footage, old and contemporary photographs, letters, inscriptions and photographs from a camp Year Book – fragments of information are juxtaposed and layered, building up a collage that appears not only representative of memory, but also representative of the partial story that Ima has inherited, the clues to be assembled but never fixed in one configuration. While *The Interlude* does bear testimony to the 120,000 Japanese-Americans interned in camps in the USA, it also testifies to the impossibility of ever fully capturing what that was like, as lived reality. Perhaps Ima's father's silence is, then, a wholly appropriate testimony to that impossibility (rather than a symptom of trauma). The structure of the performance, however, bears testimony to the affect of trauma, the incoherency of traumatic experience. As we shall see, in this respect *The Interlude* bears certain similarity to Lisa Kron's *2.5 Minute Ride*, its form also that of a 'traumatized text' (Walker, 2003, p. 111), which in this case both witnesses and testifies to persistent silence. Ima allows that silence to be heard, and therefore to speak, by resisting the urge to talk over it, neither presuming nor assuming her father's speech.

Whilst Ima's father's silence might be a response to the indifference and lack of 'witnesses' ready to solicit and hear his testimony, a number of critics have importantly attempted to resist the fetishisation of 'talking', which comes at the expense of 'keeping silent'. Luisa Passerini, for example, reminds us that, in contrast to the Jewish enterprise of 'remembrance' in relation to the Holocaust, the Roma practice 'an art of forgetting'. This 'forgetting' is not complacent, 'rather, it suggests sometimes buoyant defiance' (2003, p. 242). Passerini insists that 'it takes strength, sometimes, to keep silence' and that on some occasions there are 'silences which are connected with remembering, and not forgetting' (ibid., 2003, p. 248). Offering another perspective on the appeal of silence, this time from within a context of suicide, Louise Woodstock resists the 'cure' proffered by 'talking' where talking is seen to function 'as a necessary step toward forgetting' a traumatic event (2001, p. 25). For Woodstock, it is precisely the forgetting of her dead mother that is feared. To remain silent is to remember: silence is an act of testimony.

Present-ing the Past: *Sally's Rape*

Describing Ima, Kron and McCauley simply as 'secondary witnesses' is somewhat misleading, for the experiences of Kron's and Ima's fathers and of McCauley's great-great-grandmother have an impact on the artists' lives and life histories. The past and the present interact in tangible ways, pointing also to the future. As Sue-Ellen Case has written, 'performances are both portals into an unknown future and kinaesthetic and oral reserves of the past' (2006, p. 106). Ima's performance performs witness not only to her father's experience of the camps, but also to his complete silence about them – a silence that Ima herself felt and by which she was undoubtedly affected. Ima bears testimony to the affect that her father's story has on her as the 'aftermath' of trauma 'lives on in the family' (Miller and Tougaw, 2002, p. 9). Marianne Hirsch describes the inseparability of one generational story from the next as 'postmemory', which can be 'distinguished from memory by generational distance and from history by deep personal connection' (1997, p. 22).

Postmemories are 'traumatic memories that precede one's own life narrative, but which nevertheless define it' (Hirsch, 1999, p. 8). Hirsch further explains that while all memory is mediated, postmemory is somewhat different in that 'its connection to its object or source is

mediated not through recollection but through an imaginative investment and creation' (1997, p. 22). McCauley draws on the experience
of 'postmemory' to determine a line that connects the institution of
slavery, as experienced by her ancestors, with her own contemporary
experiences of being a black woman in the USA, putting 'flesh to
ghosts' (Pollock, 2005, p. 12). Ann Cvetkovich pointedly reminds us
that 'Genocide, slavery, and the many other traumas of "American"
history', though 'buried more deeply in the past' than those traumas
that can be spoken about by first-hand witnesses, nevertheless 'continue to haunt the present, and they take surprising forms, appearing
in the textures of everyday emotional life that don't necessarily seem
traumatic and certainly don't fit the model of PTSD [Post Traumatic
Stress Disorder]' (2003, p. 6). Though not talking about her own
experience of slavery, McCauley is, at the same time, precisely talking
about her own experiences that arise from the history of slavery. The
affect of traumatic historical experience extends also to those 'who
have not stood directly in the path of historical trauma, who do not
share bloodlines with its victims' (Miller and Tougaw, 2002, p. 9; see
also Hirsch, 2002; Schneider, 1997, p. 159).

Sally's Rape was first shown in the East Village's experimental
performance space PS122 in 1989 and is part of McCauley's series
titled *Confessions of a Working Class Black Woman*, which also
includes *Indian Blood, My Father and the Wars* and *Surviving Vir-
ginia* (Patraka, 2000). The specific context for *Sally's Rape* was the
ongoing experience of racism and tensions between races in the USA
that often had disastrous consequences. Despite progressive changes
to civil rights legislation, the last decade of the twentieth century, with
respect to race relations, was perhaps not so different from previous
decades (or indeed the decade that followed). In the year in which
Sally's Rape was premiered, for example, an African-American youth,
Yusef Hawkins, was killed by a group of whites in New York. The
brutal beating, two years later, of Rodney King by four white police
officers seemed to epitomise institutionalised racism. The subsequent
acquittal of the officers, whose actions had been captured on video,
served merely to confirm the depth of racism within American culture, sparking riots in Los Angeles that matched the infamous Watts
riots of 1965.[13] Another event in 1991 that received international
news coverage was the Crown Heights riots in Brooklyn, where racial
tension flared up between the black and Jewish communities of the
area following the death of a young black boy, Gavin Cato, by a
Jewish driver, and the subsequent fatal stabbing of a Jewish student,

Yankel Rosenbaum.[14] Important within such a context is the fact that for *Sally's Rape*, McCauley collaborated with a white actress, Jeannie Hutchins. McCauley explains in her author's note that 'some of the scripted dialogue in this piece came out of my conversations over tea with Jeannie Hutchins. Some of it emerged from improvisations during our performances' (1994, p. 218). Choosing to confront the racial tensions in wider culture, and most particularly the existence of racism, McCauley conducts that exploration within the making and performing of the piece itself.

Taking as its primary subject the story of McCauley's great-great-grandmother, *Sally's Rape* might be considered both a literal and a Foucaultian genealogical practice. In its earlier manifestations, *Sally's Rape* carried a subtitle that made explicit the intention of the piece: *The Whole Story – The Past Becomes the Present in this Portrait of Survival within Today's Plantation Culture* (Schneider, 1997, p. 174). McCauley and many other commentators have noted that the work of *Sally's Rape* is to provide a counter-history to the 'story' of American culture, while making clear the connections between the past and the present in this story (Whyte, 1993; McCauley, 1996, 2001; Patraka, 1996; Thompson, 1996; Nymann, 1999; Young, 2003). For McCauley, 'the survival of black people in the United States is full of war stories, real war stories, not just the official ones' (1997, p. 253). Focusing on the enslavement and rape of her female ancestors, McCauley reverses cultural assumptions and stereotypes about black people, particularly the pervasive myth concerning the 'black male rapist' and the white female victim (Thompson, 1996, p. 134), a myth that continues to resonate in contemporary culture. Challenging the perception of black people as the victimisers, in McCauley's version of history it is the white people who were feared. In *Sally's Rape*, explicit attention is drawn to the 'practice' of history and of history's effects:

> Robbie: In 1964 at the library job a U.S. history major who'd graduated from Smith College said –
> Jeannie: I never knew white men did anything with colored women on plantation.
> Robbie: I said, "It was rape." [. . .] The point is that Smith College, all those colleges, are places that people should go to learn things that help the world. All right? And if she went there and studied U.S. history and came out sounding dumb about what went on during slavery time, I don't understand.
>
> (1994, pp. 225–26)

'History', McCauley has insisted 'is who's telling it. It's political, rhetorical, and personal at once' (cited in Whyte, 1993, p. 282). Her aim is to teach history differently – and to teach different histories, not just histories of black people but black women.

McCauley 'remembers' the rape of her great-great-grandmother not simply, only, or even to provide 'healing'. *Sally's Rape* also develops a genealogy of racism, a colonial discourse dependent on the historical construction of 'black' and 'white' subjects, a history that includes the slavery and systemic rape of African women. As such, *Sally's Rape* provides a useful example of engaging with 'experience' in a non-foundational way (Scott, 1992). Experience here is not held forth as 'evidence', or as referential guarantee. McCauley does not, therefore, fall into the trap of challenging one (presumed empirical) version of history with another (presumed authentic) version. Drawing on 'memories' not her own, she works outside of 'the disciplinary framework of history', thereby opening up 'the possibility of examining [the] assumptions and practices' of orthodox history 'that excluded considerations of difference in the first place' (Scott, 1992, pp. 24–5). Attending to difference as 'constituted relationally', *Sally's Rape* forges connections between the historical event of slavery and the contemporary experience of racial oppression being careful to locate 'black' in its 'historical, cultural and political embedding'. Her practice resonates with Stuart's Hall's insights:

> 'black' has never been just there either. It has always been an unstable identity, psychically, culturally and politically. It, too, is a narrative, a story, a history. Something constructed, spoken, not simply found.   (cited in Scott, 1992, p. 33)[15]

So of course is 'white', although this location and construction is often unremarked. *Sally's Rape* is not about the 'power' or domination of whites over blacks, but about the historical (neo-colonialist) structural conditions that enable and perpetuate that domination.

Tracing her ancestral roots, her bloodline, one branch in her family tree is the result of the rape of her great-great-grandmother Sally by the white 'master'. Robbie McCauley literally carries the body of her raped great-great-grandmother within her. This history of rape is directly and literally her own, present story (Young, 2003, p. 146). McCauley bears and lays bare for us the wounds imprinted by the institution of slavery through which both men and women were turned into commodities, and within which rape was simply another feature of the commodification of the black female body, a body – or object – that by 'right' belonged to its white owner. McCauley's body resembles Foucault's 'body' then, 'imprinted by history and the process of history's destruction of the body' (Foucault, 1977a, p. 148). The history of slavery of African-American women is inseparable from the history of rape (Phelan, 1993, p. 7). The central scene in *Sally's Rape* is McCauley's 'acting out' of the rape of Sally. The 'reverberations' of that act of rape travel from past to present, both literally and figuratively (Young, 2003, p. 146; Schneider, 1997, pp. 155, 174–5). In *Sally's Rape*, then, 'the past is living rather than dead; the past lives in the very wounds that remain open in the present' (Ahmed, 2004, p. 33). McCauley carefully figures that reverberation through a structure of repetition and fragmentation, so that one can almost feel the experience rebounding (see Young, 2003, pp. 147–78).

> In the dream I. I am Sally being (*An involuntary sound of pain*) b'ah. Bein' being' I . . . I being bound down I didn't I didn't wanna be in the dream, bound down in the dream I am I am Sally being done it to I am down on the groundbeing done it to bound down didn't wanna be bound down on the ground. In the dream I am Sally down on the groundbeing done it to. In the dream I am Sally being done it to bound down on the ground. (McCauley, 1994, p. 231)

The grandmother's 'ghostly performance' is fleshed out in McCauley's live performance (see Case, 2006, p. 105). McCauley's dream, as traumatic symptom, returns unwanted and unbidden. The relationship between traumatic event, memory, dream and performance is, however, more than usually complicated here because McCauley's dream concerns an experience belonging to someone else. In the dream it is Sally, not Robbie, who is being raped. The dream, then, is a dream of transference where McCauley becomes Sally. McCauley *is* Sally in the dream, so it is also McCauley that is being raped. The 'trauma' is not so much relived in the dream, but experienced for the first time, through the dream. The 'dream' is, in itself, a traumatic experience – McCauley does not want to be dreaming she is Sally being raped. This acting out of Sally's experience makes clear the cross-generational inheritance of trauma; McCauley is haunted by her great-great-grandmother's experiences. Cathy Caruth explains trauma by suggesting that 'the pathology consists [. . .] solely in the *structure of its experience* or reception', by which she means that 'the traumatic event is not experienced fully at the time, but only belatedly' as the event repeatedly possesses the one who experienced it (1995, p. 4). McCauley's dream of Sally's rape is the staging of this 'belatedness' and 'possession', a belatedness and possession that stretches across four generations.

The term 'acting out', used to describe McCauley's act, is problematic within a therapeutic, psychoanalytic frame where it is pitted against 'working through', the former understood as a symptom of 'melancholia', the latter as evidence of 'mourning'. A melancholic response refuses to let go of the 'lost object', thereby denying any reconciliation with the real event of loss, whereas the work of mourning allows the subject to renounce the ties and accept the situation of loss. Mourning facilitates the acknowledgment and remembering of an event, leading to its transformation; melancholy consists of the unconscious repetition of an act that is not remembered; or more precisely, the repetition of an act 'replace[s] remembering' (Freud, 1953 [1914], p. 151). However, I have chosen the term 'acting out' specifically because the repetition of Sally's rape, as repetition, denies 'closure', although not transformation. Considering McCauley as a 'time traveller' (Case, 2006, p. 106), her aim is to connect the present to the past, and to recognise the affects of trauma inscribed within present experiences of being black in the USA (and not only the USA). It is important that the continuing affect of rape remains preserved within the dream-memory, 'making the experience of trauma present' (Bennett, 2002, p. 339). The repetition of trauma, as Freud notes, 'implies conjuring up a piece of real life' (1953 [1914], p. 151). Maximising the potential of live performance, the memory of trauma is 'confront[ed . . .] within the realm of the senses' (Bennett, 2002, p. 339). Trauma here appears embodied and real (and really felt), thereby enabling history to carry the mark of trauma (ibid., p. 340). The repetition of this trauma keeps an eye on the future as much as on the past. 'Acting out' may not always be pitted in opposition to 'working through' and certain (expressive and performative) forms of 'acting out' might offer alternative modes of response to trauma.[16] However, I would argue that McCauley's 'acting out' of Sally's rape is both a repetition which foregrounds the presentness of the trauma for the spectator, *and* a 'working through'; McCauley's 'acting out' of this scene is a self-conscious representation of the repetition of traumatic history rather than a repetition of the event itself, and it is intended to transform the future.

The 'I' in 'You'

The rape of Sally was not, of course, an exception. Raising into visibility the rape of the millions of other 'Sallys' that reside in the history of slavery, McCauley prompts us to reconsider our assumptions or certainties about our own racial identities. Her statement 'Almost everybody in my mother's family was half white' (1994, p. 220) might be equally true for any number of twentieth-century spectators; as might the corollary – 'almost everybody in my father's/mother's family was half black', although of course the impact of these familial genealogies is not the same. The construction of 'race' depends on the construction and maintenance of otherness, and any concept of 'whiteness' depends upon a construction and then exclusion of 'blackness' (Mullen, 1994, p. 72). If one is either white or not-white, a familial identity of 'whiteness' must constitute itself by denying the 'others' in its history. However, an acknowledgement of the practice of systematic rape, endorsed within the institution of slavery, renders any belief in the 'purity' of racial lineage difficult to sustain (Phelan, 1993, p. 7). For Rebecca Schneider, as for each of us, 'implicit in the visibility of my "whiteness" is a host of invisible bodies – a host of counter-memories that reverberate between us' (1997, p. 159). It is these 'invisible' connections between us that *Sally's Rape* works to reveal. In one scene, McCauley stands naked on a table, as if on a slave auction block, and Jeannie asks the spectators to chant 'Bid 'em in'. Many critics have reflected on how painful this moment is for them: Schneider 'wanted to choke', and 'had to fight to keep the words crawling out of my mouth [. . .] like my own guts turned to stone and spat out' (ibid., p. 174); while Deborah Thompson 'was particularly and personally horrified' (1996, p. 135). As a spectator at *Sally's Rape* during its presentation in the ICA, London (1995) I recognised, like Patraka, that participating in this event meant acknowledging my 'complicity' or 'connection' to it (1996, p. 212), which serves in turn to bring this history closer. Of course, as both McCauley and Schneider make clear, an actual, literal genealogy is not what is at stake here. Rather, the connections are to be found in 'historical' events, 'regardless of bloodlines' (Schneider, 1997, p. 159) and it is those shared histories that continue to supply the blood flow to our still troubled contemporary veins. The 'auction scene' might be thought to stage what Jill Bennett calls 'the sense memory of grief', which 'touches the onlooker who understands at a certain point the implications of his/her presence at the scene' (2002, p. 348). In such moments the spectator experiences an 'affective "prick"' which accompanies 'the realization "I am in this scene," it affects me, I am a witness' (ibid.). In *Sally's Rape*, however, one is not only implicated because one is called upon to be a witness, rather the 'prick' is also a realisation that one is bearing witness to one's own historical past. Sara Ahmed's reflections, offered in the context of Australia's 'stolen children', have some resonance here: 'Knowing that I am part of this history makes me feel a certain way; it impresses upon me, and creates an impression. [. . .] I cannot learn this history – which means unlearning the forgetting of this history – and remain the same' (2004, p. 36).[17]

There are, however, other possible relationships with this historical event. *Sally's Rape* played to diverse audiences across the States. Where Schneider and Thompson felt choked or horrified, at the Crossroads Theatre in New Jersey the mostly black audience enacted the auction block ritual 'with relish. They knew what playing an auctioneer meant' (McCauley in Patraka, 1996, p. 233). For such spectators, and for McCauley, the role-playing perhaps allowed a direct confrontation with a painful past whilst simultaneously robbing this past of its power through communal appropriation of it and the playing of the role within the safe space of theatre. McCauley is 'not on exhibition' but is 'doing it as part of a ritual' (ibid., p. 213), and ritual, if successful, enables transformation. For McCauley, 'To face the oppressive elements, to understand and move through them *is* change. It's where an artist is useful because the audience can share that kind of release' (ibid., p. 206).

The Limits of Memory

As we have noted, Kim Ima's intention with *The Interlude* is not only to acknowledge the silence surrounding a particular historical event, it is also to prompt talk around contemporary events. Ima includes in her performance a powerful propagandist documentary film made during World War II, which justifies the internment of Japanese-Americans. She follows this with contemporary footage relating to concerns around 'national security' and the potential threat of 'Arab Americans'. In her programme note she urges us to 'remember the past in order to keep the legacy as an active tool for the present'. *The Interlude*, recalling historical events and their resemblance to the contemporary situation, aims to construct a public that will not remain silent in the face of racial injustice (as it did previously), but will rather speak out against it. Ima's reconstructed memory becomes 'a site of resistance' (Apel, 2002, p. 58). In this respect, *The Interlude* employs past history for moral purpose or, in the words of Roger Simon, strategically constructs a 'moralizing pedagogy' drawing on a discourse which ascribes 'learning' to remembering (Simon, 2000, p. 3; cited in Apel, 2002, p. 5). We learn from past actions, our own or others. Though *The Interlude* refuses to fix Ima's father's story by filling in the gaps, it does, nevertheless, at least in its stated intentions, offer itself as a potential 'cure' for the ills of the present by interpolating the spectators as 'agents for the future' (Apel, 2002, p. 57).

'Never again' has become the 'sublime command of this early twenty first-century' while 'the guarantee against repetition is held to be remembrance' (Huyssen, 2003b, p. 18). Understandable though this strategy is, it might also be considered problematic given that it assumes the 'past' can be read unequivocally, and that such a reading can then be transferred to another context, the future (see Jordanova, 2000, p. 167). Such strategic remembrance erases the historical specificities, subsuming or collapsing the past into the present. Equally, what is the mechanism for learning from the past? How does that transference take place? The transparent problem with the phrase 'never again', of course, is that since it was first issued atrocities have happened over and over again. Though we might indeed 'remember', memory, nevertheless, appears dramatically to fail us. As Huyssen bluntly puts it, 'unspeakable repetitions occur all the time. [. . .] Remember Rwanda. What good was memory here?' (2003b, p. 18). Rather than seeing memory as a tool against repetition, Huyssen reads the command 'to remember' as a 'veil covering ongoing atrocities in our present world':

> We have to face the hard question: to what extent are the public memory rituals of our culture at the same time strategies for forgetting?   (ibid., p. 19)

We erect monuments as evidence of our remembering, but such monuments, in their continual physical presence, suggest that we no longer personally have to take responsibility for consciously or actively remembering. This, of course, begs the question of whether performance, an ephemeral and impermanent act, functions as a monument. In these testimonial performances, the performer must consciously, actively and literally remember, again and again, in order to perform and repeat the testimony so as to make it momentarily present. And in attending a performance, a spectator has usually made an active choice *to* attend it. The spectator of theatre necessarily notices it – or takes note (rather than simply walking by an unnoticed monument). Equally, after the event, the only way that the spectator can access the performance is through exercising his/her own memory of it although he/she must first make the choice *to* remember, must take responsibility *for* remembering. Perhaps, then, it is precisely the ephemeral nature of performance that proposes it to be an appropriate and alternative mode of memorialising since to be realised it requires the active agent, or embodied agency, of both performer and spectator. Equally, the impermanence of performance – in distinction, say, from a built and concrete monument – allows it to be rewritten, or performed differently, always open then to a shift in the narrative, to the possibility of other voices telling other stories.

The relationship between memory and historical events is configured somewhat differently in *Sally's Rape*. The performance strategically avoids setting up an equation between 'telling the story' and 'providing the cure' through the use of a particular dramaturgical structure that refuses to allow McCauley's testimony to lead towards closure. Contrary to her own subtitle, the theatrical form that McCauley devises ensures that she deliberately resists offering, or assuming, the 'Whole Story' – a teleology of beginning, middle and end: in this *Sally's Rape* is similar to *The Interlude*. Though Harvey Young has suggested that McCauley 'locates the misplaced and mislaid body of black history, listens to its story, channels it through her, and then prepares to properly memorialize it' (2003, p. 151), his reference to channelling and memorialising might suggest that McCauley's performance enacts a cathartic exorcism. However, McCauley insists that her work is rather the catalyst for a beginning, providing an 'opening for movement' and creating 'the groundwork for dialogue'. Confronting cultural and historical taboos, including the admission of shame and guilt, for example, or in McCauley's words, 'speaking the unspeakable', the work of her performances is to get each of us to share our own stories in response to hers (see Patraka, 1996). This belief in the necessity of dialogue in order to move forward is reflected in the structure of the performance in a number of ways. First, throughout the performance, McCauley and Hutchins themselves stage dialogue around experiences relating to race, including the experience of engaging in open, and often difficult, dialogue. Most crucially, this dialogue is improvised in performance and its outcome is not known in advance. In the version of the performance published in *Moon Marked and Touched By Sun* (1994), for example, Jeannie admits that what upsets her is the underlying assumption that Robbie is going to 'unmask' her: 'That you're gonna get underneath something and pull it out. That you can see it and I can't' (McCauley, 1994, p. 228).

The spectators are also directly included within the dialogic structure as they are asked to contribute to the performance by offering scripted exchanges at key moments. McCauley and Hutchins mark this interaction as belonging to some communal ritual structure by allocating parts to the spectators at the same time that they distribute food. Establishing *Sally's Rape* as a ritual means that the spectators are active participants, rather than merely passive observers. Whilst McCauley might claim the status of witness for herself, she also insists that 'what's important about the witnessing is that the audience is doing it with me' (in Patraka, 1996, p. 215). The cast-list of players in the published script even includes 'AUDIENCE, those who are there, who witness and talk back' (McCauley, 1994, p. 218).

The participative element of the performance continues to the 'end' of the piece which, matching McCauley's perceptions that the work is in fact an 'opening', sets the stage for the beginning of dialogue *between* the spectators. Mirroring the praxis of McCauley and Hutchins, the Epilogue, entitled, 'Leaving the Audience Talking', provides the opening for the actual work that the performance hopes to have prompted. Before walking off stage, the audience is instructed to 'turn to somebody else and find out something' (ibid., p. 237).

McCauley recognises that speaking about the difficult issues circulating around race relations is itself a useful act (ibid., p. 213). Resisting closure, *Sally's Rape* also, however, resists presuming that dialogue will simply result in the overcoming of differences. The 'effective history' that McCauley performs for us is not that of 'reconciliation to all the displacements of the past', not a 'completed' or 'continuous' development' (Foucault, 1977b, pp. 152–3). McCauley is not, then, 'talking about "we shall all hug and overcome everything" ' (McCauley, 1994, p. 214). Nor is dialogue proffered as 'cure'. Becky Becker makes the point that examining differences might, in fact, result in 'misunderstandings' (2000, p. 523), although she recognises, after Peggy Phelan, that such misunderstandings could themselves be considered 'generative and hopeful', providing 'opportunities for conversation' (Phelan, 1993, p. 174). Admitting this, it is also apparent that critics, desiring (and hoping for) the utopian potential of live performance (see Dolan, 2001), refuse to consider the spectators' total failure to stage dialogue. The 'potential' realised by such a failure is harder to propose. I remember that in London's ICA, the conversation never really began as we (polite) spectators sat awkwardly next to each other, hesitating to even make eye contact. Any potential effect of autobiographical performance can change dramatically from night to night and cannot be presumed in advance.

Resisting the Archive: *2.5 Minute Ride*

In contrast to *Sally's Rape* and *The Interlude*, both of which were first presented in East Village venues in New York City, *2.5 Minute Ride* premiered at La Jolla Playhouse, University of California in San Diego, in 1996. Nevertheless, Kron, an experienced solo performer as well as member of the collective, The Five Lesbian Brothers, often performs in downtown New York spaces. At the time of writing, Kron continues to tour *2.5 Minute Ride*. Where the context of *Sally's Rape* was the continuing experience of racism in the USA, the context for *2.5 Minute Ride* was/is partly that of 'testimonial culture' and of how to give testimony within such a culture. *2.5 Minute Ride* also shares some of the same challenges and strategies as Kim Ima's *The Interlude*, testifying to the difficulty of being a secondary witness, and of recounting the life-story of another. However, where Ima's difficulty revolved around acknowledging a history that had been hidden and shrouded in cultural and personal silence and secrecy, Kron's difficulty resides in telling a story about her father, exiled from Germany during World War II, in a culture that appears to be already saturated with similar stories. Moreover, the greater the temporal distance from the event, the more interest there appears to be (Apel, 2002, p. 9).

The Fortunoff Archive is a notable illustration of the proliferation of Holocaust testimonies experienced in recent years. Begun in 1979 as a local grassroots venture called the Holocaust Survivors Film Project, the now international Fortunoff Archive has amassed over 10,000 recorded hours of videotape. The Fortunoff is not alone in its endeavours either. Following the filming of *Schindler's List* (1993), director Steven Speilberg founded the Survivors of the Shoah Visual History Foundation, which collected nearly 52,000 testimonies over six years.[18] Holocaust museums have been established internationally, located in places as diverse as South Africa, Canada and Croatia, not to mention the numerous museums in America and Germany.[19] Published memoirs and diaries of the Holocaust, which first appeared in the 1960s, also show no signs of losing their public appeal. Apel records that in 1995 alone more than a hundred books dealing with the Holocaust were published in the USA (2002, p. 16). Second-generation testimonies also take their place in this testimonial literature, including the well-known *Maus* (1986) by Art Spiegelman (and it is perhaps not incidental that this is one of Kron's 'favorite pieces of Holocaust literature' [Carr, 1999]). The production of films engaging with the subject matter of the Holocaust has continued following Spielberg's Hollywood blockbuster and includes *Life is Beautiful* (dir. Benigni, 1997/8), *The Last Days* (dir. James Moll, 1998), *Jakob the Liar* (dir. Kassovitz, 1999), *Conspiracy* (dir. Pierson, 2001) and *The Pianist* (dir. Polanski, 2002). Over the same period a new discipline, what we might call 'Holocaust Studies', has also become firmly established. Centres for Holocaust and Genocide Studies exist at various institutions, including the University of Minnesota and the University of Vermont. Critical texts, prompted by and responding to the sheer mass of cultural productions available, have also flourished. Exemplary are *Holocaust Testimonies: The Ruins of Memory* (Langer, 1991) and *The Texture of Memory: Holocaust Memorials and Meaning* (Young, 1994). 'Dedicated' journals have also been launched, including *Holocaust and Genocide Studies* and *History and Memory*. More recent explorations of Holocaust testimonies, such as Dora Apel's *Memory Effects: The Holocaust and the Art of Secondary Witnessing* (Apel, 2002), tend to be inflected by contemporary critical concerns, including the relationship between trauma, representation and personal and cultural memory.

While one would not argue for 'silence' in the face of historical atrocities, 'the Holocaust', which Ludmilla Jordanova refers to as 'a reification if ever there was one' (2000, p. 139), has become, through the sheer scale of its cultural representation and circulation, the paradigmatic example of cataclysmic or traumatic event (Miller and Tougaw, 2002, p. 3). Contradicting the sense that the atrocities perpetuated by the Nazis remain 'unrepresentable', testimonies of Holocaust experiences are now packaged for mass consumption, as the huge popularity of *Schindler's List*, *Life is Beautiful* and *The Pianist* testify, a situation captured in the well-known bleakly comic quip, 'There's no business like *Shoah* business'. Claude Lanzmann, challenging the relationship of 'talking' to 'healing' in a way that resonates with Andreas Huyssen's insights regarding memorials, suggests instead that 'To talk too much about the Holocaust is a way of being silent, and a bad way of being silent' (1995, p. 208). Arguably, the glut of iconic images relating to or representing the Holocaust endangers a desensitisation to the reality of the events; the impact of such saturation is an inability to really listen or to fail in our role as the witnesses of witnesses.

Lisa Kron is acutely aware of the context in which she performs *2.5 Minute Ride*. As she writes in the preface to the published script of the performance,

> It seems to me that in this age of Holocaust museums and memorials we have developed a way of responding to this most horrible of tragedies that, in fact, prevents us from ever approaching its horrors. We come to it with a prescribed attitude of reverence and awe. We know the outcome. (2001, p. xiii)

Like Lanzmann, Kron recognises that sometimes talk is in fact silence because 'when you do a show about the Holocaust, the audience just doesn't hear what you're saying' (Carr, 1999). One consequence of our 'culture of testimony' is that testimonial acts become ritualised; 'we surround survivors' speech with so much hype, so much ceremonial and rhetorical fencing, that we are almost able to seal it off completely' (Greenspan, 1998, p. 29). In a key scene of *2.5 Minute Ride*, Kron directly addresses this mass production and consumption of what are by now iconic Holocaust images. Recounting her experiences of visiting Auschwitz with her father she suddenly stops and confronts the audience as if no longer 'in character':

> I don't know why I'm telling you this. You already know what this looks like right? You've seen these images before. You don't need me to describe this to you. . . . Even if you've never been there you've seen these images before, right? In the movies – *Sophie's Choice* . . . *Schindler's List!* Is there anyone sitting here right now who *didn't* see *Schindler's List? (Scans the audience for takers.)* Really. Really. And you know what? That's exactly what it looks like when you go there. That movie was really well done. That's exactly what it looks like. If you missed the movies you've seen it on TV, right? On public television or the movie channels. Sometimes I feel like they show these images every fifteen minutes or something. You know the ones I'm talking about, the films from the liberation of the camps with the bulldozers and the bodies. Right? You all know what this looks like. I feel like a cliché. (Kron, 2001, pp. 26–7)

The 'Holocaust' as a signifier has become a simulacra, with *Schindler's List* acting as the 'real' (or original) ground for comparison.

Kron's challenge, as recognised by Cathy Caruth, is that she needs to find a strategy of 'listening and responding to traumatic stories . . . that does not lose their impact, that does not reduce them to clichés or turn them all into versions of the same story' (Caruth, 1995, p. vii). While Kron refers to herself as a cliché in the pivotal scene cited above, 2.5 Minute Ride tactically refuses to enter into the proliferation, repetition and circulation of this image bank, this 'hypperrepresentation of the Holocaust' (Cvetkovich, 2003, p. 23). Bucking what might be considered a trend in autobiographical performance (as seen in Ima's The Interlude), Kron does not employ authenticating images. Though using the structural device of a slide show, Kron projects empty space. The very first scene of the performance opens with the sound of a slide projector clicking but we are confronted only with a square of coloured light. Kron then describes for us the absent image:

These are my grandparents. My father's parents. This, as you can see, is their wedding picture.   (2001, p. 5)

Kron's assumption that we can 'see' what is visibly not there thematically places seeing and recognition – or the difficulty of these acts – at the heart of 2.5 Minute Ride, in contrast to Ima's focus on silence. Throughout 2.5 Minute Ride Kron's father's particular disability is foregrounded. He has only peripheral vision: 'All of a sudden the middle was gone. Only the edges remained' (ibid., p. 19).

Kron's decision not to use photographs stands out in a context in which the photograph has become an almost fetishised authenticating tool of the past. Lawrence Langer captures the ambiguity of the photographs of family members killed during the Holocaust when he asks whether the point of such photographs is 'to remind us that [those photographed] once were or no longer are alive. Is it an effort at rescue or an avowal of loss? Are we gazing at presence – or absence?' (1991, pp. 59–60). As we have seen, Kron herself is only too aware of the archival image-bank that already exists in our minds in relation to the repeatedly circulated images of the Holocaust. Seeing more slides of the Holocaust does not necessarily make that event any more real.

Kron's use of the empty slide frame in 2.5 Minute Ride might also literally signify that there are no photographs in existence, that neither Kron nor her father possesses such physically solid mementos.

Kron's next statement about her grandparents is that she 'never knew them, actually'. Marianne Hirsch reads photographs as 'stubborn survivors of death', and as 'precisely the medium connecting first- and second-generation remembrance, memory and post-memory' (1999, p. 10). The photograph, though documenting a past, is nevertheless in its materiality an object of the present and exists in the present. As 'instruments of memory . . . they expose its resolute but multi-layered presentness' (ibid.). But what if there are no photographs, what if that ' "umbilical" connection to life' (Hirsch, 1997, p. 23) has been cut? If photographs 'affirm the past's existence' (Hirsch, 1999, p. 10) what happens to that past when no photographs remain to bear testimony to its 'having-been there'? Arguably, the lack of photographs indicates not a present absence, but more simply absence. One response to this is to project creatively into the empty space, to construct mementos that are able to testify to and validate a specific past, specific people, which is perhaps what we witness Kron doing as she describes the 'missing' photograph to us. Is such a projection any greater than the projection we routinely apply in our engagements with photographs, as we look back across time and place?

The 'blank screen' constructed by the not-present photograph is also a blank screen for the spectator, and the square of light might well be Tim Miller's 'window' for the audience (Miller, 1991/2, p. 140). Kron insists that, although her work is autobiographical, her aim is always that it transcends the narrowly personal, and, therefore, has wider significance. In particular, she writes of *2.5 Minute Ride* that her intention for the stories is that 'they serve as a template, a framework into which audiences project their own relationships and experiences' (Kron, 2001, p. 3). In the space of the blank slide the audience have no option but to project their own image of Kron's grandparents on their wedding day. The blank slides, then, demand an inter-subjective relationship, between the spectator and the subjects of Kron's performance. For Kron, it is this relationship between the stage world and the viewer's imagination that generates the dynamism of the performance (ibid.). Refusing to present the actual images of her grandparents, they become more representative and less specific; this could have been your grandparents. This is not to deny the danger implicit to such a tactic. While withholding actual images of her grandparents prompts identification, and perhaps reduces the possibility of passive consumption or appropriation, identification via projection might equally be so complete as to erase totally Kron's grandparents' story, generating 'an overap-propriative identification that makes the distances disappear, creating too available, too easy an access to this particular past' (Hirsch, 1999, p. 10). Kron limits this danger, however, by keeping the specifics of time and place in the spectator's mind's eye. In the second 'slide', she describes her father's home town. While the lack of photograph perhaps enables it to be any town, the provision of details simulta-neously anchors it to one specific town. The spectator seems then, to exist in two places at once, and this is perhaps an example of what Kaja Silverman and Marianne Hirsch call 'heteropathic mem-ory', 'the ability to say, "It could have been me it was me, also" and, *at the same time*, "but it was not me"' (ibid., p. 9; emphasis in original).

Producing Affect

Aware that photographs, memoirs, testimonies, documentaries and museums of the Holocaust do not render the reality, the lived experi-ence of the Holocaust, in the introduction to the published script of *2.5 Minute Ride* Kron admits that she 'wanted to create a primary experience rather than a reflection of past experiences' (2001, p. xiv). Considering her father's history she became 'fascinated with [. . .] the difference between the stories describing the events of the Holo-caust, and what it must have been like to actually experience those events' (ibid., p. xiii). While verbal or textual language is always an inadequate substitute for lived experience, we need to remember that theatre is always more than verbal. For Kron (2004), the potential of theatre is that it enables the audience to have an embodied expe-rience, rather than just be told about an event, and Kron devises a dramaturgical structure that allows for just such a primary experience (see Cvetkovich, 2003). The performance rapidly and unexpectedly switches between three different narrative tracks: the visit that Kron and her father took to his home town and to Auschwitz; the annual pil-grimage that the Kron family make to a theme park, Cedar Point; and, her brother's wedding to his Jewish bride. Switching tracks repeatedly means switching not only narrative line and context, but also emo-tional atmosphere, an experience equivalent, perhaps, to feeling our hearts in our mouths as the roller coaster descends at rapid speed. One of many examples of such a switch is the movement from Kron's father recalling the literally chilling moment when he realised that his own parents were actually dead (a recollection performed by Kron), to the warning signs erected at the entrance to one of the roller coaster rides (which Kron humorously narrates for us):

> 'I don't think I accepted it until a few years ago, in Lansing. It was the winter and it was so cold and I was shivering. In my coat. And I realized this would happen to them once. They were old and they stood outside, lined up in the cold and they were of no use to anyone and they were killed.' (*Cross to center.*)

> At the entrance to the Magnum there are signs all over which say under no circumstances is this ride suitable for people who are elderly, diabetic or have heart conditions. I look at my father. He can't read the signs because, in addition to having all the conditions listed, he is also legally blind.   (2001, p. 7)

The journey that *2.5 Minute Ride* takes the audience on symbolically mirrors the emotional complexity and turmoil that Kron and her father experienced during their trip to Poland, both in relation to each other (irritation, protectiveness, comfort, sadness, love . . .) and in relation to the experience itself (horror, humour, boredom, hunger, fear, loss . . .).

In addition to the emotional and psychical affect of the performance structure, the unexpected switches also serve to jolt us from the already- or over-familiar Holocaust testimony, crossing the sentimental with the irreverent, and the serious with the comic. For example, a group of Israelis visiting Auschwitz, carrying huge Israeli flags, are in one moment 'a reminder that the world of Auschwitz is no more' and in the next moment are simply annoying: 'I'm just irritated all day with these irritating Israelis. If I get shoved one more time . . . ' (ibid., p. 23).

In the context of the pervasive mediation of representations of the 'Holocaust', witnessing seems always in danger of being far removed from the complexity of lived, embodied life, a life in which her father is both a Holocaust survivor and her father. Every time Kron tries to tell her father's stories she hears 'the myth and the awe creep into' her voice, 'and that makes me feel sick because I don't know what that has to do with him?' (ibid., p. 28). The 'mythologisation' of the Holocaust swallows up her real father and her experience of him as her father rather than as some mythical, iconic survivor. Talking us through 'slides' of her father, Kron switches from the scene of Auschwitz, to her father's everyday world of dinners and supermarkets, and from this material register to one of the imagination or psyche, where we learn that the performance might be her own memorial to her father, but also testimony to the performance's failure (and hers) to really 'capture' him and her own genealogy:

> This is a picture of my dad getting his insulin shot. *(The slide changes.)* This is a picture of me not being able to hold his world in my head. *(The slide changes.)* This is a picture of my father's funeral – which is odd because my father's still alive. *(The slide changes.)* This is a picture of my hands. And here you can see I'm holding my grandfather and my grandmother and his students from the Jewish school and the chairs they sat in and the streets that they walked on and the way they held a pen and [. . .] and all these things have slipped through my fingers because *I couldn't remember any of it.*   (ibid., p. 29)

Kron attempts to capture the everyday, the mundane, the details and the idiosyncrasies that keep people real, such minutiae exceeding the historical symbols that are imbued with mythical stature. Before her grandparents were deported to the Ghetto and then to their deaths, they had lives, everyday lives. It is these quotidian details that make them proper subjects. Living subjects. Painfully, Kron acknowledges that such details 'must have slipped through my fingers because *I couldn't remember any of it'*. Of course, Kron could never hold such details because she never knew them in the first place. If she did, they were passed down to her by her father. And if you cannot remember something, does it cease to exist? If, as Paul Ricoeur insists, we each have a duty to remember, does forgetting inevitably make us feel guilty? And yet, we can only ever fail in this duty, because memory always and inevitably fails us. Kron cannot hope to hold the details of anyone's life in her hands, not her father's, not her grandparents, not even her own, because no 'record' of a life can fully represent its depth and multiplicity.[20] What she (and we) can do, though, is imagine, and through this deliberate act of creativity, we each of us takes responsibility for filling in those empty squares of light – and doing so responsibly. Though Kron interrogates the practice, efficacy and even ethics of archiving and of testimony, bringing into focus the representational inadequacies of performance, *2.5 Minute Ride* nevertheless reveals performance's potential to still move us, and to move us into the realm of others (while still remaining ourselves). This capacity of the emotional should not be underestimated:

> What moves us, what makes us feel, is also that which holds us in place, or gives us a dwelling place. Hence movement does not cut the body off from the 'where' of its inhabitance, but connects bodies to other bodies: attachment takes place through movement, through being moved by the proximity of others.   (Ahmed, 2004, p. 11)

In all three performances discussed here, testimony is intended as a prompt to movement; though the head turns to look back at the past, the feet stay resolutely pointing forwards, waiting for the heart to lead us towards other possible futures.

3 Place: The Place of Self

In Chapters 1 and 2 we have been variously concerned with autobiographical performance practices which take a self as the foundation for story-telling and which, simultaneously, render that self less than stable. Learning from the experiences of the second-wave feminist movement, the 'authority' that accrues to the self – and to some selves more than others – is powerful. In this chapter, the negotiation between authority and authoring applies to place as much as self. As we shall see, the politics of place are as complex as the politics of identity and the two are, in fact, related.

The experience of living is rendered not only in temporal metaphors, but also, frequently, in spatial terms. Indeed, it becomes difficult to describe life without bringing space into the picture. We talk of 'mapping a life' and 'patterns of experience', of life as an 'odyssey' or 'journey' or 'path' or 'course', marked by trajectories, up-hill struggles, things going downhill, taking wrong turns, turns for the worse and arriving at dead ends; we change direction, lose our way and find ourselves.[1] Sidonie Smith's analysis of traditional written autobiographies discovers that they move in two directions, expanding horizontally (taking the self along for the ride) or delving vertically (to find the hidden self at the centre) (1993a, p. 18). We might think of autobiography as cartography of self.

Our interest in this chapter is not only with the spatial metaphors that accompany lived experience, but also with an actual literal focus on space because, obvious though it may be, lives do actually and necessarily take place; they happen somewhere. In this instance, to be 'located' means not only to be embodied as a gendered, sexed and raced subject, but also to be embodied in and through specific spaces (though these play no small part in gendering, sexing and racing bodies). In the words of Edward S. Casey, 'just as we are always with a body, so, being bodily, we are always within a place as well' (1997, p. 214). We might also reverse this insight; just as bodies are in place, places are bodied. And some bodies are out of place, just as some places appear to be without certain bodies. As Yi-Fu Tuan writes, 'Body implicates space; space coexists with the sentient body' (1974, p. 215).[2] The performances explored here set place and identity in relation to each other. For *Bubbling Tom* (2000) Mike Pearson returns to his childhood home of Hibaldstow, Lincolnshire, and performs a guided tour, with his 'mam' as one of his witnesses. Phil Smith's *The Crab Walks* (2004) similarly returns to a place of childhood, of happy summer holidays on the beaches of Devon. Pearson and Smith make space personal. Bobby Baker's *Kitchen Show* (1991) meanwhile, takes us inside, but renders the seemingly private public. After hospitably welcoming the spectators to her own kitchen, she proceeds to share her coping mechanisms for 'surviving' in the domestic sphere. Curious' *On the Scent* (2003) similarly publicises the private by allowing us into stranger's homes in order to tell us different stories of home, using the powerful mnemonic of smell to transport us – perfume, frying meat, cigarette smoke, whisky, medicine. Where Pearson and Smith court the nostalgia of their pasts, notably Baker and Curious proffer a different kind of home-sickness. My broad interest in all of these performances is in the interrelation of place and identity that they perform, in the sorts or types of places configured in them and the identities enabled through them. All foreground the place of lives but these 'places' are ultimately no more grounded than lives are fixed. The autobiographical slant of each performance allows us to consider not only the way they map or spatialise lives, then, but also how that mapping simultaneously renders place.

Autotopography: Autobiography and Place

The significance given to place in all of the works discussed here is best registered by the descriptive term 'site-specific', which gained currency in the UK in the mid- to late 1980s (Wilkie, 2002, p. 141). The category, though serving in this context to underline the importance of place, is nevertheless problematic. Debate continues as to what 'site-specific' might properly encompass or exclude (see Wilkie,

2002; Pearson and Shanks, 2001). Mike Pearson and Michael Shanks have offered an almost 'purist' definition, proposing that 'site-specific performances are conceived for, mounted within and conditioned by the particulars of found space, existing social situations or locations, both used and disused' (2001, p. 23). Site-specific performances within this frame are deemed 'inseparable from their sites, the only contexts within which they are intelligible' (ibid.): Pearson's own *Bubbling Tom* fulfils this criterion. Other performances, though, such as *The Crab Walks*, made for particular sites (a beach hut), do not make significant reference to the actual sites of the performance. In fact *The Crab Walks* was performed in two different beach huts in Devon; while Baker's *The Kitchen Show*, which does make reference to her actual kitchen, was subsequently relocated for the Magdalena Project to a large tent. Similarly, Curious' *On the Scent*, billed as an 'intimate performance for domestic spaces', though relying on the real homes in which it is staged, is an international touring piece, taking up residence in different and strange(rs) houses.

Recognising the nuances, gradations and differences of performance practices and opinions coalescing around the term 'site-specific', I nevertheless want to retain that reference point here because of the stress it places on specifically chosen sites, however these are then engaged with. We might consider the works explored in this chapter as doubly site-specific since not only do they take place in specific locations but the autobiographical nature of each of them is also, inevitably, specific. In fact, as we shall see, the 'specificity' of any site is dependent on the specific bodies that inhabit it, and vice versa, since the relationship between identity and place is one of mutual construction.

In thinking about performances that fold or unfold autobiography and place, particularly outside places, I have conceptualised them as being autotopographic, a neologism used for more than its fleeting allusion to autobiographic. *Topos* comes from the Greek word for place, while *graphein* means to scratch, to draw, to write; *topography*, then, signifies the writing of place. (Scratching the surface also comes to mind.) Dorset poet William Barnes has proposed replacing topography with the word 'placewrite' (cited in Trezise, 2000, p. 13), while scholar Simon Trezise, also from the UK's West Country, understands that both topography and placewriting 'face both ways: towards the territory we can touch and see and towards the mind with which we respond to that territory' (ibid.). *Autotopography*, in line with Trezise's insights, intends to foreground the subjectivity involved in plotting place; autotopography is writing place through self (and simultaneously writing self through place). Autotopography, like auto-biography, is a creative act of seeing, interpretation and invention, all of which depend on where you are standing, when and for what pur-pose.[3] With its stress on the *auto*, perspective is foregrounded in a way that distinguishes it from dominant (contemporary and Western) forms of mapping. This sort of mapping also allows you to 'write' the unknown or unrecognised route (functioning, then, like the local or counter-histories explored in Chapter 2).

Michel de Certeau's inscription of the authorising and controlling 'view from above' is probably one of the best known passages to capture a practice of mapping where a literally elevated viewer 'sur-veys' the scene below without actually partaking in it. In this process, 'he' is turned into a voyeur (1988, p. 92). (The gendered pronoun used by de Certeau to describe this elevated viewer is perhaps not accidental.) The cartographer in this position 'manufactures power' by creating 'a spatial panopticon' (Harvey, 1997 [1989], p. 159). De Certeau acknowledges that such a 'vantage point' exposes the 'lust to be a viewpoint and nothing more' (op. cit.). A viewpoint is, though, a point of view and, in fact, a very specific and embodied point of view. In de Certeau's example, it is the view from some body at the top of the World Trade Center. Feminist geographer Doreen Massey reminds us that there is nothing intrinsically prob-lematic about this view from above, since it is after all only another perspective (2005, p. 106). However, in the production of maps, too often the act of 'seeing' *as* an embodied point of view is hidden and the fact that it is but one 'perspective' is, if not denied, at least not made explicit. Employing de Certeau's metaphor, the actor or stagehand is pushed 'into the wings', leaving the map 'alone on the stage', suggesting that it got there all by itself (de Certeau, 1988, p. 121).

This lack of transparency in relation to the subjective production of maps might prompt us to (mis)take the map as a singularly 'truthful', accurate reflection of the scene surveyed, forgetting also that the flat dimensions of the map make such accuracy impossible from the outset. Massey, alluding to Magritte's iconoclastic painting, puts it well: 'a map of a geography is no more that geography – or that space – than a painting of a pipe is a pipe' (2005, p. 106). We forget, too, that since our very act of seeing or surveying is inevitably embodied, *contra* de Certeau's 'God', we can never be totally removed from the scene or the seen. (Deb Margolin's epiphany, recounted in the

Introduction, resonates here too.) In short, all maps are partial and selective. Specific people produce them from specific places, within particular historical and cultural contexts, and usually for specific reasons. We need only to encounter the 'new names' given to 'newly discovered' countries to recognise this; colonised lands are rendered the same as 'home' through their mapping and naming. The strange is made familiar: translated and at least metaphorically conquered through the already-known (see Loomba, 1998, p. 101). Such acts of naming are also performances of claiming ownership; this is, after all, 'my name'.[4]

As with all discursive productions, some people are more authorised than others to produce 'authoritative' maps; Dorling and Fairbairn wittily note that 'a picture is a map when it is drawn by somebody with the authority to draw maps' (1997, p. 71). Authority in this sphere, as in most others, is conferred by the support of powerful institutions and the display of competence in the particular rules that adhere to the 'language game', here the routine application of standard geometric grids, measurements, scales, symbols, etc. (Massey, 2005; Harvey, 1997 [1989]). These function as the hard (and cold) data, hiding the contaminating presence of the warm body that produces them. Ordinance Survey Maps are representative of such authority, and we should recognise that this authority has material effect. What is represented on a map and in what manner contributes to the construction of knowledge about places and people, signifying, for example, their level of importance, centrality or marginality. What is not represented has an equally material effect. Thus, mapping is a powerful technology which might stand comparison with autobiography. Autobiography traditionally provided a way of shoring up a cultural belief in a 'deep' and 'inner' self, particularly the bourgeois subject, who could then be controlled and regulated. Only some people's lives were held to be representative of 'a life', and, therefore, only certain 'selves' were written (historically male, white and middle class); others remained marginalised or invisible. Importantly, maps similarly help produce and maintain the social relations that *take* place (and here again we might consider colonial mappings). Both Pearson's and Smith's performances engage with maps; recognising the discursive effect of maps we most certainly want to ask what sorts of mapping practices they perform. In my application of the term an autotopographic practice brings into view the 'self' that plots place and that plots self in place, admitting (and indeed actively embracing) the subjectivity and inevitable partiality or bias of that process.

'The Lure of the Local'

'The lure of the local' is the title of Lucy Lippard's influential monograph on place, specifically local place. Concepts of place and of the local in Lippard's work, as in others', are synonymous:

> Inherent in the local is the concept of place – a portion of land/town/cityscape seen from the inside, the resonance of a specific location that is known and familiar. Most often place applies to our own 'local' – entwined with personal memory, known or unknown histories, marks made in the land that provoke and evoke.   (Lippard, 1997, p. 7)

Place, for Lippard, is a lived-in landscape, a concept shared by anthropologist Marc Augé who regards 'place' as composed of the 'unformulated rules of living knowhow' (Augé, 2000, p. 81); place is a habit. In such formulations place and the lives that take place in it are inseparable, leading to a profound sense of relationship between who we are and where we have been (or come from), a sense of 'belonging'. Place is also, as Augé makes clear, in most instances shared, in which case the 'identity' arising from place might be thought of as communal, best captured by the phrase, 'I'm local'. In all of this, we can see that place is not something that simply exists, but is rather something that we bring into existence through our relationships with it and our relationships with others in, on or around it.

In an attempt to identify (and perhaps fix) its co-ordinates, place is also often distinguished from space. Yi-Fu Tuan's early proposal for place understands it 'from the perspectives of the people who have given it meaning' (1974, p. 213). Place is the experienced and inhabited:

> What begins as undifferentiated space becomes place as we get to know it better and endow it with value [. . .] From the security and stability of place we are aware of openness, freedom, and threat of space, and vice versa.   (Yi-Fu Tuan, 1977, p. 6)

Where place is local and inhabited, 'space' then is conceived of in more abstract and often oppositional terms. Thus Augé opposes 'anthropological place' to 'non-symbolized space' (2000, p. 101), while Lippard defines place as 'space combined with memory' (1997, p. 10) which is similar to Carter et al.'s description of place as 'space to which meaning has been ascribed' (1993, p. xiix; see also Cresswell, 2004, p. 7; Stewart and Strathern, 2003, p. 4). Tuan's early reckoning of place is important also for its inscription of place as secure and stable in contrast to the dangerous openness of space, which brings us back to Lippard's 'lure'. 'Place' exerts a 'pull that operates on each of us . . . It is the geographical component of the psychological need to belong somewhere, one antidote to a prevailing alienation' (Lippard, 1997, p. 7). Place, it seems, is a safe harbour.

Lippard perceives that a sense of 'placelessness' and the corollary need for 'place' is a result of globalisation (1997, p. 33; see also Lowenthal, 1975; Relph, 1976; Huyssen, 2003b). Other theorists similarly point to the compression of time and space and its effect on our sense of the local and particular.[5] Tuan, as early as the 1970s, proposed that dominant modes of transport, fast and individualising, serve to detach people from place. For Tuan, 'Time is needed to create place' (1974, p. 245), time as experienced through our everyday habits which 'establish a sense of place' (ibid., p. 243) and genealogical time conferred by remaining in one place, by being 'rooted in location' (ibid., p. 236). The forces of rampant global capitalism are perceived by many to appropriate and render everything the same, producing a culture of homogeneity (see Tuan, 1974; Solnit, 2000, pp. 9, 255; Augé, 2000). Miwon Kwon captures well the link between alienation and place when she writes, 'The intensifying conditions of spatial indifferentiation and departicularization – that is the increasing instances of locational *un*specificity – are seen to exacerbate the sense of alienation and fragmentation in contemporary life' (2004, p. 8). Against such a backdrop of alienation, Lippard proffers place as therapy.

The problems associated with these ideas of place and space are, by now, well rehearsed. If place is set in opposition to space, with the former imagined as closed, fixed, secure, stable, etc., and the latter as open, free, mobile, and risky, then it is easy to consider 'place' as reactionary and its operations exclusionary (see Massey, 1997 [1991]). The feeling of being a local is easily matched by the sense of being an outsider. (One could also refract these conceptions through a gendered lens, with place equating the 'private' and 'space' the public.) Other critics, though, would encourage us to rethink radically the local *as* global; as open, complex, shifting and networked. David Morley recognises that 'almost everywhere in the world, experience is increasingly "disembedded" from locality and the ties of culture to place are progressively weakened by new patterns of "connexity"' (2000, p. 14). The local, then, is not separate or cut-off from the global but is implicated in, and impacted by it, and 'space' may well be 'in place'. The local is also unavoidably heterogeneous. Peoples, cultures and goods have crossed territory for centuries. Nevertheless, understanding the continued desire that many have for outmoded or 'nostalgic' concepts of the local, Massey rightly proposes that 'the question is how to hold on to that notion of geographical difference, of uniqueness, even of rootedness if people want, without it being reactionary' (1997 [1991], p. 319).

Where Lippard's 'lure' lies in place, Andreas Huyssen has identified a similar lure residing in the past. Recognising the contemporary impulse of 'musealisation', Huyssen understands that this appeal to memory is an

> attempt to slow down the pace of life, to resist the dissolution of time and space in the synchronicity of the electronic archive, to recover a mode of contemplation outside the universe of simulation and fast-speed information and cable networks, to claim some anchoring space in a world of puzzling and often threatening homogeneity, non-synchronicity of cultures and information overload. (2003b, p. 28)

Perhaps then Lippard's sense of place is really a sense of the past: 'The faster we are pushed into a future that does not inspire confidence, the more seductively a past world beckons in which life seemed simpler, slower, better' (ibid., p. 24). In a culture experiencing rapid and continuous change, Huyssen perceives memory as an anchor by which to 'secure a space' (ibid., p. 25). Memory, then, rather than place, is the safe harbour. Huyssen is also right to propose the link between memory and place; in fact, memory is literally placed, 'inscribed in the landscape' (Cresswell, 2004, p. 85). Place serves as a mnemonic, and an affective one embracing the multiple senses (Lippard, 1997, p. 34). We might even consider that it is the memories of place that perform the lure of the local, serving to remind us where we have been and what we have done, which in turn brings us back to a sense, not of place, but of ourselves. *Nostos* is the Greek for 'to return home'; *algai*, 'a painful condition'; *nostalgia* is homesickness (Davis, 1977, p. 414). In the 'place' of nostalgia, 'one remembers feeling a sense of wholeness and belonging' (Steinwand, 1997, p. 9). Nostalgia (like autobiography) is also a means of engendering a coherent and continuous identity as we remind ourselves in the present of who we were in the past. It is, then, one of the processes at hand for 'constructing, maintaining and reconstructing our identities' (Davis, 1977, p. 419). Though nostalgia no longer refers solely to 'place', the 'return home' (both imaginary and actual) remains a nostalgic gesture. For Dietmar

Dath, 'homes are "origin stories" constructed as retrospective sign-posts . . . they are made for coming *from*' (quoted in Morley, 2000, p. 16). I am surely not alone in taking intimate lovers back to the places I once lived, as if that will somehow explain who I am. And in some senses, of course, it might, because there on the hill remains the rural school I attended, with its single class-room. But the grass field we used to play in at break is now tarmac. And the adjoining house where the teacher lived is now an office. And the shop where I bought my playtime snack has closed and become a house. And it is not the same place at all. But the same as when? Surely, day by day, as I lived in it, the place changed? The place I take you to is not, nor has it ever been, fixed in time. And neither, of course, have I. So where is this place of my origin then, and which me are you supposed to be finding?[6]

Bubbling Tom: Relocating the Self/Place

Mike Pearson's *Bubbling Tom* (2000), a performance which takes him 'home' for the first time, seems a good place to start our own plotting of place and identity in performance. Pearson, though an archaeologist by training, is a seasoned performance practitioner, involved first in the experimental performance scene that evolved in the UK during the 1970s, specifically the laboratory work in Cardiff, and later with the hugely influential Welsh company, *Brith Gof*. In spite of his expansive *curriculum vitae*, the vast majority of it connected to site-specific practice, Pearson had curiously never performed 'at home' before. In the year 2000, it would seem that the 'lure of the local' made itself felt and reeled him in. Participating in the national creative project *Small Acts: Performance, the Millennium and the Marking of Time*, a series of performances commissioned to 'mark' in small and personal ways the millennium, Mike Pearson chose to return to Hibaldstow, the home of his childhood.[7] Notably, the millennium was, from the outset, as much a personal mark of time than a public one given that in the year 2000 Pearson also turned fifty.

Working with the evocative Welsh notion of '*y filltir sgwar*', the square mile of our childhood, a place that we know intimately and 'in a detail we will never know anywhere again', Pearson performed a guided tour of Hibaldstow, stopping at ten sites that had childhood significance (Pearson, 2000, p. 181). Given that in earlier chapters our focus has been on the means by which performers negotiate 'identity' and 'experience', our interest here is similarly in the ways *Bubbling Tom* engages with concepts of 'place', 'home', 'origin' and 'self'.

With its focus on the familiar and intimate, it is easy to read Pearson's return to 'origin' as symptomatic of the 'alienation' identified by Lippard and others. In his reflections on making *Bubbling Tom*, Pearson reminds us that the 1950s (the time of his childhood) was an era of change – of increased consumerism, greater mechanisation, and a wider reach of mass media. However, alongside such 'developments', the older ways survived too: 'here face-to-face communication still had currency' (ibid., p. 174). Such practices though, as we approach the new millennium, have 'gone' (ibid.). In this light, *Bubbling Tom* might be considered as Pearson's attempt to return not only to the place of his childhood, but to retrieve an earlier mode of practice now vanished or vanquished. Adopting the form of a tour, Pearson's concern was to find 'ways of telling', luring the spectators in through the 'grain of the voice' – 'chatting, lecturing, reciting, orating, seducing' (ibid., p. 175; see Barthes, 1977). In this we might be reminded of Huyssen's recognition of the appeal of a different mode of archival recovery, 'the seduction of the archive' (Huyssen, 2003a, p. 5) which enables 'some anchoring of space' (Huyssen, 2003b, p. 28). Pearson and his colleague Michael Shanks acknowledge a similar appeal in the telling of shared history in performance, a communication which exists as an oral record and in fact which serves to 'hold it, and us, in place' (Pearson and Shanks, 2001, p. 120). Accompanied on the tour by only a small number of spectators, the majority of whom are from the village, the performance space Pearson engenders enables close encounters, drawing on the memories of those present to 'read' or 'write' the landscape.

Reflecting on the work Pearson explains that

> it began with a work of archaeology: to reveal and record the memories of those who recall my actions up to the age of eight, particularly non-family members, and to record interviews relating to particular events. I set out to uncover records and photographs of me in this place to discover the physical marks I left in the landscape, in order to re-embody the traces the landscape has left in me: to relocate myself.   (2000, p. 175)

Key here is Pearson's phrase 'relocate myself', which we might understand as symptomatic of nostalgia; perhaps Pearson, turning fifty, is 'lost', and a return to his origin will allow him to find himself? However, 'relocate' in its typical usage actually means to move. Performing in Hibaldstow, paradoxically, is not a gesture of return then but in fact is the moving of self to a new place, or even the moving of (past) place to a new place (in time). This is to perform nostalgia differently and the strategy, though specific to Pearson and the context of *Bubbling Tom*, adds to recent critical attempts to wrest 'nostalgia' from its reactionary position.

Critics have proposed that one affect of nostalgia is an active 'resistance' to the present, rather than simply a romanticisation of the past. Such resistance might be regarded as political – to assimilation, to the erasure of difference, to present privations, etc. In such a vein Marianne Hirsch and Leo Spitzer suggest that 'a past reconstructed through the animating vision of nostalgia can serve as a creative inspiration and possible emulation within the present', providing what the present lacks (2003, p. 83). Catherine Wiley (1998), writing of Chicano theatre, similarly proposes nostalgia as a regenerative model. Understanding the past as an 'in-between' space serves to both innovate and interrupt the present. This nostalgia, a model of 'past-present', can be carried as a guide rather than a burden, using 'what we have learned of the past to construct a future for Chicano identity' (Wiley, 1998, p. 102). Jennifer Ladino, meanwhile, proposes nostalgia as a potentially useful tool of progressive politics, suggesting that in 'some contexts, nostalgia can be a mechanism for social change, a model for ethical relationships, and a useful narrative for social and environmental justice' (2004, p. 89). Pearson's nostalgic gesture and return might similarly be considered a way to rewrite the past and future of Hibaldstow.

Pearson has had a long critical interest in reading the past. In *Theatre/Archaeology* (2001) he and Michael Shanks note that archaeology crafts and mediates the past; archaeology – like autobiography – is a production and interpretation of the past in and therefore through the present, 'informed by present interests and values' (2001, p. 11). Given this perspective, the archaeological processes undertaken by Pearson for *Bubbling Tom* are unlikely to propose the past – land or self – as in any way fixed or authentic, or indeed 'discoverable'.

Plotting Place

SE 97990257

It's 1953 again and I'm on the move. We're whizzing down East Street and I'm clinging onto Dad's handlebars, perched on the small saddle fixed to his crossbar. He recently brought home a tortoise in his saddle-bag. Found it on Station Bridge, where Grandad Pearson once met a red light swinging in the fog. Gingerly, he pedalled forward, to find that the lamp was tied to the tail of an elephant.   (Pearson, 2000, p. 179)

The published document of *Bubbling Tom*, though a different text to that of the live performance, nevertheless serves to suggest the multiplicity of 'tellings' and 'selves' that Pearson performs, with place inscribed in bodies, accents, local habits and the micro-physical environments (the feel of the doorknob in the hand, like 'the iron of the school fence' whose 'coolness and resistance' is 'stored subliminally' in our memory [Santmyer, cited in Tuan, 1974, p. 235]). Just as his Nan's kitchen resounded with different types of talk, all given equal footing, so too does *Bubbling Tom* juxtapose the factual with the fictional, event with imagination, history with story, narrative with fragment, past with present. In the guise of storyteller (and here Pearson is influenced by Walter Benjamin's storyteller [Benjamin, 1968]), Pearson weaves 'together history, geography, genealogy, memoir and autobiography, and including anecdotes, traveller's tales, poetry, forensic data, quotations, lies, jokes, improvised asides, physical re-enactments, impersonations and intimate reflections' (Pearson, 2000, pp. 175–6).

Mike Pearson, *Bubbling Tom*. Photo Hugo Glendinning

Though each of his chosen locations can be marked on the Ordinance Survey Map of the area (and the grid references are included in the published document), Pearson's storytelling transforms the fixed and anonymous co-ordinates into an inhabited and lively place, where the touch and feel of place is as important as sight. The jumbled mix of lived events, taken from across time, and as the elephant testifies, from across expansive space, exceed the rigid grids. The 'map' performed by *Bubbling Tom* is more akin, then, to the story maps that preceded those of the Enlightenment. In earlier times, maps recorded actions, itineraries, events, actual bodies moving through space. The 'actor' or stagehand takes a visible position, centre stage.[8] The Aztec map, for example, did not depict a 'route' but instead presented a 'log' and in Michel de Certeau's words was 'not a "geographical map" but "history book"' (1988, p. 120).[9] Pearson himself works with the concept of 'deep maps', a term borrowed from William Least Heat-Moon who coined it to capture the 'accumulation of narratives' that adhere to sites (Pearson and Shanks, 1997, p. 51). Such 'maps' produce places very different than those constructed by OS cartography. For Doreen Massey, one troubling effect of the more typical 'scientific' map is that it gives the impression of space as a fixed surface, a 'sphere of a completed horizontality' (2005, p. 107). Such a conception of space serves to render it as whole and discrete, a 'multiplicity of inert *things*' and a firm ground where 'you never lose your way, are never surprised by an encounter with something unexpected, never faced with the unknown' (ibid., p. 111). Massey encourages us to think instead of space as 'a heterogeneity of practices and *processes* . . . an ongoing product of interconnections'. This arena of space is necessarily 'unfinished and open' (ibid., p. 107) When the map is conceived as an account of stories, there are, inevitably, loose ends rather than a singular end (ibid.).[10] Though the representation of the story might stop at the edge of the page, we know that its trajectory must continue.

In 'going home' and performing there, what Pearson in fact brings home is that place, even local or intimate place, is fractured, layered, multiple and contested. While Pearson might propose a return to his 'origins', there can be no original place. What any space 'is' depends on who occupies it, when and for what purpose, and this can shift continuously. Social practices imbue space with meanings (McDowell, 1999, p. 168); in this sense, rather than conceptualising space as either simply given and fixed, we should recognise it as continually practiced or performed (Cresswell, 2004, p. 39). And also, then, as potentially practiced – or performed – differently.

Where *Bubbling Tom* Leads to Babbling Tom . . .

Pearson had hoped that his own stories would prompt other stories of the places passed through. In the event, and perhaps even to Pearson's surprise, those other stories were offered during the performance itself. Pearson admits that this might have been because the place of the performance, its location outside of the theatre building, meant that the spectators were not circumscribed by the behavioural rules that adhere to theatre spectatorship (see Bennett, 1990). In fact, Pearson believed that 'few people there . . . had this sense that I was performing' (2001). At each stop on the route Pearson's largely scripted performance would be spontaneously and unpredictably added to, interrupted and challenged with other stories offered by the spectators. The already layered performance became even more so, with the real-time element of performance enabling the layers to exist contemporaneously rather than discretely (see Massey, 2005, pp. 109–13). *Bubbling Tom* unwittingly became a model for ethical community or participatory performance where the content or 'script' of the piece is largely dictated by the spectators (Pearson, 2001). Spectators become equal participants in the performance event and in the performance of place, charged with replotting and reshaping both.

Given the interrelation between representation and materiality, an abiding political problem for auto/biographical performance relates to the choice of stories told. If places are in part imagined and sustained by memories, then it really does matter which memories are circulated (Cresswell, 2004, p. 85). Who are the mapmakers? The performance structure of *Bubbling Tom*, though devised by Pearson, is an 'aesthetically produced instance of democratic sociability' (Jackson, 2005, p. 62) that provides the space for different and often unexpected memories. While *Bubbling Tom* might be considered part of the negative trend of musealisation identified by Huyssen, for Pearson and Shanks, place continues 'not only to commemorate but also to animate' (2001, p. 159). *Bubbling Tom*, prompting memory, inspires such animation and the further reinvention of this place called Hibaldstow. Those walking with Pearson in April 2000 collectively performed the public memory of Hibaldstow – a memory and, therefore, a place contingent to that time and event and the people in it, place (and museum) as an ephemeral and live act.

Massey's invigorating proposition of imagining space 'as a simultaneity of stories-so-far' seems uncannily suited to Pearson's performance of place in *Bubbling Tom* (Massey, 2005, p. 9).[11] de Certeau also tells us that, potentially at least, 'stories diversify, rather than totalize' (1988, p. 107). The simultaneity and diversity of stories told in *Bubbling Tom* renders the community diverse also. Like *Fingerlicks* (see Chapter 1), *Bubbling Tom* creates community through its practice rather than assuming it in advance.

The title, *Bubbling Tom*, refers to a stream called Bubbling Tom, where lore has it that if you sip from its source you will always return to the village. The final stop on Pearson's tour was this source, or 'origin'. To mark the end, Pearson had planned that everyone would congregate in this 'significant' place. In fact, what actually happened was that 'whole groups of people [were] heading off in different directions saying, "No, it's here", "No, it's here"' (Pearson, 2001). In the event, it became apparent that there was no agreement on where Bubbling Tom actually was. While *Bubbling Tom* unashamedly flirts with nostalgia, this lack of local consensus about source and origin, a lack revealed entirely through chance, seems to be a supremely fortuitous symbol for Pearson's engagement with the place of Hibaldstow, with where he has come from and with who he 'is' (or was). The kind of nostalgia that Pearson performs is perhaps a 'counter-nostalgia' which 'envisions the "home" as fractured, fragmented, complicated, and layered; to "return" to this sort of home is to revisit a dynamic past' (Ladino, 2004, pp. 90–1). And, of course, *Bubbling Tom* will itself become another story of and about Hibaldstow, a moment of the past to be retold in the future, with such retellings filled with gaps and slips in memory, different perspectives, creative imaginings. In 2020 we might well overhear the following: 'Do you remember, oh, it must be twenty years ago now, you were only a kid, that man, what was his name, Peterson, Mark Peterson, took us round the village on a tour . . . '.[12]

The Art of Walking

Both Mike Pearson's and Phil Smith's performances involve some element of walking: Pearson's guided walk around Hibaldstow; Smith's performance about his walking activities undertaken during one summer. The 'art' of walking has something of a history, best epitomised in Richard Long's *Line Made by Walking* (1967) which, as its name suggests, was a line made in grass by continually walking the same path. This 'line' was then documented in a black and white photograph. Whilst Long's action, contextualised in the late 1960s, embodied a certain challenge to the status of art – as product or process, as object or ephemera – earlier focuses on walking saw within the activity itself a radical creative potential. Baudelaire's *flâneur* of nineteenth-century Paris, for example, strolled and looked (Tester, 1994, p. 1), his 'landscape' the crowded streets of the urban city (and the *flâneur* was decidedly male, a point we will return to shortly). Walking leisurely, but nevertheless conscious of his surroundings, the *flâneur* was an unhurried and detached spectator of, even if dependent upon, the bustle and business or busyness of others, 'the secret spectator of the spectacles of the spaces and places of the city' (ibid., p. 7). The *flâneur's* looking was active; he consumed and savoured (but never actually bought). The ostensible 'aimlesseness' might not, then, be quite so aimless in its effect, since 'such inoccupation belies intense intellectual activity' (Ferguson, 1994, p. 26). The *flâneur*, we might propose, though 'lingering', was not in fact a malingerer, but rather the producer of 'new and unexpected connections in a serious kind of play' (ibid., p. 30). As Walter Benjamin writes,

> basic to flânerie, among other things, is the idea that the fruits of idleness are more precious than the fruits of labour. The flâneur, as is well known, makes studies.   (1999, p. 454)

Rob Shields (1994) also makes the point that the *flâneur's* activity was more directed than the word strolling would imply. He notes that *flânerie* is 'a crowd practice' and 'a spatial practice of specific sites: the interior and exterior public spaces of the city'; moreover, the *flâneur* would be open to diversions provided by interesting sights (1994, p. 65). *Flânerie*, then, shared something with the later Situationists (other than the Paris setting), who within the same urban context in the 1950s and 1960s practiced the *dérive*, which literally translates to the suggestive term 'drifting'. For a set period the usual motivations of spatial movement are replaced by motivations prompted by the space itself (see Debord). In this respect the word 'drift' is perhaps slightly misleading, since the *dérive* is not left entirely to the operations of chance – not least because the idea of total 'chance' was considered a red herring. Rather, Debord recognises that one is emotionally drawn to or repelled by a place: 'cities have psychogeographical contours, with constant currents, fixed points and vortexes that strongly discourage entry into or exit from certain zones'.[13] (Certain bodies, I would propose, detect certain 'currents'.) The rather stern instructions offered by Debord in fact impress the *dérive* as a structured activity. One outcome of the *dérive*, with its attention to the psychogeographic makeup of a city, was to be the production of maps of 'influence'.

Michel de Certeau, who perceived 'the ordinary practitioners of the city' as walkers, *Wandersmänner* (1988 [1984], p. 93), in turn owes something to the Situationists. De Certeau has stressed the walker's radical potential to realise literally a city:

> If it is true that a spatial order organizes an ensemble of possibilities (e.g., by a place in which one can move) and interdictions (e.g., by a wall that prevents one from going further), then the walker actualizes some of these possibilities. In that way, he makes them exist as well as emerge. But he also moves them about and he invents others, since the crossing, drifting away, or improvisation of walking privilege, transform or abandon spatial elements.   (1988 [1984], p. 98)

The interventionist potential of walking has been inherited by a number of contemporary practitioners, including the company Wrights & Sites, whose recent work shares something with Mike Pearson's *Bubbling Tom*. Interacting with the 'genre' of the guided tour, the company has published imaginative *Mis-Guides* which make no distinction between historical fact and subjective responses to place. In these *Mis-Guides*, as in *Bubbling Tom*, the spectators are in fact participants, with each Mis-Guide simply being a set of instructions to be interpreted and enacted. Some of these court autobiographical reflections, such as the 'Nostalgic Drift (for those who know the city well)':

> Revisit scenes from your past and see how they're getting along without you. Look into the back gardens of houses you used to inhabit. Commemorate in chalk special places on the pavement where you said 'Goodbye' or had a memorable conversation, or kissed. Lay a wreath on the site of a memory you want to put to rest.   (Hodge *et al.*, 2003, p. 37)

From the *flâneurs* to Wrights & Sites, each instance of walking cited here is potentially 'resistant' – to habit, to capitalism, to rules, to expectations. Within the context of assumptions about time–space compression, walking is also considered to have radical potential. Rebecca Solnit's engaging book, *Wanderlust: A History of Walking* (2000), maps walking practices across history and space, but, in each time and place, walking is rendered in some senses 'wholesome'. For Solnit, a sense of place 'can only be gained on foot', a mode of transport through which 'everything stays connected' (2000, p. 9). Walking is also proposed as an activity that enables us to stay in contact with ourselves. For phenomenologist Edmund Husserl, the body is always, no matter where we are, 'here', present; moving through place, our body, nevertheless, serves as an anchor. In Solnit's words, 'it is the body that moves but the world that changes', an experience which enables us to retain a sense of a coherent self amidst 'the flux of the world' (ibid., p. 27). This phenomenological quality of walking is one that is stressed; we 'know' the world through our physical, bodily experience of it and our literal contact of body with environment is thought to provide a privileged mode of knowledge (and, of course, different bodies produce different knowledges).

The separation of self and place might be deemed problematic; place is proffered here as a stable object of study. We do not, though, so much walk through place as make places through our walking (and we might think here of Richard Long's 1967 artwork as a literal example of 'placemaking'). 'Placemaking' is also as imagined as it is physical. Alongside the literal markings of places enacted by the daily habits of tramping bodies, our lived experiences of places imbue them with meanings, narrativising them. We have already noted that life is often thought of as a 'path'; Solnit further recognises that this life journey is in turn most often imagined as 'a journey on foot, a pilgrim's progress across the landscape of our personal history' (2000, p. 73). In many autobiographical performances, the literal and the metaphorical are combined as certain places take on particular and personal resonance.

The Art of Crab Walking

Phil Smith, member of Wrights & Sites, performed his solo show, *The Crab Walks*, at Devon's seaside during the summer of 2004. Like Pearson's *Bubbling Tom*, the work was intimate, usually performed for an audience of six at a time. Again like *Bubbling Tom*, the root of *The Crab Walks* is the walking of a route linked to childhood, in this case Devon's seascape. Over the course of the summer, Smith revisited places on the coastline that he had first visited with his grandparents. *The Crab Walks*, performed in a beach hut at Teignmouth and at Coryton Cove (Dawlish), offered an account of that walking.

During the course of the performance, Smith explained to his assembled audience why he was walking, in what way and to where. He also attempted to render the connections that his mind made as he traversed the land; in some senses, then, the route being explored/revealed is as

Phil Smith, *The Crab Walks*. Photo Anne-Maree Garcia

much a mindscape as a landscape, and perhaps the one really serves as an analogy to the other. Just as the mind jumps tracks, rarely getting to the end, and makes odd and unexpected connections, grasping fleeting impressions, random facts and casual thoughts, so perhaps is surrounding space equally chaotic and unpredictable – depending on how you wander it. Stories are 'spatial trajectories' that 'traverse and organize places' (de Certeau, 1988 [1984], p. 115).

Settled into my chair, in a beach hut at Coryton Cove, I am rapt by Smith's narrative. I learn that he has been walking from 'Dawlish Warren to Paignton', 'looking for something, looking for connections' (Smith, 2004a).[14] The 'map' he used was of childhood holidays when he would stay in Paignton with his 'Nan' and 'Pop', on an off-season holiday described by Smith as 'heaven', where it felt as if everything open was open especially for him:

> And this walk was about finding that precious feeling again. When this seaside was that magical playground for me.

Like *Bubbling Tom*, it is easy to read *The Crab Walks* as driven by a nostalgic longing for a rosy past where, with the benefit of hindsight, the self was known to be safe and secure (and loved). Except that Smith's walking and storying work together against this pull. The performance opens with him telling us of his attack by a mob of angry herring gulls and his attempt to escape their wrath, darting into and out of places of sanctuary that he finds *en route*. We learn that one place, now a funeral parlour with a bowling club above it, used to be a fish store for salted cod brought from Newfoundland, which had been salted in Newfoundland with salt taken from the Haldon Hills above Teignmouth. Following its spell as a fish store, it was a prison, and before any of this, it was a volcano. Global and historical movement passes through the spectral building conjured before our eyes. Smith is crying like a flock of maddened gulls and ducking out of reach of his own malicious intentions:

the gulls are going mad now and history is circling over my head.

In these first few moments the performance is already layered and complex, embracing the locality that is Teignmouth. It provides nuanced details of the landscape that sits under our feet and extends ahead of and behind us. At the same time, it becomes apparent that this locality that is Teignmouth is not just located here. The salt was taken to Newfoundland, and then brought back again, albeit transformed. And Teignmouth is not just the present: the funeral parlour and bowling alley once a prison, a fish store and, long before any of that, a volcano. The molten events of the past resist becoming lava, continuing instead to exert influence upon the present, but also feeling the influence of that present on its own flow. Teignmouth through the ages, you might say; Teignmouth continuously on the move. This is Teignmouth as 'hub', given width and depth (Lippard, 1997, p. 7).

I'm walking over the ballast from foreign ships used for the foundations of the town centre, the volcanic lava in the undertakers is flowing. Everything is originally from somewhere else.

If everything is originally from somewhere else, it is difficult to hold onto ideas of 'local', 'belonging' and 'origins'. Doreen Massey (2005) similarly notes that in those places typically considered exemplars of so-called 'natural' landscapes, such as the Lake District, everything is continuously moving. For example, 'The Lake District has been repopulated, through the movements of animals, plants and humans, in the few thousand years since the last ice age', while 'Cornwall to the west goes up and down by 10 centimetres with each tide'. Massey's point is that 'there is no stable point' (2005, p. 138).

Having run from the gulls, Smith returns to tell us about the walking that he did, the walking used to devise the stories he will go on to share. More like a Situationist psychogeographer than a *flâneur*, Smith was not so much interested in observing other people, as allowing himself to go off the map, dictated by feelings:

> . . . you get a sort of feeling when you are about to find somewhere special. It's to do with the shapes of a place. It's like you're sliding down into a basin of attraction.

This type of 'sensual' walking might be thought somewhat 'out of place' in a region that has its coastal walking routes well marked and well tramped, and Smith acknowledges that, despite appearances, he was 'not like the other walkers' met along the way. His itinerary was dictated by neither destination nor levels of exertion. His walking, then, was more leisurely and also more unpredictable:

> I was taking my time . . . doing it in bits . . . going home and starting again . . . beginning in the middle . . . I was heading off the path all the time.

As with *Bubbling Tom* and Wrights & Sites' *Mis-Guides*, history, fact, myth, local lore, intuitive hunches and autobiography rub shoulders in *The Crab Walks*. Like the crab, Smith scuttles sideways, choosing to forego the direct route; connections are to be made, but they are never simply given or assumed. A specially designed map, handed to each of the spectators at the end of the performance inviting them to undertake their own crab walks, explains the methodology behind Smith's crab walking. This is clearly indebted to the Situationists: 'follow your crab instincts and scuttle sideways into any nook that intrigues, any place that draws, any space that pulls' (Smith, 2004b). The 'crab philosophy' justifying this process is also rooted in Situationist thought:

> The crab philosopher believes that just off our usual routes – to work, to the shops – are places with intense atmospheres, accidental beauties, haunted by the everyday, often with the appearance of a dream, sometimes littered with remnants of mysterious events. That behind the municipal pleasure ground and official beauty spot, just one turning off the usual footpath is hidden treasure.   (Smith, 2004b)

In his own walking, Smith does not leave chance to chance. On one of his detours, he takes a friend, an Indian-born actress, Anjali, with him, instructing her to guide them to the Ness, even though she has neither map nor previous knowledge of the area. Sharing an affinity with his perambulating predecessors, Smith informs us that 'this is a way you can find new places, unexpected places, allow yourself to be led by someone who doesn't know where they are going' (2004a). He also advises us to find a stone that looks like our head and carry it when walking, 'to remind you to look at things from different points of view'. (At this moment we are each given a blob of modelling clay to mould into our own head shapes and to keep throughout the performance and afterwards.)

Smith's walking methodology encourages the emergence into visibility of the 'socius' that is interwoven with place: 'proper, property, propriety, appropriate' (Williams, 1998, p. vi). Of course, it is precisely against such interdictions that the walking of the *flâneurs* and Situationists was set. Explicit throughout Smith's performance is the fact that space is controlled, both in terms of who is allowed in it and the behaviour thought appropriate to it.

'Visitors always welcome' – the church is locked. [. . .]

A sign reads: 'Railtrack plc hereby give notice that this way is not dedicated to the public.'

Just as Smith cannot predict the paths his walking will take, so too are the stories he tells and the connections he makes between them chance encounters. Though this walking is supposed to return Smith to his childhood, on the beach Anjali tells him that she has been reminded of her own childhood, in Bangalore, and 'reading Famous Five adventures'. Here is another unexpected node, a marker of colonialist history spanning time and space. As Anjali remembers the Famous Five, Smith remembers that his Granddad served in the British Army in India, and that his father brought back a carved Ganesh from Calcutta in the 1970s; we also learn that the Redcliffe Hotel, opposite the guest house where he used to stay, has 'different parts based on famous Indian buildings'; and that Donald Crowhurst, who sailed his Teignmouth Electron from here in 1968, was born in India in 1932. This is not, then, in any way a nostalgic return to some past place. The places and times that Smith conjures are always multiple, reflecting his layered sense of 'self'. Hearing someone shouting out 'Phil', he thinks that it must have been for some other Phil, 'Maybe the one I was becoming'.

The Extroverted Self

In spite (or because) of all his crab walking, Smith admits to us that he has not located his memories. Instead, he has 'found all these layers'. In this, *The Crab Walks* is exemplary of the practice of place that Doreen Massey (1997 [1991]) seeks – a practice that embraces an outward-looking or extroverted sensibility. This conception of space seeks to dissolve the binary between local and global, understanding that connections found in the so-called local are expansive. In this understanding, place is a specific *meeting* place of 'networks of social relations and movements and communications' (ibid., p. 322). As with *Bubbling Tom* the present to which Smith returns is populated with ghosts, confirming de Certeau's proposition that 'There is no place that is not haunted by many different spirits hidden there in silence, spirits one can "invoke" or not' (1988 [1984], p. 108). Those that Smith chooses to invoke include Donald Crowhurst, Oswald Moseley, Lady Florrie Westenra, the Mad Monk, his nan and pop and other versions of himself:

> The countryside is riddled with these spirit possessions, these old lines, these wild haunts . . .

Place as a meeting place is made tangible as Smith walks not only with his friend Anjali, or his sound recordist Tom, but with all the other people encountered, raised and imagined, and the stories that each of these had to tell:

> I realise now this has never been an autobiographical walk. I've been walking for other people. The memories I have – are not mine. They're not just the past [. . .] No – this walk through nostalgia is a walk into the future, a pioneering wander through the familiar, only to find everything changed and full of endless wonder.

Smith and Massey both know that you 'cannot go back home or to anywhere else' because by the time you get there, 'that place will have moved on just as you yourself will have changed' (Massey, 2005, p. 124). Where the uncertain source of Bubbling Tom provided a neat symbol for the uncertainty of place, the train station at Dawlish Warren offers a symbol of place continually changing. The train station is the first place that Smith intends to visit in search of those special feelings from the past; when he arrives, though, he is confronted with a burnt shell, and learns that the fire happened only the day before. In a similar vein, the literal disappearance of houses to the encroaching sea and the expanding coastline bear testimony to the fact that time does not so much pass through space (as if one was intangible and the other material) so much as create space (see Massey, 2005). A fitting if somewhat poignant post-script is that one of the beach huts in which Smith performed *The Crab Walks* was washed away during a powerful storm a couple of months later. Both it and *The Crab Walks* now ghost the landscape, waiting for the next meeting place – and maybe that meeting place is here and now.

Whose Place?

Conceiving of place as 'performed' and made is politically important. Space is produced through relations that we are always in the process of constructing (Massey, 2005, p. 111). If place is produced through relations, is 'throwntogether' rather than simply present (ibid., p. 141), then it demands our continual negotiation. And herein lies the politics of place, since the social relations that produce places are rarely equal. Cresswell is not being overly hyperbolic when he writes that place 'is right at the centre of humanity' (2004, p. 123).

That space or place are not solid or fixed does not make being in space a less tangible experience. I agree with Elspeth Probyn that 'space is a pressing matter and it matters which bodies, where and how, press up against it' (1995, p. 81). Though space is 'performed', it is nevertheless also material, existing simultaneously then as both 'real' and 'representational'. As Henri Lefebvre puts it, 'This pre-existence of space conditions the subject's presence, action and discourse, his [*sic*] competence and performance; yet the subject's presence, action and discourse, at the same time as they presuppose this space, also negate it' (1991, p. 57).

Having lived for some years in the south west of England, an area of the UK named 'The English Riviera' and packaged either as a beach resort or as a picture post-card rural idyll, replete with palm trees and thatched-roof cottages, I have experienced feeling both invisible and 'out of place' (see Heddon, 2002). Identifying as a lesbian, I have not only felt mis-placed, I have also felt inappropriate; place functions as a 'moral geography' and is used to demarcate or mark those who belong from those who do not (Cresswell, 1996, 2004). People then, are also 'placed'. Many cultural geographers have noted that most space is heterosexualised through the repeated performance of heterosexuality that takes place within it (Bell *et al.*, 1994; Valentine, 1996; Duncan, 1996; Myslik, 1996). A sense of 'out-of-placeness' is not, though, unique to sexuality. I would imagine that, when held against the iconography of Devon and Cornwall (or the Highlands of Scotland or the Lake District, etc.), a black or Asian person would feel similarly out of place. Space is also as gendered as it is raced, and the vast majority of women will have felt out of place at some time, 'public space' having been historically constructed as masculine, with so-called 'private space', typically domestic space, perceived as the domain of the feminine (Duncan, 1996).

Places, like the bodies located in them, are embedded within and produced by historical, cultural and political vectors. In planning this section, I realised that all of the performances I was familiar with, which featured walking in their execution, had been created by men (in addition to Pearson and Smith's work, Carl Lavery's *Mourning Walk*, Graeme Miller's *Linked* and Simon Whitehead's and Lone Twins' various walking projects came to mind). Of course, many women do make site-specific work. Nevertheless, I have struggled to locate many women who include walking practices in their *oeuvre*. This is not to deny that much site-specific work by women is sited in public places, but many of these resonate with the contained or the domestic(ated). Bobby Baker, for example, has made work for her own kitchen (*Kitchen Show*) and her own local church (*Box Story*).[15] Geraldine Pilgrim, co-founder of the influential group Hesitate and Demonstrate and founder of site-specific company Corridor, has devised many site-specific works including *Deep End*, staged in a disused Soho swimming bath, *Dreamworks 3* at St Pancras Chambers, *Spa* at the Elizabeth Garrett Anderson Hospital and *Hotel* in a 1930s' Midland Hotel on Morecambe Bay. If 'sited' practices are gender differentiated, the reasons for this are not difficult to surmise.[16] Returning to that still influential nineteenth-century walker, the *flâneur*, we already confront the fact that where men could walk the streets at will, 'women were (are) fated, thanks to men, to be only streetwalkers' (Tester, 1994, p. 18).

The development of separate spheres in the mid-nineteenth century severely curtailed middle-class women's activities in public (see Massey, 1991; Wolff, 1994) (although working-class women were always obliged to travel the public thoroughfares – space is also 'classed'). Indeed, representations of the *flâneur* depict him as the classically disembodied male subject: 'suspended from obligation, disengaged, disinterested, dispassionate' (Ferguson, 1994, p. 26). As we have noted, the primary activity of the *flâneur* was watching.[17] Priscilla Parkhurst Ferguson, characterising the modern stroller, writes that 'Good legs [. . .] are essential equipment. But the most essential appendage is the eye' (ibid., p. 27). Many critics have drawn attention to the fact that this specular activity implicitly disbarred women from *flânery* since they were always the object of the (male) gaze, and never its subject (see Ferguson, 1994; Massey, 1991).[18]

This sense of the objectification of women in public spaces remains strong more than a century later. Where Carl Lavery can walk for fifteen miles alone in *Mourning Walk* (see Mock, 2007), retracing the path his father used to take, I know that if he were me he would continuously be looking over his shoulder and scanning the horizon ahead, rather than contemplating his father. I resent this, of course, and want to rebel against such circumscriptions of place, but like Rebecca Solnit 'having met so many predators, I [have] learned to think like prey' (2000, p. 242). I resent this also. Even though statistics will propose that men are more likely to be attacked by strangers than are women, and that women are more likely to be attacked by people that they know than by strangers, the potential threat of place nevertheless makes itself felt. The fact that the violence women encounter is most often sexual undoubtedly has an added impact. Again using Solnit's words, 'fear of rape puts many women in their place' (ibid., p. 240) – and arguably keeps them there.

Comments surrounding many incidences of rape suggest still that 'public' places are not really public at all (women should not go into parks alone, after dark; women should not walk down dark or quiet streets alone, etc.). And women's behaviour in all public places is strictly monitored for its appropriateness – how often are we advised to wear clothes that will not encourage or attract unwanted attention? Remembering Suzanne Lacy's site-specific political performance *Three Weeks in May* (1977), we might be forgiven for arriving at the depressing conclusion that little has changed in the intervening thirty years. For *Three Weeks in May*, Lacy and her collaborators presented a number of performances and performative actions in Los Angeles, in an attempt to highlight the extent of sexual violence perpetrated against women in the city. A 'rape map' recorded specific instances of rape on a daily basis and made rape visible as a social (public) phenomenon by stamping the word RAPE in red ink onto the map on sites where rapes had occurred during the three-week period. Outlines of women's bodies were also marked onto pavements, a flower placed within each with the words 'A woman was raped near here' written next to them, and the date on which the crime was committed (see Loeffler, 1980; Lacy, 1978).

The continued fear that women experience in all sorts of so-called public places suggests that place, then as now, still does not belong equally to all. The explicitly political agenda of *Three Weeks in May* remains as relevant today as it did thirty years ago. Sections of Forced Entertainment's *The Travels* subtly engage with these issues. In this studio work, the performers recount their experiences of visiting different streets with suggestive names, first selected from 'A to Z's of the UK but then chosen randomly by each member of the company. Their journeys are made by chance refusing to be bound by any predetermined itinerary. Their map of the UK is a story map, a point made in the show itself when attention is drawn to, and comparisons made with, older systems of cartography (as well as de Certeau's urban walkers):

> Each map a new mix of stories, each mix, a new version of the world. And I'm thinking that's how we're working, on the ground, building space out of rumours.   (Forced Entertainment, *The Travels*, 2003)

The performance is minimal; performers sit behind tables and simply read their reflections aloud to us (reflections about themselves, about the places visited, about the world). One of the three female performers, Terry O'Connor, in spite of the variety of places to which she travels, seems continuously to place herself in situations where risk might be inferred, and her actions and sentiment appear almost as challenges to our assumptions about safe or appropriate behaviour (for women). Terry has to go to 'Rape Lane'. She tells us that it is a pretty lane. It is also, however, quiet and it takes Terry thirty minutes to walk down it (during which time she encountered no one). I think about how I would have felt doing that. In another scenario, Terry needs to get to 'Time Park'. Ironically, she realises that she won't make it there in time, and so instead looks for a hotel to stay in. Asking people she meets where she can find a hotel, she is first advised to avoid the north, which is unsafe, and then to avoid the east, at night time. Terry ignores such warnings, going where she is advised not to, and spending quite a lot of time in bars on the way. During her travels she meets a number of different men. She is offered a place to stay by one of them and is escorted back to her hotel by another. On yet another search for a specific place, Terry enters a house on a deserted cul-de-sac, where she has a cup of tea and a chat with three workmen who are renovating it. As I listen to Terry recounting her escapades, I can't help but think how reckless she is. In each of these tales, I am acutely aware of Terry's female body in these places (its seeming out-of-placeness) but I also get the impression that Terry is determined not to behave like prey (and not to treat the men she encounters as predators). Her performance is a challenge – a risky one? – to cultural assumptions.

No Place Like Home

Where 'public' space is often and at various times represented as and felt to be threatening, 'private' space is equally often deemed to be 'safe' space, so much so that a sense of place and the literal home are frequently taken to be synonymous. Of course, the place to which 'home' refers can be geographically variable, spanning from the house in which one was born, to the village or town and from there to country and nation. Common to each of these is Lippard's idea of intimate knowledge and familiarity (even if only 'imagined'). Philosopher Gaston Bachelard takes the first home as the primary essential model that structures our relations to all subsequent places since 'the house we were born in is physically inscribed in us'. For Bachelard, this first house continues to exist as 'a group of organic habits' long after we have left it, to the extent that 'all really inhabited space bears the essence of the notion of home' (1994 [1958], p. 5). Bachelard conceives of this model of the house (even if existing only in imagination) as a haven of stability and protection:

> In the life of a man, the house thrusts aside contingencies, its councils of continuity are unceasing. Without it, man would be a dispersed being. It maintains him through the storms of the heavens and those of life. It is body and soul. It is the human being's first world. Before he is 'cast into the world' [. . .] man is laid in the cradle of the house. And always, in our daydreams, the house is a large cradle. [. . .] Life begins well, it begins enclosed, protected, all warm in the bosom of the house.   (ibid., p. 7)

The inscription of gender is unmistakable in such conceptions of home, and even Bachelard mentions directly its 'maternal features' (ibid.). For Bachelard, drawing on and expanding psychoanalytic notions of the 'self' through 'topoanalysis', our idea of this first home is most pronounced because within it lodges the fantasy of a time of 'well being', of fullness (in which case we might consider the first 'home' as the womb; one can see why 'home' and 'nostalgia' – home sickness – fit together). Yi-Fu Tuan draws directly on Bachelard when he too proposes that 'Home is the outstanding example of a strong and rich sense of place', one 'redolent of fresh baked bread and unwashed linen, dust and waxed furniture' (2004, p. 46). Such sensuous renderings of home serve as markers of intimacy. And, though Tuan admits that most people (at least in the West) now live in several homes during their lifetime, he nevertheless proposes, like Bachelard, that 'the place where we grew up is home in a special sense' (ibid.). In fairness to Tuan he does also recognise that such frequently recited impressions of home, though enduring and appealing, are more fantastical than real (and therefore, perhaps symptomatic). Whilst home may be figured as safe and stable, it might also in reality be confining and limiting.

Home, with its suggestion of rooting, is, like place, frequently held against a more 'liberated' idea of movement. Such an opposition assumes rather than comments on the idea of home being stable and/or fixed, thereby also neglecting to read the potential for self-growth or development within this sphere. Moreover, if one considers 'home' from within the context of post-colonialism and migration, then we might be reminded that *being grounded is not necessarily about being fixed; being mobile is not necessarily about being detached*' (Ahmed *et al.*, 2003, p. 1; emphasis in original). Reading one as intrinsically reactionary and the other as implicitly liberatory neglects the difference made by specific details that lead to a 'variegated texture of habitation' (Ahmed *et al.*, 2003, p. 3). Equally, a sense of home, depending on one's experiences, may lie in continual movement rather than in a single place; home does not necessarily have to be tied to geographical territory. David Morley, indebted to John Berger, posits home as not 'so much a singular physical entity fixed in a particular place, but rather a mobile, symbolic habitat, a performative way of life and of doing things in which one makes one's home while in movement' (2000, p. 47). 'Home' may also transcend sentimental concepts, as Morley makes clear when he recites an interview with a Turkish migrant worker who pragmatically stated that 'Home is wherever you have a job' (ibid., p. 44). Tuan does also recognise that home might be less stable than is often proposed, since most homes are the sites of 'internal divisions and contradictions' (which in turn renders the 'self' that arises from such a home also less than 'whole') (2004, p. 54).

Though drawing attention to 'home' as more complex than some concepts of it allow, and to its potential as a site of conflict rather than of safety, Tuan nevertheless refuses explicitly to address the gendered experience of home. The social conception of home as a safe place has been enabled by perceiving and treating it as private, in distinction to the (assumed to be more dangerous) public space. Women's 'place', since the nineteenth century, has been the home. The home is also a sign of the historical 'privatisation' of life, and is, moreover, linked to the concept of the 'interiority' of the self (see Morley, 2000, p. 23). While the 'dangerous' social space is policed, what happens in the home is deemed to be a private matter. As many feminists have adduced, this division of private and public has served to make the private home a place that is 'protected' from public intrusion, but which as a result fails to protect its inhabitants from violence and abuse. Statistics for so-called 'domestic' abuse powerfully bring home the fact that home is not always homely.

What 'home' means will depend on what one's experiences of home are. For the harried full time mother or father (though it is still most often the mother), home is perhaps not quite a place of rest or sanctuary; rather, it is a place of full time work (often a second job). For the woman or man battered by her or his partner (though it is still most often women who are physically and sexually abused by male partners), the home may be associated with fear and pain rather than safety and sanctuary. For the gay son or lesbian daughter, home may be a discomfiting closet where one is always dissembling rather than a place of relaxation and relief from the daily 'public' stresses. However, home may also be, for some, a place of radical political resistance, as bell hooks insists (1991). When read against a history of slavery (and placelessness), and from within a context of black segregation and black menial labour (where many in fact served in the homes of white people), domestic work undertaken by black women in their own homes was not 'drudgery' but rather the active making of a place of recognition, really 'homemaking', where the homeplace 'in the midst of oppression and domination' is 'a site of resistance and liberation struggle' (hooks, 1991, p. 43). hooks carefully and radically inscribes the domestic site as a site for and of conscious political action by women (rather than domesticity as a sign of woman's 'natural' role). Home has no essential meaning in advance of its making. Rather, 'homes are always made and remade as grounds and conditions (of work, of family, of political climate, etc.) change' (Ahmed et al., 2003, p. 9).

Home Sickness

Having made reference, in Chapter 1, to the hugely innovative *Womanhouse* project (1972), where the 'age-old female activity of homemaking was taken to fantasy proportions' (Chicago and Schapiro, 1972), it seems appropriate to close this chapter by returning home. Mike Pearson's return home to Hibaldstow does not neglect the literal home, and the text of *Bubbling Tom* consciously inscribes women at its centre, recognising the cultural collusion between the domestic and gender, but also recognising the cultural work carried out at home. David Morley's citation of Richard Hoggart's portrait of working-class culture in the north of Britain in the 1950s has much resonance with Pearson's performance. Morley notes that, 'at the epicentre' of the local was the mother, or 'Ma', who in Hoggart's words is 'the pivot of the home, as it is practically the whole of her world [which] she, rather than the father, holds . . . together' (Hoggart [1957], cited in Morley, 2000, p. 63). In Pearson's text, homage is paid to the female figure of the homemaker, where the making of home is bound up with the maintaining and transmission of local knowledge. Thus, Pearson tells us that

> some people seem everywhere here, women in particular . . . Grandma Pearson, who through some extraordinary process involving the visitation of family and neighbours, glimpses of the street from behind her curtains, the daily perusal of the obituary column in the local newspaper and some almost mystical divination, accumulated, processed and held together vast bodies of information: histories, geographies, genealogies. She knew who lived where, who was related to whom, what was happening over dozens of square miles, constantly up-dated and cross-referenced. A world picture, a world in which to live.   (2000, p. 184)

Bobby Baker and Curious propose quite different engagements with 'home', showing that this supposedly 'private' space is thick with cultural (and therefore shared) assumptions and prescriptions. *Kitchen Show* (1991), first performed in Baker's own kitchen in London, both renders explicit and resists the gender operations that typically 'reside' at home. For Marcia Blumberg, *Kitchen Show*

> expose[s] and resist[s] stereotypical representations of domesticity and the normative positioning of a woman in a kitchen. This 'kitchen' theatre radically re-c/sites the engendering of place as contestatory space. (1998, p. 195)

As in her other work then (see Chapter 1), in *Kitchen Show* Baker appears to occupy the stereotypical role of housewife/mother in order to then deliberately transcend this (see Baldwyn, 1996): in the process, however, she, nevertheless, reveals the very real restrictions brought to bear by being located as a housewife and mother (though again, as in her other performances, Baker occupies a shifting and resistant subjectivity, being also comedian, story-teller, performer, cook, cat and believer).

Throughout *Kitchen Show* Baker is the perfect hostess, offering spectators the quintessential British cup of refreshing tea. (We, then, are the source of her work – and in more ways than one, since as an audience we also solicit her work as a performer.) As she stirs the tea, very precisely, she literally marks this gesture on her body by taping together her thumb and forefinger, just as they are positioned when holding a teaspoon. The role of hospitality is one that seems to constrain and bind her; the fact that she must perform the entire show with one hand bound tightly only serves to reinforce this perception. Baker will make a total of thirteen such marks on her body throughout the piece (a Baker's dozen), each signifying a daily activity that she professes to carry out regularly whilst in her own kitchen and each bearing testimony to the impact of 'being' a housewife-mother, a role most often taken for granted and undervalued. As Griselda Pollock puts it, 'the persona in the piece functions as the visible crossover point between the action of culture upon this woman and the cultural action of this artist' (1991, p. 7).

In *Kitchen Show* the specifically female body is as important as the site in which the work is placed, and this body is also the site of agency. Baker's performance manages to bring to the surface – often literally – what is so often invisible or denied (because it is felt inappropriate to the 'role'). The kitchen, like any other place, is rule- and role-bound. Making the kitchen a site of 'struggle and disruption' (Blumberg, 1998, p. 195), Baker's frustration and, sometimes, rage is performed here. Listening to her insist on the beauty to be found in peeling carrots under a running tap, we cannot help but admire her resilience; the kitchen, as a place, is seemingly as layered with signif- icant details as the place of Hibaldstow, and here too it appeals to all of our senses. Acknowledging this revaluing of the commonplace, I simultaneously admit to resenting the constraints apparently placed on Baker's creativity which oblige her to so persistently transform her everyday into moments of aesthetic pleasure. (Oh, if she could only go for a walk around the streets of London . . .) And when she (comically) demonstrates how she throws a ripe pear at the kitchen cupboard, to release some of her (pent up) anger, we might first applaud only to then feel deflated as we are instructed that the cupboard is the perfect target because it can be wiped clean afterwards (the sign of her anger once again swept under the carpet).

The fact that Baker performs in her actual kitchen, the real site of her frustration, surely adds to the effect since it brings in to sharp relief that this is not some stage set or fictional life; this *is* the everyday, filled with mundane tasks and creative acts of coping. (This is not to deny that the effect is partly rhetorical, because although Baker *is* a housewife and a mother, she is also a successful, international touring artist. Even in this 'non-set', Baker is strategically, tactically and skilfully playing her 'self' [see Chapter 1].)

At the end of *Kitchen Show*, Baker stands on a cake stand, slowly circling, her body displaying the thirteen different 'marks'. Her movement is poignantly accompanied by a recording of her daughter playing the piano. Her position on the cake stand is obviously precarious, as she struggles to balance, her body literally and metaphorically weighted down by the marks she has inscribed upon it. My response to this ricochets between humour and sadness. She looks comical, and faintly ridiculous. She looks burdened and teetering on the edge. Lesley Ferris marks the historical connection and intervention:

> Women on pedestals have been served up to us as artworks created by men. They have neither autonomy nor self-definition. But here, standing precariously on a cake stand overtly used for consumption, Baker connects her body to her domestic life and to her artwork.   (2002, p. 201)

Either way you, or she, turns, the housewife-mother on display before us is far removed from the 'ideal' representation, while the kitchen is figured as an ambivalent place of entrapment and resistance.

Curious' performance *On the Scent*, like *Kitchen Show*, is also performed 'at home', although the home in which it takes place is not the performers' (or spectators) and, in this sense, the picture of 'home' that we are offered is made strange.[19] Curious turns other people's homes into its personal theatres. Though the physical space is intimate, this is not a place of intimate knowledge, of deep connection for the performers. Already 'home' is dislodged from its usual place of familiarity. And yet, at the same time, something of the familiar remains for the spectator, because the idea of 'home' is a shared cultural discourse that surpasses the specific. Whether in Baker's home or in this home, I understand, anticipate and know the everyday practices that work to create and maintain this space.[20]

Performed for an audience of three, who are given a key to let themselves into (to intrude upon) the house, different stories about home unfold in three different spaces – the living room, the kitchen and the bedroom. Understanding that home is not just a matter of physical location but is 'lodged' within the senses, home is conjured through smell. Where Pearson remembered place through the intimacy of familiar touch, each room here is filled with the different smells that signify home for each of the performers. Irrespective of where we might be in time, smell has the capacity to transport us back to other times and places, dislodging vision as our primary mode of knowledge.

The living room of this particular home in Newham, London, is a space of sensuous luxuriousness, where Lois Weaver tempts us with violet and rose-scented chocolates and engulfs us with the 'Allure' of the past, literally with sprays of perfume, and metaphorically with tales of longing. Her tale hints of 'Obsession', of desires first provoked by the Avon Lady with her case of enticing bottles; bottles that could not be had right away, gratification stalled. Though the Avon Lady moves on, the desire she ignited remains unsatisfied, lingering like the scents sprayed in the room in which we stand and inhale. Home as unfulfilled, simmering longing . . .

In the kitchen, Leslie Hill cooks up a tale of mass destruction, evoking the spirits of her grandmother, grandfather and mother. Within this home, the *unheimlich*, Freud's 'uncanny', haunts every nook and cranny. Layering smells one over the other, a sense of the complexity of both 'home' and 'past' is conjured. The incense signifies the Native American 'home' of New Mexico, where Hill once lived (and, though Hill's father's mother was Cherokee, that tribe is not from New Mexico, leading Hill to wonder what it means to be 'a native'). A chop frying, combined with the wafts of cigarette smoke and a quick blast of hairspray, signifies Hill's other grandmother, a woman who understood that though you could not change the past you could rewrite it. (Her grandfather, a Marine Sergeant unable to cope with his commission in the South Pacific Islands, drank himself into an early grave; but this is one story that is edited out of the family history.)

Hill's childhood home was in New Mexico, and in the scenario painted for us here (through smell as well as through words), this home could not be further from safety or closer to danger. Hill was seven years old when she discovered that she 'was living right on top of the largest nuclear arsenal in the entire world', a discovery that petrified her. The term 'nuclear family' has a different ring to it in this context. The bombs invented and tested here were later dropped on Japan and, in addition to familial spirits, Hill also invokes the spirits of the hundreds of thousands of Japanese killed by 'Little Boy' and 'Fat Man', burning her own hair to signify that mass, pointless destruction claimed by the White House as the 'greatest scientific achievement in the history of mankind'. As the pictures so often broadcast on television make clear, warfare brings the inevitable destruction of other people's homes, bodies crushed under collapsing masonry. 'Home', for Hill, an exile in the UK, is also the USA, and as she hospitably invites us to drink a shot of tequila and toast 'home', her sentiments are clear:

Here's to Home – Sickness.

Hill's rendering of 'home' is, like Phil Smith's performance, extroverted in its outlook, crossing time and continents. Hill also deliberately confronts ideas of nostalgia and homesickness. Wresting 'sickness' away from the concept of longing for (a past) home, she revisions home as rather the source of sickness, making it a place to which one would rather not return. When she earlier conjured her grandmother and mother in the same space through the nauseating mix of cigarette smoke, frying meat, cheap hairspray and pop corn, Hill cheerily informed us that this 'smell[s] like old times', but then comically confuses 'neuralgia' with 'nostalgia'.

This challenge to homesickness is continued in the final room, the bedroom, where Helen Paris lies in bed and tells us that she's 'home, sick'. The smell of medicine is overwhelming. Paris too shifts the focus from being physically ill to suggesting that home itself is an ill place, a place of dis-ease where lies are told, acts of treachery are committed, a place where the past has fossilised and aspirations lie festering. Her alcoholic uncle, taking advantage of the fact that his wife has no sense of smell, pretends to have stopped drinking whilst continuing to drink himself to death. Paris's family home is pervaded with the smell of time passing, a passing that her mother refuses to acknowledge, instead clinging to the past. In this 'home', the future appears to have been banished, and home instead signifies stasis and atrophy:

It's remembrance of things past that have all been kept on way past their sell by date, things she should have let go of but still clings to, burying her face in the soft powdered folds of her long grown up children just trying to inhale back the years, through their school uniforms [. . . .]

Doreen Massey (2005) warns us that one danger of nostalgia is that it transfixes people into a past, rather than allowing them to have moved on with their lives. One cannot return home, for home has always moved on, as have the people in it. In this performance, however, it is not Paris's nostalgia that serves to transfix her mother, but her mother's own entrapment in the family home and her role within it. The gendered activity of homemaking is often the provision and maintenance of a home for others, as is evidenced in Bachelard's equation of home with womb. When the children leave home, does the home/mother/self cease to exist?

On the Scent, in its separate parts and cumulatively, offers visions of home that are far from enticing. In the homes of others, these conjured personal homes are subjected to critique rather than a nostalgic return. In place of a longing for home we smell, instead, frustration, fear, stagnation. At the end of the performance, the spectators are transformed into participants as we are each invited to share a memory about smell with Weaver, who 'captures' it on camera. Curiously, even though 'home' has been reframed for us over the duration of the performance, the vast majority of these remembered smells that we offer are nostalgic in their affect, taking us back to the 'good old past'. My own memory was of the smell of pine trees that in turn conjured before me an able and physically active forester father, invincible and still king of his own domain. The lure of the local, the fantasy of home, seems to be – as Bachelard proposed – an embedded habit that is hard to break (see Wheeler, 1994). Yet each of the performances discussed here works to make 'place' and 'self', and the relationships between these, complex. As place shifts, so it becomes impossible to ever finally locate or anchor the self either here or someplace else. Just as Massey prompts us to consider place as 'extroverted', as outward looking, existing not in some pre-given essence but through specific interrelations and interactions, so too might we want to consider the self as such a specific, but nevertheless extroverted subject, 'waiting to be determined' (Massey, 2005, p. 107); and perhaps even self-determined. The 'self' as a meeting place. If loose ends and ongoing stories are challenges to cartography, so too are they to be welcomed as challenges to autobiography.

4 Ethics: The Story of the Other

In the preceding chapters, our focus has been primarily on the political intentions and potential efficacy of autobiographical performance. What we have yet to address are the politics of making the work, or the ethics of praxis (Nicholson, 2005). The performances discussed in Chapter 2, 'History', all explicitly embraced more than autobiography by performing the stories of others at the same time as performers told their own stories. In those instances, the biographies were of close, familial or proximate others (Eakin, 1999, p. 176), specifically mothers and fathers. What such performances implicitly reveal is the relational status of the 'self'. The 'self' not only a historical and cultural construct but is imbued with, and indeed is inseparable from, others. In this instance, such inseparability does not refer only to the psycho-analytic understanding of the self as being dependent, structurally, on the other, but rather points also to more material connections between subjects. Our actions and experiences are never isolated; our stories are intertwined. As Nancy K. Miller asks, can autobiography ever be a story 'separate from the significant others – parents, lovers – with whom we continually make and remake ourselves'? (2000 [1996], p. 123).[1]

The extent of such relationality is plain to see in the majority of performances included in this study. Tim Miller cannot perform his demands for equality without also telling stories about Alistair; the lesbians in *Fingerlicks*, to record their experiences of survival and agency, must simultaneously bring into focus the rejections by children and parents and abuse by husbands; Mike Pearson, in conjuring his past of Hibaldstow, must also conjure spirits into existence, bringing them to life once again through the tales he tells; 'his' Hibaldstow is also reauthored by those others who walk with him on his guided tour.

In and through our everyday practices the self exists in relationships with others. The question that I want to ask in this chapter is whether this unavoidable relationality of selves brings with it a burden of responsibility. I am prompted in this exploration by Paul John Eakin's confident insistence that 'Because our own lives never stand free of the lives of others, we are faced with our responsibility to those others whenever we write [perform] about ourselves. There is no escaping this responsibility' (1999, p. 159). What might such a 'responsibility' mean in the field of autobiographical performance?

In this final chapter, I intend to propose neither a moral theory nor ethical principles that then prescribe an ethical model of autobiographical performance. I come to the question of ethics not as a moral philosopher but as a practitioner and spectator and the questions I ask here have announced themselves in the auditorium and in the practice studio where I have experienced ethical challenges. My application of the term 'ethics' is anchored within this lived space, and not in the realm of abstraction. Nevertheless, I do want to take seriously Eakin's insistence on 'responsibility' in order to consider the ethical dilemmas that arise in the unavoidable practice of representing others when performing autobiography, or more accurately, performing auto/biography. Particularly, I hope to prompt self-reflection on the part of those who create auto/biographical performance in order that they at least know what it is they potentially do, to others, every time they tell their 'own' story.

Though G. Thomas Couser's monograph, *Vulnerable Subjects: Ethics and Life Writing* (2004) refers exclusively to written texts, the series of questions he poses translate into the performance realm and are worth quoting at some length:

Where does the right to express and represent oneself begin to infringe on another's right to privacy? How shall the desires of the self be weighed against the demands of another, concern for aesthetics with concern for ethics? Is it necessary, or at least desirable, to obtain consent or permission from those to be represented? [...] Are autobiographers obliged to 'do good' – or at least to do no harm – to those they represent? Can harm to minor characters in one's autobiography be dismissed as unavoidable and trivial? If life writing necessarily involves violating the privacy of others and possibly harming them, what values might offset such ethical liabilities? Further, since published life writing is, after all, a commodity – in today's market, often a valuable one – is it necessary, or at least desirable, to share any proceeds with one's subject? What constitutes appropriation or even expropriation of someone else's story?   (2004, pp. x–xi)

Couser rightly identifies that the act of life writing, in which the self and the other are always implicated, is simultaneously a mimetic and a political act (ibid., p. 33).

The ethical models that Couser presses into service are utilitarianism, where individual desires are set beside a concept of social (that is majority) 'good'; and Kantian-based libertarianism, where individuals exist as ends-in-themselves and rationally perceive others as equal ends-in-themselves (rather than 'means'). Whilst these dominant models have increasingly come under criticism from many feminist moral philosophers (to whom we will turn at the end of this chapter), they undoubtedly continue to hold considerable sway in general debates concerning ethical practice, and are still used to 'weigh-up' choices.

Self/Other

While the self/other relationship is implicit to every auto/biographical act, there are a multiplicity of ways in which the relationship is structured in performance. Spalding Gray's best known monological work was self-evidently autobiographical but, as he admitted, it did also include the *bio* of another:

> Renee Shafransky I lived with for 14 years – an incredibly long time. [...] I would tell stories about our life together and that would make the monologue. So in a way Renee was a cowriter because I would often be quoting her. She'd be a central character, not only my life partner. The monologues were about those two characters, Renee and Spalding.   (Gray in Schechner, 2002, p. 164)

Another of Gray's shows, *Interviewing the Audience* (1980), offers a different model. For this, Gray would invite a number of spectators to the stage and interview them about aspects of their life, after which they could then ask him questions. Watching *Interviewing the Audience*, Michael Peterson admits to being concerned 'about the potential embarrassment or even heartbreak of his guests, and could not shake the feeling that they were being "used"' (1997, p. 64). In particular, Peterson worried that participants, whom he refers to as 'the sacrificial spectator', incited by the situation would divulge more than they should. He asks, 'How often do participants regret what they say? Isn't this thoroughly immoral?' (ibid.) Whilst *Interviewing the Audience* ostensibly facilitated the empowerment of 'ordinary' people (the everyman and everywoman of the audience), in fact these people, at least in Peterson's opinion, were transformed from subjects into objects though a verbal 'ritual thrashing' intended to reflect Gray's own stage power (ibid., p. 65).

Performances explored in Chapter 2, where epic familial stories become a primary motivating factor to give testimony, provide yet another model. In spite of their political intentions, these works are not immune from ethical considerations; indeed, Robbie McCauley admits that someone once asked her whether 'it is fair to stir your fathers in their graves'. Her reply was 'I'm not sure they are resting there' (in Patraka, 1996, p. 214).

Works tightly focused on inequality in relation to identity, such as those explored in Chapter 1, though primarily *auto*biographical, are again often auto*bio*graphical, as the 'personal' is related to the wider cultural and social context, making reference to others almost inevitable – mothers, fathers, lovers, friends, enemies. Perhaps at the other end of any auto/biographical spectrum there is the model called 'verbatim theatre', akin to 'oral history performances' (see Pollock, 2005). In verbatim theatre, interviews with people provide a foundation from which a script is developed that is then performed by actors. The term auto/biographical is entirely apt here since the words spoken are taken from people's reflections on events connected with their own lives (their autobiographies, then), whilst the representation of these by writers/actors casts the process as biographical. This might seem quite far from the autobiographical act which unavoidably enacts others in the process of performing the self but, in fact, the form's deliberate focus *on* others prompts some useful considerations that might then be reckoned with in relation to different models. Moreover, in some examples of verbatim theatre the performers also incorporate elements of their own lives into the production, employing a self-reflexive mode.

Verbatim Theatre

The term 'verbatim theatre', coined by Derek Paget in 1987, refers to a form of theatre which places interviews with people at the heart of its process. The genre is also popular in the USA, where it may be called theatre of testimony or documentary theatre. Wishing to distinguish verbatim theatre from the testimonial performances discussed in Chapter 2 (though nevertheless admitting to certain crossovers), in this section I am going to use the British term of reference.

Practiced in the UK since the 1970s,[2] the past decade has seen a remarkable increase in – or at least public recognition of – performances that might also be called performances of solicitation and/or appropriation. The performance of personal life experiences by the subject of those experiences has increasingly given way to performers who explicitly and deliberately solicit and perform others autobiographical testimonies in order to create a 'theater of public dialogue' (Jackson, 2005, p. 52); in distinction to the work explored in Chapter 2, the 'others' in these examples are not intimately related to the performers. This turn to 'others' might be understood as one response to the accusation that autobiographical performance is necessarily limited and solipsistic; these performances are ostensibly *not* about the performer (although I will go on to challenge this assumption). There are numerous examples of verbatim works in the USA including those by Emily Mann, Anna Deavere Smith, Eve Ensler and Tectonic Theater Project (to name only the most well known).[3] Britain has also recently experienced a flurry of highly visible verbatim performances, including works by Tricycle Theatre, Out of Joint, 7:84 Theatre Company and Liverpool Everyman.[4]

Though there are wide variations in terms of form and practices, a point made forcefully by David Hare who reminds us that we would be 'silly' to think that the performances had 'a single, common character' (2005, p. 112), I would, nevertheless, argue that many productions do share a dramaturgical structure. Typically, they create a collage that enables multiple points of view, represented through multiple voices, but anchor this to a single or central storyline or thematic, offered up 'for social deliberation' in an 'alternate public sphere' (Jackson, 2005, p. 52). Though these voices remain those of individuals, in many examples such a structure allows the spectator to 'shift their discursive conceptions of the subject from the single protagonist to the greater community' (Claycomb, 2003, p. 95). Verbatim plays, whilst consciously nodding towards a mode of realism, place people and their spoken thoughts side by side in order to imagine or stage conversations that have not yet happened. In this sense, we might consider them aspirational and even inspirational.

Hare describes verbatim drama as giving 'a voice to the voiceless', and this seems to be a recurring rhetorical trope used in relation to the form, often coupled with an associated duty to 'listen'. The programme note to Liverpool Everyman's *Unprotected* (2006) is typical when it explains that 'Verbatim Theatre enabled us to go to the heart of the issue, giving a voice to those most involved with and affected by street sex work' (Wilson *et al.*, 2006). Hare actually aligns verbatim drama with a practice of democracy (2005, p. 112). Given that verbatim dramas often represent untold stories, this positioning is understandable; it also implicitly signals the fact that theatre is not usually the site for these stories (the marginalised), and the verbatim model might therefore itself be perceived as a democratising force within the theatre industry. Verbatim work shares much with the testimonial performances previously discussed. Practitioners solicit the unsolicited, giving those unheard voices a public place, and perhaps then rewriting the dominant narratives in the process (narratives of history, social justice, community).[5]

Recognising the political motivation behind much verbatim work, we might nevertheless want to ask whose voice is spoken in verbatim productions and with what other potential effects? The typical process of creating verbatim dramas causes me to think that Hare's formulation might more accurately be phrased as 'voicing the voiceless', since talking out is replaced in this act of ventriloquism by talking for or talking about. For Linda Alcoff, as for me, 'Who is speaking, who is spoken of, and who listens is a result, as well as an act, of political struggle' (1991/2, p. 15). As we have explored in Chapter 1, it was precisely the lack of voice that prompted many women during the second-wave feminist movement to embrace autobiographical performance as a useful political platform. Those women also had to reckon with the politics of speaking 'as' and 'for'. I want to engage a little more with the practices and implications of performances considered 'verbatim' in an attempt to get under the rhetorical clichés of empowerment and liberation. Here again I am guided by Alcoff who recognises that 'the problematic of speaking for has at its center a concern with accountability and responsibility' (ibid., p. 16). To whom is one responsible or accountable in the production of verbatim performances?

Constructing the Other

The practical methodology of verbatim performance, though it might vary in detail, generally includes the conducting of interviews by performers, which are often recorded.[6] These are then used as the basis of the performed script (sometimes composed by a playwright and/or dramaturges), with performers taking on the words of the interviewees, and often key physical characteristics or what might be thought of as *gestus*. Anna Deavere Smith's work is typical of this approach, utilising a performance mode that Carol Martin labels 'hypernaturalistic mimesis' (1993, p. 45). Smith has been developing a series of performances since 1982, entitled *On the Road: A Search for American Character*, and commentators make frequent reference to her 'verbatim' rendering of the interviews she conducts. However, we should remember that the process of interviewing is not at all accidental. For example, Smith actively searches for specific kinds of people to interview (Martin, 1993, p. 46). Writer Rony Robinson similarly admits that his interviewed 'samples' were far from random. Reflecting on one interviewed subject, he discloses to Paget that he 'actually knew of her and found her and interviewed her. Because I wanted...that kind of voice' (Paget, 1987, p. 324). This might be considered problematic because the use of the term 'verbatim' deliberately aligns it with some notion of the 'authentic' and 'truthful'. 'Verbatim', and indeed 'documentary', as signifiers, operate like 'autobiography' proposing a relationship of veracity to the supposed facts.

In addition to sourcing and selecting interviewees, verbatim practitioners also construct the questions that are then posed, arguably thereby prompting certain answers. Finally, more people are interviewed than can possibly be included in a single performance. Though Smith might interview two hundred people for a project like *Twilight Los Angeles*, she actually only represents about twenty-five of them (Smith, 1994, p. xvii). Having decided who to interview, then, the practitioner also decides which interviewees to represent. Smith admits that

> The challenge of creating *On the Road* works is to select the voices that best represent the event I hope to portray. *Twilight* was a particular challenge in this regard due to the number and diversity of the voices I had gathered through interviews.   (ibid., p. xxii)

For *Unprotected*, 1000 pages of transcripts were transformed into a sixty-page script. Who decides what representation of an event is the 'best'? And how is that decision arrived at? The Tectonic Theater Project similarly gathered hundreds of hours of tapes for *The Laramie Project*, from which they selected the 'most important or relevant material' (Shewey, 2000, p. 18).

Verbatim plays do not, typically, provide us with the full contextual information of the interviewing process itself; speech is lifted out of context and used within a different context. Feminists have long insisted, particularly within the realm of ethnographic and oral history, that interviews and what they reveal must be treated with caution; 'interviews must be carefully contextualised, with attention to who is speaking, what their personal and social agenda is, and what kind of event they are describing' (Sangster, 1998, p. 88). Where they are speaking, when and to whom is also surely significant; as is the act of listening. These are the 'conditions of speaking' (Alcoff and Gray, 1993). As the interviewer is often invisible in the subsequently represented interview, we are unable to witness the extent to which the speech statements are jointly authored, the creation of a collaborative or interactive process (Sangster, 1998, p. 94) rather than unprompted and unmediated reflections. Where an address to the interviewer is included within the performed text, this seems only to increase the appeal to 'veracity' rather than provide any actual contextual information regarding the interviewing process and the dynamics that structured it or indeed the process by which the recorded interview was subsequently edited and restructured. In David Hare's *The Permanent Way*, 'David' is mentioned frequently, as in this extract that we presume is from an interview with the Vicar of Hatfield:

> David, I would like to see a drama of people who make things work. If Hatfield is in a play, I'd like it to be mentioned as a town of determined people. The town will regenerate and rebuild and rise up out of all this. (Hare, 2003, p. 59)

'David' might be referenced, but as I recollect, we never actually see him in the production; he is always out of view, a silent participant, which diminishes any sense of him as a 'controlling' presence in the interview (or indeed in the play – in fact, he is credited as the playwright). Rather, we might be inclined to think David is simply recording and then reporting what he heard. In fact, as Hare states in interview with British academic Richard Boon, while some of the speeches are reported directly as spoken, others are penned by Hare based on what he thinks 'the person wanted' but failed to say. Hare admits bluntly that 'The illusion is that I'm not present, but it's an illusion. I work like an artist, not like a journalist'.[7]

Tectonic Theater Project's *The Laramie Project* (2000) does draw attention to the making process since the opening lines, spoken by a 'narrator', inform us that

> On November 14, 1998, the members of Tectonic Theater Project travelled to Laramie, Wyoming, and conducted interviews with the people of the town. During the next year, we would return to Laramie several times and conduct over two hundred interviews. The play you are about to see is edited from those interviews, as well as from journal entries by members of the company and other found texts.   (Kaufman *et al.*, 2001, p. 5)

Such meta-theatrical gestures are now common in verbatim plays. *Unprotected* contains a similar moment at its opening, when Andy, an outreach worker speaking to a client, references some people in the drop-in centre (who are not represented by actors on the stage): 'Have you heard about the project that these're doing? [...] They're doing a project about managed zones'. Ali, a sex worker, asks him what happens, to which he replies 'Well they're gonna get actors and actresses to portray your words' (Wilson *et al.*, 2006, p. 2). Ali then asks the invisible writers

> My face isn't gonna be on that is it? It's just using the voices, isn't it? Okay. That's cool. Alright. Cool. Cool.   (ibid.)

We hear Ali give her consent.

The inclusion of such direct references to the process appears to make the mechanisms of that process more transparent. However, even in such examples we are rarely told or shown *how* or with what agenda the play is made, nor are the interviewing conditions ever made transparent. At the risk of dealing a no-win hand to verbatim practitioners, I share Ryan Claycomb's sense that rhetorical appeals to 'fairness', which lack detail, serve to further mask the playwrights' power (2003, p. 112).[8] Meta-theatricality does not lessen the appearance that stories are simply being told and simply being 'caught'. Baglia and Foster reach the same conclusion: 'the audience is enticed to "forget" that this play is constructed as an artistic representation' (2005, pp. 134–5).

While some productions, such as *The Permanent Way*, do acknowledge the playwright's power in relation to representation, the actual mechanisms of that power, its deployment in the creative act, remain veiled. For Couser, 'when mediation is ignored, the resulting text may be (mis)taken for a transparent lens through which we have direct access to its subject (rather than to its author)' (2004, p. 38). Rather than showing their processes of creativity, verbatim dramas, like other auto/biographical modes, more typically strategically deploy their closeness to the signifiers of 'truth' and 'authenticity', employing particular devices such as the use of the actual recorded interviews, or the projection of video recordings or photographs of the interviewed subjects.

Taking a moment to consider more fully the incorporation of such texts, the complexity of ethical practice in the field of theatre is made clear; arguably, intercutting the 'real' with the 'theatrically re-presented' *does* potentially serve to make transparent that what we are witnessing *is* a theatrical representation. The difference between the enacted voice and the recorded voice is undeniable. Second, by placing this actual recorded voice within the theatrical scene, that voice *is* given a literal place and is not being appropriated. Third, bringing the 'real' onto the stage serves as a powerful reminder that outside the theatre the real world, in all its inequality and violence, continues unabated. In *Unprotected*, for example, near the end of the performance we learn that Anne Marie Foy has been murdered. We then hear the actual recorded interview of her:

> You're never safe. Ye know out there, ye – it's it's – it is – like every car you get into ye don't know whether ye gonna get out of it. It's it's dangerous all the time, ye don't realise how dangerous. And me of all people do realise 'cos I have been in situations where I've nearly died.   (Wilson *et al.*, 2006, p. 67)

Hearing Foy's voice, having just learnt of her death, is shocking, particularly given her prophetic vision. As stressed throughout this book, this appeal to the real is precisely the powerful potential of auto/biographical performance; but this close proximity to the real also encourages a realist mode of representation (including the recordings, videos and photographs) which risks masking mediation and construction. Though the real voice may be heard, or the real photo projected, the image may nevertheless be the playwright's (and surely the fact that these plays carry playwrights' signatures is clear evidence of this). Also, what agency does Anne Marie Foy have here? Is she used, even in death, for emotional effect and impact?

Not only are subjects (people and topics) selected from the range available, but those interviews that are used are subsequently subjected to further editing since interviews are rarely replayed in their entirety. Alecky Blythe, artistic director of Recorded Delivery, informs us that it is during the edit that she tries to 'distill the characters and the key moments for dramatic effect. This is where you can control the story by being selective over what parts of the interview to present' (2005, p. 103). Emily Mann, though she would insist that she does not distort an interview or 'bend a person's testimony' to her 'personal needs' (Jordan, 2000, p. 3), nevertheless simultaneously declares that she chose, 'out of hundreds of hours [of conversation], to show these particular stories, and I chose to give this particular point of view. There's no such thing as an objective documentary' (Greene, 2000, p. 82). Blythe and Mann are, of course right since this is, after all, *theatre*, not a moment of reality. Derek Paget is blunt in his recognition of what takes precedence in the process of creating docudrama: 'the end in view in a verbatim show is very different from a sociological survey, since an awareness of *theatricality* is ultimately informing the whole operation' (Paget, 1987, p. 324). In *The Laramie Project*, for example, the interviewed residents exist as cogs in the dramatic wheel (or as a means to an end [Dolan, 2005, p. 126]), subjected to the narrative drive and needs of the story. Amy Tigner reads the play as mimicking the genre of the Western in terms of thematic, setting and narrative sweep, suggesting that individuals' 'stories become subsumed into and are often sacrificed to the larger narrative through-line' where townspeople exist 'to facilitate the hero's tale' (2002, p. 152). Such facilitation requires careful scripting. Tigner notes that the interview with Aaron Kriefels, the person who first found Matthew Shepard, 'follows the typical romance structure upon which Westerns are based – young man leaves society, encounters a conflict, succeeds in overcoming some obstacle, discovers an inner truth from the experience, and then returns to society a changed man' (ibid., p. 145). However, for this narrative to hold together, certain homophobic remarks that Kriefels made are left out of the representation. Mercedes Herrero, a member of the Tectonic Theater Project, tellingly admitted to Tigner that 'to include this part of his interview would have Kriefels "sound out of line"' , which Tigner rightly reinterprets, according to the narrative model, 'as out of character' (ibid.).

That the people represented in verbatim dramas are theatrical constructions, characters rather than 'real' people, is probably accepted by the majority of spectators who are all the time aware of the theatricality of the product. The impressive ensemble work that opens *The Permanent Way*, for example, signals clearly that this is a creative (and collaborative) endeavour. The construction of a train setting, produced entirely from the physical movements conducted in unison by the cast, and the various tableaux created, places theatricality at the centre of the experience. However, such theatricality is often then erased by the strategically deployed rhetorical appeals to veracity (see Reinelt, 1996; Tigner, 2002).

Perhaps, also, my concern with ethics in relation to the representation of others is naïve and misplaced since it assumes the existence of some 'original' or 'authentic' self that can be enacted, remaining 'truthful' to the 'source'. In reality, as we have seen, the 'self' is a historical, cultural and social construct, experienced as multiple, shifting and relational. However, whilst the self *is* a construction, every act of representing an other participates in that construction and as such extends beyond the theatrical frame, having a potential impact on the represented subject (Alcoff, 1991/2, pp. 9–10). Richard Kearney importantly reminds us of this when he insists that, 'if at the epistemological level it is often extremely difficult to establish clear referential relations between narrative and world, this does not mean, especially from an ethical point of view, that there is no distinction whatsoever' (1999, p. 21). Acknowledging theatre as a liminal space between narrative and world (and this is, after all, why so many press theatre into political service) does mean taking responsibility for representation. I am reminded here of Alcoff's insights that

> speaking should always carry with it an accountability and responsibility for what one says. To whom one is accountable is a political/epistemological choice contestable, contingent, and, as Donna Haraway says, constructed through the process of discursive action. (1991/2, pp. 25–6)

Laramie resident Harry Woods admitted to Amy Tigner that he found the experience of witnessing 'himself' on stage 'troublesome' since it reduced the complexity of his real life and his multiple subjectivity into a distilled extract, fixed in time (Tigner, 2002, p. 152). Harry, the real person, is inevitably reduced to a character in a play, with a limited number of thoughts, existing in one defined moment. The flux of life is erased. While *The Laramie Project* does attempt to represent the shifts that some people experienced over the eighteen-month period of its making, living subjects are, nevertheless, turned into stage characters, destined to repeat the same lines over and over every time the play is staged.[9] Some characters, producing what are considered 'key interviews', are given 'starring roles' in the productions and the burden of becoming in some way representative of an event, a perspective, a place or an issue, whilst others become mere one-dimensional 'sound-bites' (see Baglia and Foster, 2005; Paget, 1987). Still others, however, remain invisible, having been cut from the script. In such instances, then, these real people are doubly 'voiceless', having been initially courted, but then passed over in favour of other voices who are given time in the spotlight. This reiteration of invisibility might be considered less than empowering. As James Thompson insists (from the context of applied theatre practice), theatre practitioners who solicit stories are witnesses to those stories; which then begs the question of whether, 'by asking to hear, must we retell?' (2005, p. 25).

An awareness of responsibility, often linked to notions of trust, does not go unmarked by practitioners of verbatim theatre. Hare admits that, 'with this particular material, there is a clear moral obligation which is quite complex, particularly when you're dealing with the suffering that people have been through'.[10] In the programme for *Unprotected* we read that 'With the trust that was developing between writers and sources, many of whom were sharing intimate and sometimes harrowing stories for the first time, came a grave sense of responsibility' (Wilson *et al.*, 2006). In many examples 'responsibility' seems to be linked to unproblematic notions of truth. Thus Emily Mann notes that, in relation to *Greensboro*, she 'felt such a sense of responsibility to the survivors', a responsibility that she claims to have discharged by being 'truthful' (Jordan, 2000, p. 10). In *The Laramie Project*, only one interview is repeated throughout the production, thereby offering itself up as a guiding *leitmotif*:

> Father Schmit: And I will speak with you, I will trust that if you write a play of this, that you say it right. You need to do your best to say it correct.
>
> (Kaufman, 2001, p. 101)

Given the polyvocality of the 'community' that is Laramie, and the varying perspectives and opinions offered by its residents, what would constitute saying it correctly or saying it right? To whom is one responsible or accountable? To the people interviewed? To the murdered Matthew Shepard? To his parents, who repeatedly, throughout the play/in real life, make a plea to the media to respect their privacy? To the bare facts (as if these could be known)? To the past (as if this could be fixed)? To the people involved in the event? Must one behave with equal responsibility to all the people of this story, including the two young men who murdered Shepard? Or is the company responsible to a wider community – of gay men and lesbians? Or to the wider historical moment in the USA – in which case Laramie and its inhabitants might matter less than this greater objective? Is it possible to be responsible to all these different needs?[11]

In the majority of verbatim dramas, the performers are located as 'outsiders', which seems to translate into being able to take a different, and arguably more distanced, objective perspective on an event (see also Dolan, 2005). In Rony Robinson's words, the verbatim play is able to deliver the event 'back with a bit of *light* on it to the people who have experienced it' (in Paget, 1987, p. 317).[12] Amy Tigner, who has connections with the city of Laramie, makes a similar claim for *The Laramie Project*, arguing that the production 'had become a mirror in which the town people could view itself and could be used as a tool for Laramie to alter the way townspeople thought' (2002, p. 153). The dramaturgy of the play enabled 'a community to talk to itself' (Kelley, in Fousekis, 2005, p. 181), or at least to do so in the world of the play. The effect of this rhetoric of 'light' and 'visibility' is that it suggests that something already exists (albeit in the dark) and is simply waiting to be found. What all of this denies is that any so-called 'reflection' is a creative construction and that what is reflected or made visible is the practitioners' perspective. Alcoff warns that often the act of speaking for another is 'born of a desire for mastery, to privilege oneself as the one who more correctly understands the truth about another's situation or one who can champion a just cause and thus achieve glory and praise' (1991/2, p. 29). Inscribed in verbatim dramas are claims of gratitude. A 'Bereaved Mother' in *The Permanent Way* says

> I'm grateful to you. You've let me come in and talk about something serious. I don't want to be gobby. I don't want to go on being gobby for the rest of my life.   (Hare, 2003, p. 38)

Always remaining off-stage, so to speak, are the potential 'gains' and benefits to be had for companies (rather than participants) who devise such projects.[13] Joan Sangster's deliberation of her role as an oral historian of women's experiences translates well here: she 'gained access to women's memories not as a friend, but as a *professional historian*' (1998, p. 93). The positions occupied by the various participants are structurally different.

None of this is intended to deny that the stories told in verbatim dramas have social significance and are politically timely[14]; rather, it is to question the location and structural condition of that telling and to challenge the assumptions that are generated through rhetorical gestures, in relation to whose story is being performed. Other models of 'participatory' drama, such as *Fingerlicks* (see Chapter 1), or the 'open' script of *Bubbling Tom* (see Chapter 3), propose different approaches to facilitating the performance of auto/biography. Alicia J. Rouverol (2005), reflecting on her work with prison inmates on a collaborative oral history performance, precisely foregrounds the issue of power and where it resides. In this project, not only were the inmates' stories solicited, but they were also invited to participate in the creation of the final script and the performance. The context in which this particular performance work was made, a prison (with its own structural operations) made negotiations over the script an integral part of the process and the potential efficacy of the project.[15] Rouverol recognised that she 'was working in a setting in many ways defined by competition over power and control' and used this to insist on a different type of power, one invisible in this setting: 'the powerful right of each inmate to own their own stories, to determine how they would be seen and heard...and to be the authority in and on their respective stories' (2005, p. 25).

Laurie Lathem (2005), meanwhile, in her reflections on a project that sought to create a bridge between the young and the elderly, similarly reveals that her young performer-writers faced many of the same ethical questions that I am proposing here. For this project, a number of young people interviewed elderly people and used these stories as the springboard to writing/devising and performing other stories. The performed stories, then, were initiated by the stories that the young people had heard, but they did not try to represent these. One student, Emma, found the process ethically problematic. 'It's her story [...] Who am I to change it?' (Lathem, 2005, p. 76). Lathem's response coincides with the issues already identified: 'I told her she could be as faithful to the original interview material as she wanted, but that choice should be made on the basis of what would make for a good play' (ibid., pp. 76–7). In this project the interviews were deliberately *not* recorded. Though the young people interviewed elderly people, Lathem wanted to press upon them the need to listen closely, and the lack of recording equipment was intended as a prompt to get them to listen with their full attention. The unavoidable recourse to memory also made the play of their imaginations inevitable in the creative process that followed. In its very practice, then, Lathem's project did not propose an 'authentic' retelling and did not employ rhetorical language or devices that would suggest such an outcome; the performances were, rather, 'inspired' by the stories heard (ibid., p. 80). As Lathem reflects, watching a young woman tell 'her' story, 'the line between listening and creating had been crossed. Could anyone say where that line was any more?' The stories had become shared, and no one person could 'claim sole ownership' (ibid., p. 82). Consciously allowing a creative encounter between the story of the 'other' and of the 'self', Lathem hoped that the young people would be able to empathise with people who seemed, initially, so far removed from them:

> Through the act of repeating others' stories, the students were already creating their own stories, stories that were being told through the eyes of the 'other.' As Tania later noted, 'I had to put my own words from his [the interviewer subject's] perspective, but also from mine'. Before any writing had officially begun, the question had already been raised: whose stories were these?
>
> (ibid., p. 77)

The stories that the young people heard, which had the gloss of being 'far away', from another time and place, were brought close to them. In Lathem's opinion, the process was not one of 'vandalising' the original stories, but rather of encouraging the emerging artists to look beyond themselves by locating themselves within global and historical co-ordinates.

The National Theatre of Scotland's first 'verbatim' play, *Black Watch* (2006), written by Gregory Burke, also chooses to work with interviews in a more explicitly fictional way. Subtitled 'An unauthorised biography of the legendary Scottish Regiment', which immediately signals a distance from any assumed notion of 'authenticity', 'transparency' or 'veracity', the production makes it clear that what we are seeing is Burke's rendering of a play (an explicit work of fiction) based on interviews he held with former soldiers from the Black Watch regiment. Associate Director Davey Anderson notes in the programme that

> Although the play started off with a verbatim approach, it moved away from that quite quickly, which is useful theatrically because it means you

aren't tied down to valuing every single word or being under some moral obligation to say every word in the precise order it was spoken. What we're really trying to do is tell a story and when you stick to a verbatim approach, storytelling becomes secondary. Storytelling comes first here I think.

Though *Black Watch* does not re-present the interviews, the interviewing process is nevertheless represented, cutting into the more theatrically dramatic episodes. Through this device, we are supposedly given some insight into how this play has been made, and how Burke takes and transforms the reflections he has gathered. The distance between one and the other is marked. Simple oral replies become transformed into highly dramatic, stylised and, in places, surreal scenes, as we are transported to Iraq. The distance between the interviews and what we then see does not lead us to suppose that what we see is 'the truth' or 'real' or 'faithful' but, rather, is Burke's attempt to understand what he heard and the National Theatre of Scotland's translation of that into a highly accomplished piece of theatre. This distance is itself noted in the meta-theatrical moments woven between the dramatic story where we witness the writer, in a bar, interviewing a number of men who were once members of the Black Watch. One soldier testily asks the writer whether he has ever seen what a bullet of a particular size does. When the writer replies that he hasn't, the soldier asks him how he hopes to explain or describe that on stage. In another scene, questioning the soldiers about how it feels to lose friends in the war, the writer assures them that 'he understands', to which he in turn is told that 'No, you dinnae, but dinnae worry about it'. Close to the end of the play, one of the men (diagnosed with depression) threatens to break the writer's arm because 'If he wants to know what it's like in Iraq he should feel some fucking pain'.

The 'labour' of interviewing is also immediately apparent; questions are difficult to pose; answers are imprecise, rambling, off the point; many moments are awkward. Unlike other verbatim plays, where it seems as if people easily tell their implicitly dramatic stories, complete with a natural narrative formation, in *Black Watch* what we witness is the fragmented structure of interviews, the diversions and digressions, the moments of anger and impatience – all the stuff that is cut from the typical verbatim play. The *context* of the interview is displayed for us, and if not the actual process of playwriting, at least an acknowledgement of the distance travelled between the interviews and the 'finished product'. The power dynamic is also revealed, as in this accusation/question by one of the soldiers, made to the writer: 'You're a using cunt. You're going to use us?' When the writer replies 'No', the soldier informs him that he doesn't mind being used, as long as he's not made to look stupid. Later, another soldier proclaims that 'This cunt wants to make a name for himself by telling everyone what cunts we were'.

Of course, in a play that mixes a realist mode with heightened drama, stylised choreography, surreal images (soldiers bursting through the cover of a snooker table, for example) and popular theatre forms that 'cite' forerunners such as John McGrath's *The Cheviot, the Stag, and the Black Black Oil* (1973) and Bill Bryden's *The Ship* (1990), it is more than probable that the meta-theatrical scenes are also works of creative fiction. The 'writer', for example – stereotypically depicted as a bit of a nerd – does not bear much similarity with what we know of Gregory Burke. Whether these scenes represent what did or did not happen does not, in my mind, matter because their job, when set within the whole play, is precisely to draw attention to theatre as always a creative act, whether 'based' on interviews or not. *Black Watch* also offers commentary on the ethics and politics of the verbatim approach – its own and others. Interestingly, even though Burke does not assume a mimetic representation of the men he interviewed, the programme notes, nevertheless, make reference to the responsibility that practitioners have when they draw on the lives of other people – responsibilities to both those people *and* the work, or ethics/aesthetics: 'it's very tricky to honour somebody else's words and still make the show what you mean it to be' (Stephen Hoggett, Associate Director).

Finally, Graeme Miller's *Linked* project (2003), close in form to the verbatim dramas, provides an interesting example of ethical practice. The structure of *Linked* is an audio-walk, over a four-mile stretch. Individual participants, or walkers, are kitted out with a headset, mobile receiver and a map. Twenty transmitters fixed at different points along the route transmit recordings of people who used to live there, allowing walkers to pick up different voices linked to the specific place being walked through. Sharing features with many of the works explored in Chapter 3, *Linked* explicitly draws attention not only to the politics of place, but also to the political potential of performance. In the 1990s, Miller's locale in East London was torn apart by the construction of the M11 link road, resulting in the demolition of hundreds of homes. *Linked* is about that act of appropriation, but more productively it also serves to link the former inhabitants of the place to each other; the present to the past; and the spectator-participants to the place (and the politics).

Though inarguably site-specific, what is most atypical about *Linked* is that the site being conjured is physically absent, since it was literally made over. Where once there was a locale now there is, what Marc Augé (2000) would refer to as, a 'non-place'. When the link road was built, it not only served to demolish the material fabric of the place but also threatened the more intangible strata – of stories, histories, memories, lore – that coalesce around (and arguably make) places. *Linked*, then, is a very deliberate act of political resistance to the state-sponsored technologies of enforced forgetting and erasure (see Lavery, 2005a). Whilst the new road might destroy the physical place, Miller's sonic performance attempts to preserve place in memory and imagination. Confronting his demolished home, Miller experienced a disconnection from the past:

> We write ourselves into the landscape. We own space because we can tell stories about it. And I thought that by making a narrative piece about the neighbourhood, I could put my life back on the map and re-appropriate ten years worth of memories that had been stolen.   (Miller in Lavery, 2005b, p. 161)

Where *Bubbling Tom* collected memories relating to Hibaldstow during the performance, *Linked* was, from the outset, imagined as a 'collective memory bank' (Miller in Lavery, 2005b, p. 161). Like *Bubbling Tom*, the histories being witnessed and honoured here are those of everyday events, including acts of resistance against the impending destruction. Miller is, however, conscious of his own role in authoring and seemingly authorising this placemaking narrative artwork. Though he has deliberately created an open, fragmented and layered aural text, with voices interweaving and merging, the content of this text was nevertheless selected, as in verbatim dramas, from 'about sixty mini-discs full of material' (ibid., p. 163). In a piece about appropriation and re-appropriation, Miller must be conscious of his potential appropriation of others' stories. In what strikes me as an example of ethical practice the discs, in their entirety, are now lodged with the Museum of London. Miller's is only one potential perspective on this local history. Other tracks could easily be made from the same material, producing a map of vastly different contours. What has been left out of *Linked*, nevertheless, remains literally housed, accessible should we want to listen to it. Unlike the destructive event that prompted *Linked*, nothing has been discarded; everything has been preserved and implicitly given value. As an ongoing project, Miller hopes that *Linked*, rather than being perceived as an authoritative 'alternative' history, will instead inspire other 'remembering, counterstories, and gross omissions and alternative versions of the same event that may renew the narrative tissue of the neighbourhood' (Miller in Lavery, 2005a, p. 156). In process and product, *Linked* proposes an ethical relationship to its subjects, its spectators and to the place of performance.

Performance Rights

Surveying auto/biographies, G. Thomas Couser constructs something of a moral continuum when he concludes that in 'intimate life writing – that done within families or couples, close relationships', the degree of vulnerability between people is greater and therefore the 'ethical stakes' are higher (2004, p. xii). A sense of betrayal is, perhaps, also greater, given that trust is a key component of most intimate relationships and it is within such relationships that one can arguably become most exposed and therefore 'known' (see Baier, 1994). In the remainder of this section, I want to explore two performances that negotiate this 'betrayal', Spalding Gray's *Rumstick Road* and Lisa Kron's *Well*.

Spalding Gray: Performing Life and Death

Spalding Gray is arguably one of American's best known autobiographical performers; the fact that his 'autobiography' ends with his disappearance in January 2004, and the subsequent recovery of his body from New York's East River on the 8 March, is likely to enhance rather than diminish his reputation. This final chapter of his life encourages rereadings of Gray's life's works, applying the illuminating benefit of hindsight. However, given that Gray's monologues were consistently concerned with his state of health (physical and mental) or his search for 'the perfect moment' or with his mother's suicide, it perhaps does not take much imagination to predict the ending from what has gone before. Indeed, even before the final act, such prophecies litter the critical analyses of Gray's work: Henry M. Sayre, for example, deduces that 'all of Gray's quests are attempts to confront the specter of death' (1999, p. 261). In performance, of course, one can return from death, to repeat it again the next time (see Sayre, 1999; Gray, 1992, p. 11; Brewer, 1996) and in fact a more optimistic projected ending would have figured Gray as having successfully fought his demons through his creative practice. Gray himself appreciated the 'therapeutic' value of repetition as experienced in his repeated attendance at the funeral of Emily in *Our Town*, which gave him 'a sense of closure around the issue of having missed my mother's funeral' (Gray, 1992, p. 68). Gray has admitted that, since he did not believe in any afterlife,

> one way of coming back is to retell my life, to reincarnate myself through the story. That's very, very pleasurable, to retell it every night. 'Here I've been. I have been in the world and I am retelling this story and the repetition gives me a sense of meaning.'   (Schechner, 2002, p. 170)

Gray was also clear about the aestheticisation of his life and his sentiments echo those of Bobby Baker who stresses that story-telling is one means to respond to the mess of life (Baker, 2001b). In Gray's words,

> Life is not a story, it's a life. It's a raw and unmediated thing-in-itself. We try to make sense of what happens to us and of who we are in terms of stories. For me, meaning only exists in a story.   (Russell, 1997, p. 172)

Gray's career in autobiography properly began with the devising of *Three Places in Rhode Island* (1975–8), a trilogy that also launched the hugely influential The Wooster Group. The autobiographical impetus is already evident in the title of the first performance, *Sakonnet Point* (1975), which refers to Gray's summer holiday location when he was a child. *Rumstick Road* (1977), the second of the trilogy, refers to one of his childhood homes. Though *Rumstick Road* incorporated improvised material generated by the group, it 'was a memory piece to the extent that it dealt with my mother's suicide in 1967' (Gray, 1979, p. 37). The final play, *Nayatt School* (1978), more oblique in its autobiographical references, worked with T.S. Elliot's *The Cocktail Party*. Even here the autobiographical inferences are available to be read in the character of Celia Copplestone, 'a female character that was articulate about her "madness"' and for Gray, 'a fantasy of what my mother might have been had she had the intellectual distance to articulate her nervous breakdown' (Gray, 1979, p. 42).

After *Point Judith* (1979), an epilogue piece to the trilogy, Gray launched his more ostensibly monologic career with his solo show, *Sex and Death to the Age 14* (1979), followed by *Booze, Cars, and College Girls* (1979), *Points of Interest (America)* (1980), *Swimming to Cambodia* (1985), *Monster in a Box* (1992), *Gray's Anatomy* (1993), *It's a Slippery Slope* (1996) and *Morning, Noon, and Night* (1997). Each of these works documents a phase or event in Gray's life. James Leverett captures the dizzying interplay between Gray's life and its representation: 'It has gradually become Gray's chosen lot simultaneously to live his life and to play the role of Spalding Gray living his life, *and* to observe said Gray living his life in order to report on it in the next monologue' (1985, p. xii). When 'in' life it would seem that Gray was already accounting for it, taking stock so to speak. Gray's reflections suggest a structure of co-dependency between performance and living:

> I am in a sticky place now because *Morning, Noon, and Night* is about my family – so I am both living in it and telling about it, which makes things extremely claustrophobic. Also, once it's done, where do I go? How can I be a family man and do new material? Because to do new material would be to make an ongoing soap opera of the family – which I don't want to. (Schechner, 2002, p. 164)

Whilst recognising the potential benefits of recounting his stories, Gray was aware of the difference between therapy and performance. Following the end of his relationship with Renee, he admitted that he 'went into therapy for a while to try and figure out what the story was. What was speakable and what was unspeakable? What belonged in the therapist's office and what onstage?' (ibid., p. 172). Such self-reflexive comments as these, and his refusal to turn his family into a soap-opera, suggest that Gray had some idea of limits and of the appropriateness or otherwise of material to be performed in public. However, the closeness between Gray's lived life and his representation of it consistently raises the spectre of ethics in relation to others, not only in his *Interviewing the Audience*, but also in his early performance, *Rumstick Road*.

Rumstick Road

The second part of the *Rhode Island Trilogy*, *Rumstick Road*, is the performance that explores Gray's mother's suicide with the most focus. Incorporated into the performance are testimonies that carry 'the force of evidence' (Sayre, 1999, p. 264), including slides of the family home and of his mother, letters that his mother wrote to him and tape recordings of interviews which Gray conducted with his father and grandmothers, and also his mother's psychiatrist. *Rumstick Road* was the first of The Wooster Group's performances to court controversy, specifically for its use of 'private documents' in public (Savran, 1988). Adding fire to the oil is Gray's grandmother's specific request that the material remain private, a request that is in fact made public within the piece. Other moments in the performance prompt a similar unease with regards to the means by which it has been constructed. For example, though Gray insists in his later reflections that his relatives were prepared to help him, their uncertainty and the difficulty they experience during the recording of the material is palpable, as displayed in this excerpt from his father's interview, re-played in the performance:

> RG/MAN: ... it's the sort of thing I don't like to talk about ... I ... I don't like to be recorded you know ... [...] Well, I don't know why we go on talking about your mother, that's a very unpleasant subject you know ... I – I – I – just, uh ... I – I don't like to talk about disaster sort of things or ... things that are unpleasant in life.   (Gray, 1978b, pp. 106–7)

In spite of the emotional anguish, the father does provide his son with a description of Mrs. Gray's death, and though Gray appears to acknowledge his father's discomfort by agreeing that they should stop recording, in actual fact the cross-examination continued.

The response of Michael Feingold, reviewing the performance for the *Village Voice*, is paradigmatic in its criticism of the perceived exploitation suffered by Gray's family. Feingold registers 'a vehement protest about the morality of using private documents and tapes in this kind of public performance', arguing that he feels 'cheapened by having been made to participate in this violation of a stranger's privacy' (in Savran, 1988, p. 95). What seems to be most at stake for Feingold is his unwitting complicity in Gray's exploitative act, an experience that he claims 'brutalize[s] the audience'. A further controversial 'authentic' document included in the performance was a recording of a telephone conversation that Gray conducted with his mother's psychiatrist, which was apparently recorded without the psychiatrist's knowledge or consent.[16]

The problematic issues in *Rumstick Road* are those relating to privacy, exploitation and ownership. Gray's sharing of his mother's private letters and his playing in public a private conversation with her psychiatrist appears to flout the assumed cultural (if not legal) rights of subjects. Whilst the 'dead instantly lose their entitlement to privacy' (Miller, 2000 [1996], p. 13), this does not mean that ethical questions regarding that privacy disappear, since a certain cultural expectation to 'respect' the dead (or at least certain dead) prevails. Further, even where the recordings were undertaken with the knowledge of the participants, Gray seems to have abused the material given to him by his family by presenting publicly what was requested to remain private. Third, his use (and proposed abuse) of the material given to him would appear to turn subjects into powerless objects, and to do so in the (mere?) name of art. Gray reflects that

> *Rumstick Road* was incredible for me. To hear that material, to ritualize your relatives like that. Toward the end of the piece, I used to hear my grandmother as poetry.   (Savran, 1988, p. 94)

Adam Zachary Newton's claim that 'getting someone else's story is also a way of losing the person as "real," as what he is' resonates here (1995, p. 19). The subject is in danger of disappearing into allegory, a situation also recognised by Lisa Kron in the process of making *2.5 Minute Ride*, when she admits that she began to forget that her father was a real person with whom she had an ongoing real relationship. She states, 'I had to remind myself [to] stay actively engaged with this person. He's not just a character in your play. He is still this real person' (Kron, 2004).

Gray appears to offer some defence of his solicitation of this personal material by insisting that the recordings 'were made without any thought of how I might use them' (1979, p. 38). In another example, Gray writes that 'There was no plan or direction in the making of the tapes. I was not conscious of doing anything in the making other than asking questions as they came up' (1978a, p. 89). The discourse of 'premeditation' is conjured through its denial, a rhetoric used also by David Savran who tellingly reports that 'As Gray explains, all of these recordings were made quite innocently' (1988, p. 75). Gray's 'defence' seems to lie in the fact that, since he made all the recordings with no ulterior motive, they are not, *ipso facto*, exploitative. Leaving aside his blatant refusal to respect his grandmother's wishes – she explicitly did *not* consent to his use of her material in public – it should also be noted that, if Gray did not have any idea, in advance, of what would be on the tapes or of how he would subsequently use the recordings, his subjects could not really know to what they were consenting. One wonders whether, if they had known, they would have agreed or would have given the details they did give. Finally, the granting of permission is not, in itself, evidence of due ethical process since a subject might be motivated to help out of a sense of obligation or parental duty. Here the parent's Kantian aligned ethical duty takes precedence. This is the conclusion reached by the poet Patricia Hampl who initially thought (or at least convinced herself) that she had been doing her mother a huge favour by 'outing' her as having epilepsy. Employing a consequentialist ethical approach, it is precisely through pressing into service the rhetorical trope of 'giving voice', where speaking equates with liberation/therapy, that Hampl justifies her own actions, aligning ends with means:

> I didn't pause to think she was doing me a favor, that she might be making a terrible sacrifice. This was good for her, I told myself.... The wicked witch of secrecy had been vanquished. I hadn't simply won (though that was delicious). I had liberated my mother, unlocked her from the prison of the dark secret where she had been cruelly chained for so long.
>
> [....] My mother had been unable to speak. I had spoken for her. It had been hard for both of us. But this was the whole point of literature, its deepest good, this voicing of the unspoken, the forbidden.   (Hampl in Couser, 2004, p. 12)

Viewing the 'exchange' from another perspective, Hampl later recognised that her mother's consent was an act of maternal (cultural) devotion (ibid.).

In Gray's defence, if one is needed, it is not his mother that he presumes to be liberating (or saving) through the construction of *Rumstick Road*, as much as himself. Gray admits to using *Rumstick Road* as a way 'to develop some meaningful structure into which I could place the meaningless act of this suicide' (1979, p. 38). The performance would not enable him to make sense of his mother's suicide but rather provide a container within which he could place it – and perhaps thereby establish some control over it. The performance was

> an act of distancing. At last I was able to put my fears of and identification with, my mother's madness into a theatrical structure. I was able to give it some therapeutic distance. I was not looking to understand it, only to get it out of myself and give it some perspective.   (ibid., p. 39)

We might read *Rumstick Road* as an attempt by Gray to 'put his mother to rest' but also to deny his likeness to her. The creative act of making a performance piece provided distance; creativity was the therapy. Gray insists that *Rumstick Road*

> is a piece of art, an entirely new thing that stands on its own. Finally, if it is therapeutic, it is not so much in the fact that it is confessional but in the fact that it is ART. The historic event of my mother's suicide is only a part of the fabric of that ART. Finally, the piece is not about suicide; it is about making ART.   (ibid.)

Nancy K. Miller's illuminating thoughts on the 'betrayal' of children writing about their deceased parents has significance here. Miller considers such writings as necessary attempts by children to 'reauthor', or in fact give birth to, themselves. Her insights into writer Phillip Roth's memoirs might equally apply to Gray's apparent betrayal of his kin, particularly within the context of a suicide: 'What weighs heavier in the balance, a father's desire for privacy or a son's need to tell [....]?' (2000 [1996], p. 39):

> To separate from the other, father or mother, requires the enactment of one's own difference; the more likeness is asserted, the more difference is displayed. In this sense, betrayal – as an act of differentiation: there are two of us – seems to come with the territory of the family memoir. This is where I come from but not what I am.   (ibid., p. 29)

It is notable that Gray's conversation with his mother's psychiatrist explicitly makes reference to inherited medical conditions, revealing his anxiety about that possibility.

Gray was not present at his mother's death or her funeral and, therefore, missed the communal and ritual act of familial mourning. We might then also consider *Rumstick Road* as Gray's personal act of mourning after the fact. Although Miller's analysis is of written memoirs, her conclusions might also apply to Gray's live performance:

> Writing a parent's death in literary form displays both the steps toward separation and the tortuous paths of reconnection, after the fact. Grieving and release.   (ibid., p. 7)

Corresponding with Gray's own reflections on the performance therapeutically enabling or enacting distance from the event, Miller suggests that 'When we write abut the dead we write them into our lives, put them in a place from which we can move on' (ibid., p. 19).

David Savran, working against the grain of those critics who found Gray's process and content exploitative, rejects the 'outraged' readings of *Rumstick Road*. He interprets *Rumstick Road* as being a critique of objectification. The key to this reading lies in the only section of *Rumstick Road* not based on Gray's auto/biographical sources. 'First Examination' displays the process by which a person – and in fact this is very specifically a woman – is objectified into a body which is then worked on/worked over in the interests of 'diagnosis' and 'cure'. Savran describes the scene in performance as 'both frightening and sardonic'; in appearance the experience looks 'closer to rape than therapy' as the woman is 'dehumanised' and subjected to 'discomfort and disgrace' that 'must be endured because they are all for the patient's good' (1988, p. 87).

Employing a form that would become something of a trademark for The Wooster Group, *Rumstick Road* enacts what Linda Hutcheon (1989) refers to as a 'complicitous critique' – in this case objectifying subjects in order to critique objectification. Just as Gray's mother becomes subjected to the gaze of the medical profession, so too does she (and the rest of his family) become subjected to the gaze of the spectator.[17] But, in order for this to happen, and for that point to be inferred, LeCompte must, really, objectify them. In Savran's words, '*Rumstick Road* draws attention to the invasion of privacy, not for sensational ends, but to make the passive and silent spectator aware of his [*sic*] complicity with the act of violation, to implicate him in an exploitative way and voyeuristic act' (1988, p. 96). LeCompte admits that she 'always felt a little embarrassed that I came in and took it over, [the private material], that I objectified it' (ibid., p. 89). As Savran acknowledges, LeCompte's equivocalness in this matter arises as a 'result of her realization that the *mise en scene* submits the raw material to the same process that the piece is examining' (ibid., p. 90). The tactic of complicitous critique, however, demands that this deliberate objectification is made transparent rather than denied; hence, perhaps, the decision to include Gray's grandmother's request that her personal testimony remain private, a request that is blatantly denied. The question of the ethics of the piece is confronted directly in and through the piece itself, although we might still ask whether this cost (in trust) was worth it. In the end, for LeCompte,

what was most interesting about *Rumstick Road* [...] was the confrontation, the moral issue of the material. [...] As with *Route 1 & 9*, I still don't
understand its ramifications.   (ibid., p. 94)

Perhaps, though, LeCompte also forces us to confront the betrayal
that theatre, always and unavoidably *re*presentational, enacts. How
could Gray ever 'do justice' to his own and his family's pain, sense of
loss, anger and bewilderment, or to his mother's death?

Ethical Alternatives

Dominant models of ethics – utilitarianism and libertarianism – share
with the historical concept of autobiography a particular conception
of the 'self'. Autobiography has traditionally been understood as an
unearthing or revealing of the deep (typically hidden) self. Ethical
appeals to 'tell the truth', or to 'say it correct', are similarly appeals to
a knowable, fixed subject. Yet, as discussed throughout this text, such
a 'self' – an individual, autonomous subject – is itself a discursive construct. Every self is also, as I have argued here, relational. Perhaps, then,
as stated, appeals to ethics in the field of representation, particularly the
representation of others, problematically assume in advance some idea
of the 'original', to which representation can then remain 'faithful'.

The (historically male) disembodied and detached subject of philosophy has become as problematic as the 'self' of autobiography. If every
self is necessarily relational then appeals to 'autonomy' become problematic and the 'rights' assumed to adhere to individuals are subject to
critique. To take just one example, while Couser might ask, 'to what
extent [...] is our freedom to narrate our own lives restricted by the
rights of others to privacy?' (2004, p. 7), Eakin might respond that a
relational model of identity 'makes it more difficult to demarcate the
boundaries of self upon which a privacy-based ethics can be founded'
(1999, p. 160).[18]

Recognising that 'autonomy' is a problematic concept, some feminist philosophers now place stress on relationships of interdependence
and contexts, or an 'ethics of care', also arguing that understanding
morality as codifiable is misguided (see Gilligan, 1982; Baier, 1994;
Walker, 1998; Cooke, 1999). Margaret Walker, for example, criticises
the juridical-theoretical model for its inability to recognise particular
bonds, histories and expectations that exist between people (1998,
p. 51); universal moral codes leave no space for the specific. Walker
reminds us that:

Ours is a society pervasively segmented and stratified by gender, class, race, age, education, professionalization, sexual practice and other hierarchies of power and status. [...] Differently situated people may face different moral problems or experience similar ones differently. They will have reasonably different understandings of costs, risks, and relevance. They will see different responses realistically open to them in responding to these problems, and find different ways of resolving them to be successful or sane. They may well grasp their responsibilities as different in scope, content, kind, or stringency from those of others differently placed and experienced.   (Walker, 1998, p. 50)

Whilst we might be tempted to regard Walker's proposed ethical stance as being dangerously relativist, in fact we need to recognise her sensitivity to contextual determinants. It is not, then, that 'anything goes', but that each situation is located within a matrix of determining conditions, and that each of these conditions makes a decision more or less likely to be ethical. This is the distinction, then, between 'indeterminate' and 'undecidable'. Jacques Derrida clarifies,

Undecidability is the competition between two determined possibilities or options, two determined duties. There is no indeterminacy at all [....] When I say that there is nothing outside the text, I mean there is nothing outside the context, everything is determined.   (1999, p. 79)

Feminist philosopher Diane Elam, embracing the concept of 'undecidability' within the field of ethics and ethical activism, similarly insists that we look for 'the rule that may do justice to the case', rather than simply applying pre-existing rules. For Elam, 'we must judge where we are, in our pragmatic context, and no transcendental alibi will save us' (1994, p. 108). Operating in the domain of the 'undecidable', a decision has to be made each and every time. To apply accepted knowledge is, on the contrary, a refusal to accept ethical responsibility since no decision is required. As Derrida writes, 'if we knew what to do, if I knew in terms of knowledge what I have to do before the decision, then the decision would not be a decision' (1999, p. 66). Whilst every decision must of course be grounded in and informed by knowledge, 'the moment I take a decision it is a leap, I enter a heterogeneous space and that is the condition of responsibility' (ibid., p. 73).

Cognisant of the importance of context, in place of the juridical-theoretical model Walker instead proposes an 'expressive-collaborative' model, placing at its centre the practice of negotiation between people in deciding appropriate ethical behaviour. For Walker, 'determining responsibilities in the concrete usually involves grasping histories of trust, expectation, and agreement that make particular relationships morally demanding in particular ways' (1998, p. 69).

Lisa Kron's Well

I want to end this chapter by turning to Lisa Kron's performance, *Well*, in order to consider the relationship it is dependent upon. Specifically, I want to explore how that relationship is negotiated, both in process and product. Premiering at the Papp Public Theatre in 2004, *Well* transferred to Broadway in 2006. Kron's previous show was *2.5 Minute Ride* (see Chapter 2). Veering between humour and pathos, the comedy of *2.5 Minute Ride* is often at the expense of certain members of Kron's family, particularly her Aunt Francie. Tellingly, Kron admits that her aunts and cousins never came to see the show, and that she chose not to perform it 'in places where they might see it' (Kron, 2004). Kron was sensitive to the potential sense of hurt certain family members might feel if they witnessed her representation of them.

Where the protagonist of *2.5 Minute Ride* was Kron's father, the focus of *Well* switches to her mother. Though *Well* is not, as Kron herself says at the start of the production, about her or her mother, or indeed about their relationship, it is also not *not* about them; or rather, it is about them, but not simply nor singularly. The storyline of *Well* addresses the fact that both Kron and her mother, Ann, have experienced ill health related to allergies; however, where Kron got well again, her mother never did. At the heart of the play lie questions significant to this general discussion of ethics: how to experience or practice empathy without judgement or appropriation. In the play, one of the performers/characters advises Kron to stop 'trying to make sense of her [mother] through your experience' and instead to 'try just listening to her directly'.[19] I am reminded here of Sara Ahmed's insight that being unable to feel the pain of others does not mean that their pain is not my concern. Rather,

the ethical demand is that I must act about that which I cannot know, rather than act insofar as I know. I am moved by what does not belong to me. If I acted on her behalf only insofar as I knew how she felt, then I would act only insofar as I would appropriate her pain as my pain, that is, appropriate that which I cannot feel.   (2004, pp. 30–1)

A larger theme of Kron's performance precisely concerns the ethics of representing others in the moment of self-representation. Adopting

Lisa Kron, *Well*. Photo Michal Daniel

a self-reflexive, meta-theatrical dramaturgical structure *Well* aims to show the process by which an 'other' becomes subjected, appropriated, interpreted and constructed – or 'storied'.

Kron, always interested in experimenting with theatrical form and extending the boundaries of autobiographical performance, not only blurs the genre of autobiography by talking about both herself and her mother, she also unsettles the expected autobiographical form by really bringing the fiction of auto/biography into view. Like Kim Ima's *The Interlude*, discussed in Chapter 2, *Well* employs a number of actors to play the characters that populate Kron's auto/biography, including her mother, performed in the original production by Jayne Houdyshell.

At the beginning of the play, Kron's mother presses her to admit that she is undertaking a 'theatrical exploration of issues of health and illness both in an individual and in a community'. Asked which individual she is using, Kron replies, 'I don't know what you mean by "using"?' and then,

> Okay. Look. It's not ABOUT either one of us. I work using autobiographical material but ultimately this is a theatrical exploration of a universal experience. So it does utilize details about you. But it's not that big of a deal. I mean, I certainly wouldn't be the first person to write a play about her mother. I'll tell you, I wish I was that original.

Ann replies that though she does not like it, she can deal with it. However, with a nod towards Pirandello's *Six Characters in Search of an Author*, Ann thwarts Kron's attempt to tell the auto/biographical story by disputing her facts and memories of events, as well as her perspective and conclusions. In a key line, Kron admits that Ann doesn't 'make any sense as a character'. Ann/Houdyshell replies, 'Well, I guess that's the problem with using someone else's real life for your play'. Finally, the actors walk off stage, including Houdyshell, who stops performing as Kron's mother. Kron is, once again, the solo performer that she is best known to be. By the end of the performance Kron is left only with questions: how, with what right, why and whether she can tell her mother's story (Stevenson, 2004, p. 674).

Ethical practice is located not only in the finished 'product', but also in the process. In order to write *Well* Kron did, in fact, interview her mother about certain events, and according to Kron a lot of the words in *Well* are her mother's (Kron, 2004). Throughout the writing process, Kron would have frequent discussions with her mother about the play, giving her drafts of the text to read. Kron admits to having to confront her mother's terror in order to reassure her that the portrayal would not be negative. She also had to remind her mother that she was not the 'Lisa' represented in the play (who is distinctly lacking in empathy) but was, in fact, the whole play (Kron, 2004). Whilst we do not know Kron's particular history with her mother, we do know that she has been making solo, autobiographical work for many years and that *Well* is not a new or surprising departure. Moreover, *Well* follows on from *2.5 Minute Ride* and within this familial, historical trajectory might then be perceived as a balancing of eulogies rather than an act of appropriation or exploitation. While Ann Kron was reportedly 'terrorized' by the process of producing *Well* (Kron, 2004), is it possible that she would have felt under- or unvalued if her daughter had chosen only to pay tribute to her father? Thinking of Carol Gilligan's 'ethics of care', perhaps *Well* might be thought of precisely as a performance of Kron's responsibility to her mother, a responsibility of recognition discharged in the collecting of her mother's personal history. Whether it is appropriate for this history then to be made public of course begs another question. But there is no doubt that the making of this work would entail very specific collaboration with her mother, revolving around discussion and negotiation. Sensitive not only to hers and her mother's shared history but also to their shared future, the narrative of which was in some senses being written during the process of playmaking, Kron would have had to decide what was appropriate within this context. We might imagine that such an embedded relationship would make it impossible to ignore questions of responsibilities – where and to whom. While we must not forget the wider cultural–structural daughter/mother relationship that presses its own demands and expectations into service, *Well* at least addresses such relations and their negotiation, making it impossible for us to forget the power and privilege that enables one person to 'story' another.

Though I have chosen to focus on what I consider to be helpful self-reflective devices used by Kron, *Well* could alternatively be thought of as a double bluff. In the play, Kron's mother is allowed to disrupt and rewrite the script, and, in fact, to tell her own story. Nevertheless, ultimately, this *is* still a play, written by Kron and the 'own story' is, in the end, Kron's. Ann is a representation, created by Kron. In this *Well* is not so far from the verbatim dramas. Employing an alternative model, Kron could have invited or facilitated her mother to write and act her own story. In spite of Kron's stated desire to question her omniscience as a narrator (2004) it is telling that when asked whether she would ever consider having her parents on stage with her, perhaps in the vein of Ursula Martinez's auto/biographical show *A Family Outing* (1998), Kron replies that 'What I do on stage is way too tightly controlled for that' (Kron, 2004). While *Well* is about Kron's mother, it is also about Kron, just as *Rumstick Road* is about Gray and *The Laramie Project* is about the members of the Tectonic Theater Project. They are all, also, of course, about much more besides. And more simply, they are all, primarily, acts of theatre.

Conclusion: These Confessional Times

My interest in autobiographical performance is driven by its political potential, a potential that is writ large throughout this text. As we have seen, autobiographical performance may variously be an act of invention, intervention, contestation, revelation. The performance of personal narratives might bring hidden, denied or marginalised experiences into the spotlight, proposing other possible life paths. Bearing witness and giving testimony to others' life-stories might serve to make more complex our historical knowledge or bring the past into the present as a means to inform our futures. Performing stories about ourselves might enable us to imagine different selves, to determine different scripts than the ones that seem to trap us. Devising a performance out of the material of personal experience might enable new insights into the relationship between experience and structures of power, between identity and its formation (and reformation). Performing the personal in public might allow a connection between the performer and the spectator, encouraging the formation of a community or prompting discussion, dialogue and debate. The performance environment might well be a space of learning, the act a pedagogical one (for both performer and spectator) (see Aston, 2000b). This is just some of the work that autobiographical performance might do.

The word 'might', however, needs to be confronted. I hope that I have made as evident the dangers that always accompany autobiographical performance; dangers that include problematic essentialising gestures; the construction of limiting identities; the reiteration of normative narratives; the erasure of 'difference' and issues of structural inequality, ownership, appropriation and exploitation. We would do well to remember James Thompson's insights that 'without extreme care theatre projects that dig up narratives, experiences and remembrances can blame, enact revenge and foster animosity as much as they develop dialogue, respect or comfort' (2005, pp. 25–6). It is impossible to talk of potential without also considering failure (or failed potential), and this is the ever-present risk of autobiographical performance. In my opinion, the potential at least makes the risk worth taking; but the risk is lessened by an informed and thoughtfully critical – self-conscious – practice.

The Appropriate(d) Personal

Visiting New York in 2004, it was with some surprise (and perhaps also disappointment) that I learnt from a number of venue programmers and performance makers that autobiographical performance was not really happening any more; that it was no longer interesting as a form; that it had been seen and done. In fact, in relation to the first point at least, the number of performances that I encountered in Off-Off-Broadway venues suggested otherwise. Autobiographical performances were most certainly taking place, though admittedly less frequently in the East Village spaces where they originated. The issue was less one of disappearance than a seeming appropriation.

My visit to New York City coincided with the annual women's theatre festival, Estrogenius, which included an afternoon of 'solo' works, a number of which were ostensibly autobiographical in content. One of these, *Ayai, Yai, Yai* by Holly Rizzuto, related the tale of an Italian Lebanese woman attempting to break into the media, and failing as she is the wrong size, has the wrong shaped nose, etc. Though she moves to LA to fulfil her ambitions, in fact what she wants is 'happiness, I want love, I want food, I want family. I want to go home to New York'. The resolution of the piece is provided by her (happy) marriage to a Jewish man. Another piece, *Waiting*, a musical performed by Jenny Mercein, displayed not only her acting skills but also her singing and piano playing. The narrative recounts Mercein's experiences of being an actress who works as a waitress in the Tribeca Grill while waiting both for her big break and for the right man. The aphorism is that you must never give up hoping and trying. Though I missed the New York Fringe Festival, the rhetoric of autobiography employed in the publicity for that also suggests the programming of many performances that used personal material, including

Confessions of a Mormon Boy: 'Boy Scout, missionary, NYU-graduate, husband, father...Manhattan escort. After excommunication, divorce, prostitution, and drugs, a sixth-generation Utah Mormon reclaims his "Donny Osmond" smile. A sexy, harrowing autobiographical one-man play told with humor, song, and the Book of Mormon!'

Reflecting on these and a number of other Broadway and Off-Broadway performances which draw explicitly and primarily on personal experience, I am aware that they are formally predictable and might also be considered politically conservative. Where the use of personal material was once considered radical, these 'solo memoirs' appear almost generic. Life events are organised in relation to a particular narrative trajectory that unfolds chronologically through time to the present moment, typically represented as the 'happy ending'. Elza Zagreda's *Corn Bread and Feta Cheese: Growing Up Fat and Albanian* (2004), for example, performed at the Blue Heron Arts Centre in New York, weaves together two main strands – being Albanian in America and being a woman in Albanian culture. The politics of both are ostensible and explicit: Americans do not know where Albania is – 'Albany? Albino?', and in traditional Albanian culture women have no agency in their lives. And yet, at the end of the performance, we are assured of/reassured by the 'happy ending' as Zagreda (who is, incidentally, slim) gets married, not to an Albanian, to be sure, but her Albanian family nevertheless accepts her choice of husband; 400 of Zagreda's relatives attend the Albanian wedding ceremony:

> And there they were, my family. [...] Laughing. Happy. Nobody died or got stoned because I married a Latin American. [...] Marrying an Albanian doesn't make you an Albanian. Albanian means knowing your traditions. Giving your women a hard time and not enough credit. [...] Albanian is about family, about love, about bonds never being broken, no matter what you do.

Though Zagreda, unlike some Albanian women, is able to choose her own husband, even this radical option seems displaced since in the end family and culture remain sovereign, irrespective of whether it is precisely family and culture that are the roots of one's oppression.

In light of such work, it is perhaps understandable why so many critics consider solo autobiographical performance to be little more than a vehicle for the aspiring actor who perceives it as an easy way to 'put on a show'. The solo work, demanding a versatile performance, is considered the ideal window through which to showcase that versatility (particularly when the auto/biography represents multiple voices). The hope is that the piece will be picked up and transferred to Broadway or, at the very least, lead to the performer being cast in another production.[1] Laurie Lathem confirms this by admitting that when teaching a workshop at Highways Performance Space her 'class was filled with young actors in their twenties, most of whom sought stardom via the highly successful one person show' (2005, p. 66). In such a context, criticisms like Jonathan Kalb's seem reasonable:

> Solo performance is, of course a field rife with self-indulgence and incipient monumental egotism, and I have sat through as many shows demonstrating this as anyone – typically performed by frustrated and mediocre New York actors trying to jump-start their me-machines with sitcom-shallow autobiographical monologues.   (2000, p. 14)

That autobiographical performance has historically been considered a model of feminist praxis makes its seeming appropriation all the more troubling. This appropriation coincides with both increased social individuation – our 'society of the individual' – and the mass-mediation of the personal largely transformed into a spectacle intended for easy consumption. In these times, when the personal is ubiquitous, it is easy to forget just how radical that early feminist gesture of publicising the personal was. Michel Foucault's pronouncement on Western man, made in 1976, seems uncannily prescient from a twenty-first century perspective:

> We have [...] become a singularly confessing society. The confession has spread its effects far and wide. It plays a part in justice, medicine, family relationships, and love relations, in the most ordinary affairs of everyday life, and in the most solemn rites; one confesses one's crimes, one's sins, one's thoughts and desires, one's illnesses and troubles; one goes about telling, with the greatest precision, whatever is most difficult to tell. One confesses in public and in private, to one's parents, one's educators, one's doctor, to those one loves; one admits to oneself, in pleasure and in pain, things it would be impossible to tell anyone else, the things people write books about. One confesses – or is forced to confess.   (Foucault, 1990 [1976], p. 59)

If we were confessing animals in the 1970s, we have by now surely mutated into monsters.

The twenty-first century is the era of 'the celebrity', and we are all invited to take our fifteen minutes of broadcast fame. The number of confessional spaces available for occupancy in the mass media, and the sheer quantity of confessions elicited, is quite phenomenal and is surely so familiar that it needs no rehearsing here. Developments in digital technology, enabling the creation of blogs and use of webcams, have further increased the opportunities to publicise the private or exhibit the 'self'. In December 2004, Microsoft logged 'an average of seven million daily video chat sessions' (New York Times, 3 February 2005),[2] while the founder of Earthcam.Com estimated that by 2005 there would be thirty-six million webcams online (Andrejevic, 2004, p. 62). In June 2005, Technorati claimed to track 11.7 million blogs.[3] Not everything captured by webcam or written on blogs relates to *bio*, but a great deal of it certainly does. Confronted by such a cultural environment, it is little wonder that so many commentators talk of the commodification of the everyday.[4] The auto/biographical performance that is now standard fare on Broadway is matched by the 'colloquial turn' (Corner, 2004, p. 291) taken by television and the newer media. These too are focusing their attention on the quotidian events (both the mundane and the idiosyncratic) of the everyman and everywoman in a 'popular ethnography of the everyday' (Dovey, 2000, p. 138).[5] This cultural omnipresence of autobiography begs the question of whether a resistant autobiographical practice is even any longer a possibility. In light of continuing social inequities, I would argue that the personal does still have plenty of work to do, but that it must be put to work, must be made to work. In the face of critiques such as Jonathan Kalb's, and the frequently applied labels of 'self-indulgent', 'egotistical' and 'solipsistic', it is helpful to return to where we started (second-wave feminism) in order to re-examine the relationship of the personal to the political.

Feminist critic Imelda Whelehan reminds us that what made the Women's Liberation Movement distinct from other political movements at the time 'could be summed up in the slogan "the personal is political"' (1995, p. 13). As discussed in Chapter 1, the 'personal' here equated with the experiences of women, experiences which to this moment had been typically hidden behind domestic doors. The radical feminist act was not only the publicising of the personal but also the insistence that the personal was never only personal since it was always structural and relational. This was precisely the point about the politics of the personal. The politics of the personal is that the personal is *not* singularly about me.

In a society which predominantly focuses on the 'individual' and which lacks any discernible feminist *movement*, the slogan is admittedly little more than a clichéd sound-bite, with the repetition of 'the personal *is* political' in some ways emptying out the relationship between the personal and the social.[6] Like Bonnie Zimmerman, we might ask 'How was the personal political – by fiat or by struggle?' (1985, pp. 253–4). The personal is not implicitly political, and remains simply personal when it is removed from its cultural and historical location (Langellier, 1998, p. 210). To use Teresa deLauretis's insights, those relations which we assume to be subjective must be exposed as being social and historical (1984, p. 159). Gerry Harris rightly reminds us that 'not all of the personal is political in *exactly the same way* and to the same effect' (1999, p. 167). When a representation is 'just personal' it fails to communicate beyond the 'self' (to the audience), serving to further 'personalize and individualize meanings [...] than to open access to the sociality of experience and the politics of knowledge' (Langellier, 1998, p. 209). In some cases, the personal might just be simply that, and its publicisation – irrespective of the media – serves no wider political or interventionist end.

Given the continuing ubiquity of the slogan, we might stand to benefit from reframing the personal by proposing a more nuanced politics *about* the personal. Holly Hughes has claimed that the slogan, 'the personal is political', has 'remained a vital challenge' for performance artists, rather than 'a piece of seventies' kitsch or an excuse to pass off attending Twelve Steps groups and aerobics classes as contributions towards social change' (Hughes and Román, 1998, p. 8). The 'vital challenge' that Hughes identifies could be that of re-engaging with the politics of the personal; or rather the politics of 'the personal is political'. Such a reframing may well reclaim the personal for political – rather than niche-marketing – purposes. The work of autobiographical performance is to explore (question, reveal) the relationship *between* the personal and the political, engaging with and theorising the discursive construction of selves and experience. The personal has political purchase when its place in history and culture is examined, when its ontology is dissected rather than taken as a given, when the epistemology of experience is plotted. As Darlene Hantzis writes, after deLauretis, 'claiming discursive space for the personal is a political act that requires vigilant interrogation of both conceptual terrains – "personal" and "political" – even as their articulation remakes each' (1998, p. 203). Attention to discourses necessarily focuses attention also on discursive institutions and diffuse operations of power, including who has the right to story a life, what sort of life can be performed and what sorts of lives can be lived.

This does not, though, answer the problem of saturation. For a performance to stand out from or resist the flow of contemporary confessional outpourings, it may well be that some attention to form is necessary – a sort of re-energising of autobiography as both a medium and a message. The debate over whether a politically effective work relies on its formal structure is long standing.[7] Those performances which simply repeat known and by now conventional models (of presentational style, dramaturgical structure, thematic concerns, etc.) risk a failure of engagement.

Admitting that there may now be a formulaic 'genre' of the performed 'solo memoir', the majority of work explored in this book did or does challenge the familiar. The site-specific or site-generic work of Mike Pearson, Phil Smith, Bobby Baker and Curious places the spectator and the performer into unusual configurations and places, unsettling place as well as spectator: Robbie McCauley devises a form intended to embrace live performance as a work in progress (politically and aesthetically); Lisa Kron and Kim Ima challenge expectations by employing a multiple cast to tell their auto/biographical stories; *Black Watch* uses familiar verbatim techniques but strategically translates the results of this into a heightened theatrical form, moving away from the realist mode that 'verbatim' encourages and implies. These performances, combining formal experimentation and pressing thematic focus, at least court an active engagement.

Whilst such performances stage formal interruptions in the familiar confessional deluge, autobiographical performance is, nevertheless, unavoidably caught up in the confessional apparatus's potential effect – the production and maintenance of 'truths'. However, it is the very operation of the confessional mode that affords the opportunity for counter-discursive stories (see Chapter 1). Alternatively, in autobiographical performance the performer may not be confessing, but rather witnessing; confessing not the 'self', then, but being the watchful eye/I of the world, and seeing or proposing it differently (see Champagne, 1990; Alcoff and Gray, 1993). Is it not also possible to strategically play with the mode of confession, acknowledging its powerful role in the construction of truth? Autobiographical performance provides the means to comment *on* this historical moment of the mediation of the personal. Rather than assuming that there is a truth that the confessional can construct/reveal, one might use the confessional to challenge that foundational assumption, making what Irene Gammel (1999) has termed 'confessional interventions'. This is certainly what Bobby Baker does. Her work acknowledges the contemporary appetite for consuming others' lives through deploying tactical modes of refusal. In *Drawing* (see Chapter 1), those moments which might be more exposing, more painful, more private, are rushed over or denied as she moves us quickly along to the next section – away from childbirth, illness, depression. In this sense, Baker frustrates our desire to know, to own, her life. Though her performances appear to offer insights into her personal, private life, in fact such offers are withheld. Not only can we never be sure who 'she' is and, therefore, who is confessing, Baker often 'confesses' only the mundane. In *Box Story* these include memories of bad haircuts, rotting teeth and failed performances. Refusing to confess anything beyond the resolutely everyday, in this show Baker ultimately uses the confession as a quest for 'innocence' rather than an acknowledgement of guilt (see Heddon, 2006a).

In *Drawing*, Baker also strategically denies the spectator final consumption by holding something back, keeping her own secrets as, at the very end of the performance, she blots out her graphic testimonies with white flour, refusing to divulge the referent. Such tactics of exhibiting only the mundane or of keeping secrets recognises but refuses the voyeuristic gaze, encoding 'significant distances, disruptions, and warnings' (Gammel, 1999, p. 11). Tim Etchells, founding member and director of Forced Entertainment, captures the feeling of *Drawing* by suggesting that Baker 'builds up to this moment where you feel she's going to "tell you everything" and then she refuses [...] and I'm left wondering what is was that she might have said' (1999, p. 79). I too am left wondering. But I am also engaged in my own acts of 'making things up'. Baker's 'secrets' are not only moments of refusal, or moments of 'privacy in public' (ibid.), they also perform spaces in which I, in the role of spectator, can bring myself into (the) 'play' as I fill in her gaps with my own stories.[8] Who, then, is the confessing subject here?

Another notable example of a confessional intervention might be Forced Entertainment's *Speak Bitterness* (1995). Originally a durational piece performed over a number of hours, the performers choose sheets scattered randomly on a table and select and read from them confessions which are by turns banal, revealing, shocking, unbelievable and humorous.

We pissed on the flag. We made a soap for black people. We told long boring anecdotes. We worked for £2.90 an hour. We gave Helen 15 minutes to pack her bags and get out of the house. We never thought; we never danced at weddings. They invented a new classification of lunatic just for us. We wrote biographies without bothering to research or ask permission. We lost the front door keys.   (*Speak Bitterness* in Etchells, 1999, p. 182)

Written into Forced Entertainment's performance (which includes its temporal structure) is a deliberate uncertainty about which confessions are actual, 'truthful' confessions, and which confessions – if any – belong to which performers. Not only are the audience perhaps made aware of their own desire to 'know' or to make certain the uncertain, but they are also potentially confronted with a stark and concentrated rendition of our everyday compulsion to both confess and receive confessions. The 'glut' of confession is made concrete as the hours pass. *Forced Entertainment* consciously uses the confessional to make a comment about the confessional. So too does Third Angel in its performance *Class of '76* (2000). In its first incarnation *Class of '76* was a fantastical rendering of the lives of Alex Kelly's school class of 1976. Kelly made up stories – probable and improbable – about all the people in his school photograph from that year. In the year 2000, however, with a nod to site-specific work, the company returned to the actual spot where the photograph had been taken to perform a second version (see Third Angel, 2000). For this, Kelly tracked down as many of the people in the school photo (using Friends Reunited as one tool), to find out what in fact had happened to them in the intervening years. There was only one performance of this show, performed mostly for his old classmates. The touring show of *Class of '76*, a third incarnation of the piece, employs an illustrated lecture format and works across the first and the second, with Kelly telling the spectators about both. In the process our grasp on reality is destabilised since in this third version, Kelly insists that, whereas the first version was a fabrication, the second version was the truth. Can we/do we believe him? As the faces of the children materialise and then disappear, caught fleetingly on a blank piece of paper held in front of a projection of the school photograph taken in 1976, the status of that 'truth' is similarly as fleeting: in spite of our attempts to 'catch' and frame it, the truth, like the past, exceeds our grasp. Just as the reality tv and chat shows seem to lure me in with their promise of revelation and appearance of unmediated reality, so too does *Class of*

'76 play with my appetite to consume others' lives. In the end, those lives are left ephemeral, exposed only momentarily by my gaze.

Performance artist Joshua Sofaer confronts the mechanisms of confession (and the power/appeal of auto/biography) even more transparently in his interventionist publication, *Joshua Sofaer: A Biography by Margaret Turner* (1997). The book jacket claims it is 'a vitally important book for all those who care about the cult of personality' and carries the expert's authoritative stamp of approval, including a 'blurb' from Professor David Milner, University of Westminster:

> Impressive research, finely deployed, at last a biography which delves deep into cultural mechanisms...it is analytical and therefore reflexive; it adheres to the standard of scholarship which insists that in studying the other we learn about ourselves.   (Sofaer, 1997)

On opening the thick biography, I am confronted with nothing but blank page after blank page. In some senses, of course, Professor David Milner (if there is such a person) is quite accurate in his appraisal of this 'work'.[9] Sofaer, like the other artists discussed here, engages directly with the confessional apparatus but does so self-reflexively in order also to critique it. His blank pages are a literal refusal to enter the confessional box.

The Difference of Context

Given the mass-mediation of autobiographical gestures, it is tempting to present performance as being 'better than' mass-mediated forms. This would be to restage the 'high' vs 'low' debate. However, this would necessitate simplifying and reducing the vast range of mass-mediated outputs and their locations into one single category. The huge variety of places in which one can confess, combined with the different types of self-speaking or self-showing that are available, makes it impossible to 'contain [such moments] within a single concept of "the confessional"' (Dovey, 2000, p. 113). To presume that all mass-mediated autobiographical products are simply 'bad' or 'damaging' is also to neglect the different audiences and complex reading strategies that are undertaken by them. On the other hand, to presume that live performance is somehow intrinsically or implicitly 'better than' is to risk overly romanticising this form of mediation. To recognise the limits that surround performance is to allow a fuller embrace of its potential.

Throughout *Autobiography and Performance* I have made a great deal of the fact that performance enables a live encounter. Many mass-mediated works often incorporate live elements, while developments in broadcast technology have meant the inclusion of moments of interactive involvement from the viewer, making the mediated event increasingly immediate. The fact that a performance – any performance – is live is no guarantee of its political impact, and liveness by itself does not assure the formation of *communitas*. One can be part of an audience at a live event and feel completely isolated and alienated from the performer and other spectators. On the other hand, one can be part of an audience at a recorded event and feel part of a community in those moments when there is shared recognition (spontaneous cheering and applause at the cinema comes to mind). That moment is a live one for there is a 'liveness' that potentially adheres to all gatherings of people. For a performer, liveness, in the end, is merely a tool that they *always* have to hand. If it is to be utilised for political impact in the forging of community or in the prompting of action (even of changed consciousness) then it must be skilfully handled – as in *Sally's Rape* when we are invited by Robbie McCauley to 'Bid 'em in' or in *On the Scent* when Leslie Hill offers each of us a glass of tequila in order to make a collective toast: 'Here's to Home – Sickness' .

The 'liveness' of performance that supposedly sets it apart from other forms is to be found in the shared time and space of performer and spectator. Admittedly, the potential for the performer to sense, in the moment, and respond to the spectators' responses *is* a unique feature of live performance. Again, though, this feature has to be actively pressed into service and made to work and it demands that the performer takes a certain risk by actually being *in* each unique moment of liveness and also in this shared space. In fact, many performers continue to perform a fixed script from within a fixed architectural configuration, with the performer(s) in one area, being physically active, and the spectators in another, being physically passive and often completely disconnected from each other. After Roland Barthes, we recognise the always present mental activity of the spectator, their 'authoring' function. However, the lack of attention to the spectator's literal movement or involvement might be an oversight which misses other political potential. In considering the work that autobiographical performance does, we need to consider the structural relations that are enabled through the physical performance structure. As we have seen, when the spectators of *Bubbling Tom* walked around the village with Mike Pearson, they acted as participants, as contributors with a right to write and rewrite their location and, as such, to rewrite the 'script' of *Bubbling Tom* and the place of Hibaldstow. Pearson is firmly of the opinion that placing the performance outside a theatre environment meant that those who came to see it for the most part did not even read it within the frame of 'performance' and so did not feel the need to behave as 'spectators' (Pearson, 2001; see also Jackson, 2005; Bennett, 1990). Just as Pearson responded, in the moment, to his spectators' contributions, so did the physical architecture of the guided walk enable the spectators to leave behind the formal script that typically guides 'spectatorship'.

Recognising the inter-subjective potential of performances that erase the 'fourth wall', other performers have embraced structures of intimacy, forgoing the stage/auditorium set-up for intimate encounters with spectators/participants (see for example Phil Smith and Curious in Chapter 3). A recent trend in the UK has been the creation of one-on-one experiences, as in the work of Adrian Howells whose solo confessional performances, delivered via the persona of 'Adrienne', actively and deliberately solicit collaboration with the spectators in order to conjure an intimate exchange. Performing autobiographical revelations, Howells strategically interrupts his own monologue

Adrian Howells, *Salon Adrienne*. Photo Niall Walker

by inviting spectators to share their autobiographical reflections in turn. Howells' work, then, including his recent *Salon Adrienne* (2006) which was performed in a hairdresser's in Glasgow, formally resembles the structure of dialogue. Washing my hair and then rinsing off the conditioner, 'Adrienne' asked me when someone other than a hairdresser had washed my hair for me. Later, facing the mirror while he gently brushes my wet hair, he confides to me that he has not always been comfortable in his body and then invites me to talk about how it feels to look at myself in the mirror; how I feel about aging, about being thirty-seven. I talk about my mum, who died of cancer when she was forty-two. This unplanned dialogue continued for an hour, all the time Adrienne's memories prompting mine. Unlike the 'script' usually performed in the hairdresser's (or indeed the therapist's office), Howells gives of himself before asking of you.

The question of structural relations also applies to the performer's relationship to his/her work. Reflecting on the production of mass-mediated confession, television critic Jon Dovey notes that there are 'very few spaces [...] on television for an autobiographical mode in which the author of the representation is also its subject' (2000, p. 110). Historically, frequent reference has been made to the agency that is afforded the solo autobiographical performer who is assumed to have a degree of autonomy over her/his self-representation and the focus of the work. The subject and object are perceived to be one and the same (see Forte, 1988). We need to remember, though, that performance operates in a well-established market place and is governed by the forces of that market. Most performances exist as commodities. Certain performance markets, such as Broadway, demand certain performance products. But the experimental circuit is similarly a market, and fringe venues programme particular kinds of shows. In parallel, funding bodies and charities, which make even the most experimental or formally challenging work financially viable, also have their own list of priorities, governed by wider social concerns and political pressures. More simply, performance, for most performers, not only has a cultural and social job of work to do, but is itself literal work since it is often the performer's livelihood. The multiple demands of the performance market place, of different venues, programmers, funders and audiences curtail any simple notion of autonomy and agency.

The work of American performer Annie Sprinkle is instructive in this respect. I could write about Sprinkle's strategic performance of unstable identity as she continuously shifts who 'she' is within and between performances.[10] For example, in her best known work,

Post Post Porn Modernist, she is variously Ellen, Annie and Anya.[11] However, in spite of such shifts one aspect has remained constant. Sprinkle, as artist, appears to be trapped into selling her work on the basis of her sexuality – albeit in a performance studio rather than a porn cinema. While this does produce a potentially productive blur between art and pornography, spectator and client, it also proposes that Sprinkle will never be able to leave behind Annie Sprinkle, should she ever wish to do so. She has discovered that in the performance space sex also sells. In the show following *Post Post Porn Modernist*, called *Herstory of Porn: Reel to Real* (from 1998), Sprinkle is still called Annie Sprinkle (not Anya), and still talking about sex. That identity is quite stable. The title of Sprinkle's most recent performance, *Post Porn Love* (2005), even makes direct reference to the show that launched her nearly thirty years previously.[12] Sprinkle has found her market.

In considering the political or interventionist potential of performance – what that performance can do – the context of every show needs to be acknowledged. Context informs not only what is possible from the outset, but also reception. Autobiographical performances do not take place in a cultural vacuum, but are part of a complex network of conditions which includes a work's geographical, cultural, economic, political and historical location. Though I have explored a range of different types of autobiographical performance within the covers of this one book, each of these inevitably has its own set of particular relations (both within and outside of the work). Bobby Baker, making her solo autobiographical touring shows, assisted by her director, Polona Baloh Brown, brings into play a very different set of relations than, for example, Natalie Wilson working on the community show, *Fingerlicks*, for the Glasgay! festival.

Another informing context for this work is me, here and now. Though I have offered engagements with and analysis of various performances, it should be underlined that these engagements and analysis are *mine* (albeit informed by and indebted to a range of other performances, critics, theories and discourses). Whilst this might be obvious, the reason that I want to stress it is that the impact of any performance cannot simply be assumed, precisely because every performance is located within an arrangement of informing factors that serve to make that performance in the precise moment of its 'event'.[13] The presence of the spectator, as one of these factors, makes it impossible to determine whether and how a performance is political, since each spectator brings to the performance their own strategies of analysis and reading environment. This includes their viewing identity (admitting that this might, in fact, shift during the performance). I am guided here by Gerry Harris:

> The political effect of any given work is not a matter of authorship or form, or of individual readers, or of interpretative communities, or institutional, social or material location, theories or practices, but of the specific dynamic existing between these diverse elements at a particular moment in time.   (1999, p. 172; see also Langellier, 1998, p. 210)

Just as the majority of work explored in this text is multifaceted in its mechanisms of staging the self and autobiography, so too is the act of spectatorship. I admit that I engage with the performances discussed throughout this text as a feminist teacher, practitioner and academic who has been studying the 'form' of performance art generally, and autobiographical performance specifically, for nearly twenty years. I come to each of the performances with a sedimented knowledge (of critical theory, of other performances, of the performers themselves, of myself even, etc.). I also come to each of the performances in a specific time and place (both their time and my own, which sometimes coincide but not always). And I necessarily always write about performances after the event (and often in association with other material, including recordings, scripts, reviews and interviews). All of this serves to make my own engagement with 'the performance' much more than singular, and really I should reference each performance as being a 'plural' event, or even an imagined performance. Furthermore, the immediate context for my spectatorship, now, is the production of this book. I come to each performance with an agenda and I am looking for performance strategies and tactics that signal their political, interventionist potential. A different spectator, a different me, might look from another place and see a different show.

Context, then, of which I am a part, makes all the difference. Engaging with the politics of the personal, we should certainly consider, at the outset, 'which personal' and 'whose politics' we are talking about (Heywood and Drake, 1997, p. 23). This puts a slightly different spin on Harris's statement that 'not all of the personal is political in *exactly the same way* and to the same effect' (1999, p. 167). What is considered political in one place may seem irrelevant in another. Returning to Elza Zagreda's Off-Broadway show, *Growing Up Fat and Albanian*, and the particular context of this show (Off-Broadway, 2004), I recognise that Zagreda manages to include details about the often oppressive treatment of women in traditional Albanian society.

More importantly, in terms of *this* context (*this* time and place), she also alludes to the often oppressive treatment of Albanians in much of American society. The acceptable narrative form (which includes the happy resolution) might be read as the container through which to present the less acceptable (or more challenging) political commentary.

Zagreda's performance presses me to realise that any consideration of the political potential of autobiographical performances means also considering the questions of who, where, what, when, how and why, singularly and in combination. Our attention must encompass not only the performance, but also the 'conditions of performing' – or, indeed, of not performing. For example, though you might have 'seen it, heard it, done it', the closeted and isolated lesbian might be desperate to see it and hear it, or even perform it. Equally, in contexts in which people feel silenced, invisible or threatened (and many still do), insisting on a deep and stable 'self' might be a necessary part of their daily struggle for survival (Thompson, 2005, p. 29). Alternatively, a dogged silence in the face of coercive forces that impel one to speak might be a strategic way of 'saying' it differently, rather than a gesture of complicity. Given the variables simultaneously at play – subjects, places, histories – a singular model of politically efficacious autobiographical performance is an impossibility. What can be said, though, purposefully and without any hesitation, is that, in the face of all the evidence presented here, there is nothing 'mere' about autobiographical performances. The majority are also much more than 'merely about the self'. Rather, they are performances of aspiration and possibility, creative acts that have the potential to contribute to ongoing cultural transformations. Looking at the past through the present we are urged to consider the future and what we might choose to make there.

Notes

Introduction

1. I think I saw this performance at the Third Eye Centre in Glasgow in 1988 – although memory can play many tricks and it may be that I only ever saw a video recording of it. I have no programme or ticket that testifies to my having been there.
2. Whilst Gray might have fulfilled most of the criteria for the dominant and dominating normative subject, arguably his experience of mental health equally marginalised him from normative society.
3. The dangers that adhere to visibility include being contained and controlled and the assumption that one's 'identity' can be assumed by reading what is visible (e.g. ostensibly 'white' skin).
4. The concept of the 'universal' needs to be approached with care, though Kron's utopian aspirations could be applauded.
5. The 'live heat' of performance can be detected in the censorship legislation which has sought to control theatrical representation throughout the centuries. Alan Sinfield's citation of a report from a committee set up in 1909 in Great Britain, to look at the licensing situation, offers a prime example of the perceived threat of performance:

   > Ideas or situations which, when described on a printed page may work little mischief, when represented through the human personality of actors may have a more powerful and deleterious effect. The existence of an audience, moved by the same emotions, its members conscious of one another's presence, intensifies the influence of what is done and spoken on the stage .... The performance, day after day, in the presence of numbers of people, of plays containing one or other of these [dangerous] elements, would have cumulative effects to which the conveyance of similar ideas by print offers no analogy. (cited in Sinfield, 1999, p. 15)

6. In literary studies, many feminist critics have replaced 'autobiography' with the term 'life narrative', which is broader in its embrace and includes journals, letters, memoirs and fictional texts that are 'personally inflected'

173

174 NOTES

(Henke, 2000, p. xiii). Sidonie Smith and Julia Watson list fifty-two 'gen-res' of 'life narrative' in their introductory text, *Reading Autobiography: A Guide for Interpreting Life Narratives*, including 'Autobiographics', 'Autoethnography', 'Autofiction', 'Autogynography', 'Autopathography', 'Autothanatography', 'Bildungsroman', 'Biomythography', 'Heterobiography' and 'Testimony' (2001, pp. 183–207).

7. The connection between auto/biographical performance and self-portraits is one that is repeatedly made. Marina Warner (1998) refers to Bobby Baker as a 'self-portraitist'.

8. In fact, when I emailed Dowie to ask her about the autobiographical status of her work, I received a reply from her producer, Colin Watkeys, who explained Dowie's position on the matter.

9. Illustrative texts include James Olney (1980) *Autobiography: Essays Theoretical and Critical* and Estelle C. Jelinek (1980) *Women's Autobiography: Essays in Criticism*. Significant texts throughout the 1980s and 1990s reveal the study of the intersections between autobiography and identity such as Bella Brodzki and Celeste Schenck (1988) *Life/Lines: Theorizing Women's Autobiography*, Leigh Gilmore (1994) *Autobiographics: A Feminist Theory of Women's Self-Representation* and Sidonie Smith (1993) *Subjectivity, Identity and the Body: Women's Autobiographical Practices in the Twentieth Century*. Texts such as Kathleen Ashley, Leigh Gilmore and Gerald Peters (1994) *Autobiography and Postmodernism* also mark the poststructuralist and postmodern turn in autobiography criticism.

10. *Sally's Rape* won an OBIE in 1992, though I saw it in London in 1995.

11. Though I have seen the majority of the works I cite, I too, at times, have resorted to documentation material, including video and DVD recordings, scripts and to others' descriptions of the live experience. This is of course unavoidable when writing about performances of the 1960s and 1970s. Debate continues around the relationship of the 'live' experience to the so-called 'secondary' material. See, for example, Phelan (1993), Auslander (1999), Pearson and Shanks (2001) and Heddon (2002b).

1 Politics (of Self): The Subject of Autobiography

1. Autobiography appears even in the theatrical prologues and epilogues from the seventeenth to the nineteenth centuries, where performers often spoke in their off-stage personas, blurring the line between reality and fiction; they also made reference to contemporary cultural and political events – again, utilising the unique contemporariness of theatre. Marvin Carlson reveals that historical autobiographical performance even exceeds these relatively early moments; for example, in the thirteenth century Adam de la Halle and his 'friends and neighbours' appeared '*in propria*

persona' (Carlson, 1996, p. 599). Autobiographical performance practice can be found in the work of collective companies operating in the 1960s and 1970s such as Open Theatre's *Mutation Show* (1973) which sought to stage moments of the 'real' or the 'authentic' (see Blumenthal, 1984, p. 163 for a description). Other companies drawing on the life experiences of performers include the Living Theatre and the Performance Group (see also Sainer, 1997).

2. Peggy Phelan (2001) provides another reading of the effect of consciousness-raising activities, focusing on the power of repetition and its potential for engendering revised life stories. This is not unconnected to the potential of autobiographical performance to enable the revision of a subject.

3 The aim of collective consciousness-raising was to enable women to share their personal experiences in a non-hierarchic, safe and support-ive environment. The sharing itself was thought to be constitutive of the environment, fostering a sense of solidarity amongst women. Reflec-tions on consciousness-raising activities reveal that achieving this aim was far from easy due to the operation of 'hidden hierarchies', 'cliques' and 'coercive consensus' (Rowbotham *et al.*, 1979, p. 41). Writing in 1979, Rowbotham also recognised that the extrapolation from the personal to the general was reductively homogenising (ibid., p. 105).

4. In fact, one might consider abstract expressionist work as being auto-biographical in its content since the actions supposedly expressed the emotions of the artist. From here, one can follow the thread back to Sur-realism and the stated relationship between 'automatic techniques' and the unconscious.

5. Gerald Silk reads the 'resurgence of autobiographical impulses in the visual arts since the 1970s', not as connected to the feminist move-ment, but rather as a 'significant component of the then-fledgling postmodernism' (1998, p. 138).

6. The Feminist Art Program at Fresno and CalArts is only one exam-ple to display the intersection of feminism and the arts. Others include Women Artists in Revolution (1969), the Women, Students and Artists for Black Art Liberation (1970), the Ad Hoc Women Artists Group (1970), Women in the Arts (1971) and West-East Bag (1971). Britain experienced a similar surge in feminist art activity as indicated by the forming of the Women's Liberation Art Group in London in 1970 which mounted its first exhibition the following year.

7. See Roth (1980, 1983), Elwes (1985), Reckitt (2001), Withers (1997), Broude and Garrard (1997), Barry (1980), Wolverton (2002).

8. It is worth noting the strong echoes of this sentiment in Bobby Baker's work, most particularly *Drawing on a Mother's Experience*.

9. These examples are interesting precursors to the popular verbatim dramas of the early twenty-first century (see Chapter 4).

10. Formal theatre censorship operated in Britain until 1968, and this had a massive impact on the staged representations of gay men.

11. However, Peggy Phelan's (1993) proposition that the ephemerality of performance unavoidably stages loss might place performance in closer proximity to de Man's understanding of autobiography as akin to the production of an epitaph. Performance is a fleeting act that sits precariously between being present and absent, here and gone. Once staged, it can never be recovered, other than in memory. Performance, then, might be thought of as a rehearsal for our death. Phelan makes a case for live performance as a healthy mode through which to confront and deal with the loss (and fear of loss) that each of us inevitably experiences in our lives. Performing the 'self' might also be considered a gesture to our mortality, our inevitable absence, rather than our seeming presence (see also Gretchen A. Case, 2005).

12. On 'binary terror' see Schneider (1997), pp. 13–16; and Patraka (1992), pp. 163–85. For *écriture féminine*, or 'writing the body', see Cixous (1981, 1986) and Jenson (1991).

13. The first two productions were produced by 7:84 Theatre Company (Scotland), the second two by mct and the final one was a partnership between 7:84 and mct.

14. www.mori.com/polls/2000/sh000121.shtml [Consulted 16 November 2003]. Such polls were conducted in response to the Scottish campaign against the repeal of Section 28, led by Stagecoach tycoon Brian Souter. Section 28 referred to the Local Government Act of 1986, which was amended in 1988 with Section 2a, which provided that 'A local authority shall not (a) intentionally promote homosexuality or publish material with the intention of promoting homosexuality; (b) promote the teaching in any maintained school of the acceptability of homosexuality as a pretended family relationship'. Section 28 was finally repealed in Scotland in 2000.

15. mct stands for 'mollie's collar and tie', old euphemisms for gay men and lesbians. The company was launched in 1996 but due to a lack of funding disbanded in 2000.

16. *Fingerlicks* shares much, both structurally and in terms of content, with published anthologies of coming-out stories. See Cruikshank (1980), Hall Carpenter Archives Lesbian Oral History Group (1989), Stanley and Wolfe (1980).

17. The performers seemed to be wearing their 'own' clothes – therefore not costumes. Very little set or props were used. The aesthetic was that of the 'non-artificial' – but we must nevertheless recognise this *as* a strategic aesthetic.

18. The 'authenticity' of the documentary is equally debatable.

19. In fact, Baker's original name was Lindsey but when she was little she wanted to be a boy, so changed it to Bobby, and her adopted name stuck.

Already, then, Bobby Baker is not quite Bobby Baker (see Warner, 1998, pp. 83–4).

20. Arguably everyone is always performing and I do not wish to suggest here the presence of any 'essential' core.

21. See Aston (2000a) for a feminist appropriation of 'hysteria' as a resistant strategy, in relation to Baker's work.

22. Miller puts the figure at 100,000.

23. Nevertheless, a case might be made for encouraging more artists to show their work to a wider diversity of audiences. Cultural transformation, a broad remit, is dependent on transformations occurring across diverse communities.

24. I have extrapolated here from Mae Gwendolyn Henderson's (1998) useful identification of a 'dialogic of difference' and 'dialectic of identity' in black women's writing.

25. As a teacher and examiner in many higher education institutions in the UK over the past ten years, I have witnessed many young practitioners apply a feminist consciousness to other pressing concerns, including for example the unenviable status of refugees and asylum seekers in this country, ongoing damage to the environment, the impact of global capitalism and the politics of 'national security' and surveillance in a 'post-9/11' world. The feminist struggle for 'women's rights' rightly translates in the twenty-first century as the broader struggle for a wider range of 'human rights', or what Jill Dolan calls a 'more radical humanism' (2005, p. 2). This allows for a greater recognition of differences between peoples.

2   History: Testimonial Times

1. The production of testimony in a variety of forms including oral narratives, public performances and published memoirs is matched by an undiminishing critical engagement with testimonial practices from across disciplinary fields: Shoshana Felman and Dori Laub's seminal text, *Testimony: Crises of Witnessing in Literature, Psychoanalysis, and History* (1992), has been followed by many others, including edited collections such as Cathy Caruth (1995) *Trauma: Explorations in Memory*; Nancy Miller and Jason Tougaw (2002) *Extremities: Trauma, Testimony and Community* and Jill Bennett and Roseanne Kennedy (2003) *World Memory: Personal Trajectories in Global Time*.

2. Though the focus on this chapter is on human-made traumatic events, evidently trauma also results from natural disasters.

3. A 'politics' of trauma adheres to trauma studies in relation to which events *are* considered traumatic and which are denied that status and, therefore, also denied the response that typically accompanies it. See, for example, Ann Cvetkovich, who is 'guided by the question "Whose feelings count?" in

thinking about whose trauma gets recognised in the national public sphere' (2003, p. 278). Cvetkovich is primarily interested in affective experiences that are not the 'most catastrophic' or 'widely public events', but which are, nevertheless, experienced as traumatic. Cvetkovich is careful to point out that 'trauma' as a category has its own history (ibid., p. 17).

4. The production of autobiography might also be read as an enabling device. Indeed, early theorist of autobiography, Georges Gusdorf, describes autobiographical production in terms that resonate with Lacan's rendering of the 'mirror stage', as noted by Shari Benstock. If the 'mirror' allows the subject to perceive himself/herself as being whole and unified, when in fact he/she feels alienated and fragmented, then so too might autobiography (depending on how it is constructed). For Gusdorf, autobiography 'requires a man to take a distance with regard to himself in order to reconstitute himself in the focus of his special unity and identity across time' (cited in Benstock, 1988, p. 14). I return to this notion in Chapter 3.

5. Some have also argued that, precisely because of trauma's unrepresentability, attempts should not be made to represent it. Theodore Adorno's declaration is the most well known: 'After Auschwitz, it is no longer possible to write poems'. Adorno considered that aesthetic stylisation would transform the unthinkable into something coherent. In the process of aestheticisation the event 'is transfigured, something of its horror is removed', thereby doing 'an injustice to the victims'. However, as Shoshana Felman points out, Adorno himself revised his statement, recognising that 'It is now virtually in art alone that suffering can still find its own voice, consolation, without immediately being betrayed by it' (cited in Felman and Laub, 1992, p. 33). The issue of 'representing' traumatic events remains fraught. Recent debates over the 'phenomenon' of 'false memory syndrome' have prompted further consideration of memory's relation to experience, as well as increased anxiety around issues of memory's reliability or 'trustworthiness' (see Kearney, 1999). In addition, the incidence of 'false' or fraudulent memoirs, such as Binjamin Wilkomirski's infamous *Fragments: Memories of a Wartime Childhood* (1995), has generated much critical debate regarding ethics of representation and the ownership of 'history'.

6. Schaffer and Smith draw attention to other cultural modes of engaging with 'cataclysmic events', including 'South American liberationist theology which proves a model of resistance' and 'shamanic inscription and Daoist modes of spirit possession' from East-Asian countries which represent other performative modes of 'recovery' (2004, p. 23).

7. There have been more than twenty-one Truth Commissions, beginning with Uganda in 1974 (Schaffer and Smith, 2004).

8. Fiona Nicoll reminds me that 'reconciliation' has a double meaning, a point relevant to my argument here. Reconcile might signify coming to terms with the past. However, it might just as easily signal 'passivity' and

acceptance, for example to be reconciled to the unfolding events (Nicoll (1998), cited in Ahmed, 2004, p. 35). Sara Ahmed (2004) asks that we learn to 'live with the impossibility of reconciliation', understanding that we cannot ever feel the pain of others, and this inability is in fact the evidence of their pain. The impossibility of reconciliation stages a call for collective political action, rather than acceptance.

9. Reading Rebecca Solnit's *A Field Guide To Getting Lost* while revising this section, I am taken by the fact that she recognises that the histories she has 'written have often been hidden, lost, neglected, too broad or too amorphous to show up in others' radar screens, histories that are not neat fields and belong to no one'. For Solnit, the tidy stories of history (such as Art history) 'leave out' all sorts of 'sources and inspirations' (including those that come from encounters, dreams, poems, earlier experiences). Solnit calls these other sources 'the grandmothers' (2006, pp. 58–9).

10. These lines come from a performance given in Avery Fisher Hall, Lincoln Center, July 1989. This statement does not appear in the published version of *Sally's Rape* (1994), transcribed from a performance presented at the Kitchen in 1991. The difference in texts testifies to the fact that *Sally's Rape* continued to be a 'work-in-progress'.

11. One documentary that Walker explores is *History and Memory* (1991) by Rea Tajiri. Coincidentally, the subject of this documentary is also the internment of Japanese-Americans in American camps, specifically Tajiri's mother. For Walker, *History and Memory* 'prioritizes not so much the internment itself, but the mother's distracted experience and imperfect memory of it' (2003, p. 114). The gaps in memory here bear similarity to Ima's father's silence.

12. Citations from Elie Wiesel are from *A Jew Today* (New York: Random House, 1978, p. 196).

13. Such racism is not unique to the USA. The more recent murder of Stephen Lawrence in the UK, and the tribunal that examined police responses to that incident, found the British police force to be 'institutionally racist'. *Sally's Rape* toured to London's ICA in 1995.

14. Anna Deavere Smith has tackled the events in Crown Heights Riots and in Los Angeles in her performances *Fires in the Mirror: Crown Heights, Brooklyn and Other Identities* (1992) and *Twilight: Los Angeles, 1992* (1993). McCauley identifies certain commonalities between Deavere's work and her own 'community collaborations' since *The Buffalo Project* (1990). She also determines a major difference between them. Where Smith performs testimonies from eyewitnesses, in McCauley's collaborative projects what is presented back to the 'community' are the actors' responses to eyewitness testimonies. In McCauley's work the actors, who are located within the 'community', are more explicitly the reflecting 'mirrors' (see McCauley, 1996, p. 270.) The work of Anna Deavere Smith is discussed in Chapter 4.

15. Scott is citing from Stuart Hall's article, 'Minimal Selves', *Identity* (ICA 6, p. 45).
16. Cvetkovich (2003) offers the activist group ACT UP as one example of such an alternative.
17. As Ahmed (2004) also insists, though I am 'in' this story, the pain that I witness, which locates me here, is not mine and should not be appropriated as such.
18. http://www.vhf.org/ [accessed 6 August 2005].
19. The Israel Science and Technology website lists fifty-six Holocaust museums. http://www.science.co.il/Holocaust-Museums.asp [accessed 19 August 2005].
20. Oral historian and performer Gretchen A. Case offers a different perspective since she regards the ephemarality of performance as in fact supremely suited to the ephemerality of life. As she writes, 'Oral history pivots on morality [...]. More than fixing a life in place or saving a story from being forgotten, oral history profoundly honours ephemerality and loss by acknowledging the slipping-away' (2005, p. 133).

3   Place: The Place of Self

1. A few examples of published autobiographies which press into service these spatialising metaphors include Kevin Lewis (2005) *The Kid Moves On*; Joe Simpson (2003) *Touching the Void*; Lance Armstrong (2001) *It's Not About the Bike: My Journey Back to Life*; Edward Heath (1998) *The Course of My life: My Autobiography* (1998); Nelson Mandela (1992) *A Long Walk to Freedom*; and Harold Hobson (1978) *Indirect Journey: An Autobiography*. It is notable that these are all authored by men, and a quick search – by no means thorough or conclusive – failed to locate similar examples by women writers.
2. Though I collapse distinctions between space and place here, a discussion of those terms follows.
3. First working with this term in 2000, I subsequently became aware of its different, yet related application by Jennifer González (1995) who uses it to refer to personal objects – such as photos, tourist memorabilia, etc. – arranged by a subject as physical signs that spatially represent that subject's identity. In my application of the term autotopography, the *topos* is taken more literally (problematic as any concept of 'real' place is).
4. Brian Friel's play *Translations* (1981) remains one of the best theatrical examples of the interconnections between colonialism, mapping and naming.
5. The concept, and ascribed effect, of globalisation is not unproblematic. The use of the term itself, ironically, tends to flatten out different experiences of time and place, presenting a homogenised world. Ethnologist

James Clifford argues that the concept of 'globalisation' makes invisible the 'cross-cutting agencies and the contradictions of everyday life'. He perceives this as being a 'partial, Eurocentric view' (Coles, 2000, p. 62), an opinion shared by Doreen Massey (2005) who underlines the earlier experiences of those who were colonised and who had therefore already experienced space as incoherent and fractured. Mounting a different critique, Homi Bhabha reminds us that 'the globe shrinks for those who own it' (cited in Kwon, 2004, p. 166).

6. Carmelita Tropicana's *Milk of Amnesia* similarly engages with the concept of returning 'home', to Cuba, after many years of living in the USA, prompting questions about identity, place and memory (see Troyano, 2000). Postcolonial insights into hybrid identity, linked to notions of Diaspora, implicitly inform my analysis of identity and place since one impact of postcolonial discourse is the recognition that we are all of us hybridised.

7. Documentation of the performance was subsequently published in *Small Acts: Performance, the Millennium and the Marking of Time* (2000), edited by Adrian Heathfield.

8. Atlases used to be called Theatres (de Certeau, 1988, p. 121). Flemish geographer Abraham Ortelius first published the atlas *Theatrum Orbis Terrarum* (Theatre of the World) in 1570 while Britain's John Speed published an atlas called *The Theatre of the Empire of Great Britain* in 1612.

9. As explored in Chapter 2, the question of who wrote this history remains pertinent.

10. More recent map-makers have also attempted to stage interruptions into dominant representations of space and places, the best known being the Situationists.

11. Though Massey employs the metaphor of layers to conceptualise this space, she distinguishes it from that other popular trope, the 'palimpsest'. For Massey, layers configured through the palimpsest carry a suggestion that each layer exists in its own discrete realm, a horizontal structure. The coeval, by contrast, allows the layers to coexist, simultaneously, and it is this co-existence, this multiplicity, which opens space up to the indeterminate (see 2005, pp. 109–13).

12. *Bubbling Tom* has already achieved something of lore-status. The video recording of the guided tour continues to be shown by spectator-participants at various local events.

13. Debord wrote 'Theory of the Dérive' in 1958. A translation by K. Knabb, from the Bureau of Public Secrets, is available at http://www.bopsecrets.org [accessed 24 December 2005].

14. All citations are taken from the unpublished script of *The Crab Walks*, kindly provided by Smith. The published version of the performance text is forthcoming in Mock (2007).

15. These subsequently toured to other venues.

16. The 'if' here is important since more research on the 'places' of site-specific work needs to be undertaken to determine whether significant gender

differentiations *are* in operation. For example, it is certainly the case that many male practitioners have also used 'domestic' sites, including Third Angel with *Class of '76* set in a junior school and Tom Marshman's *Her Bungalow Heart* (2006), which though not site-specific is based on objects and memories associated with the bungalow where Marshman's 'Nanna' lived for thirty-five years. Mem Morrison's *Fuel* (2004) was made for a kitchen, whilst his new work, *Leftovers* (2007), is to be shown in cafes. There are, too, female 'walking artists'. For example, Janet Cardiff has created a number of audio walks (*Her Long Black Hair*, for New York's Central Park in 2004) and her recently published book of audio walks *The Walk Book* (2005). Black Country artist Clare Thornton recently devised a guided walk along the metro route, a 'nature corridor' stretching from Wolverhampton to Birmingham, titled *Looking for the Black Redstart* (2005).

17. Sketches of the *flâneur* often represent him with looking glasses (see Ferguson, 1994, p. 24).

18. Other feminist critics have attempted to insert the *flâneuse* into the modernist city text by proposing that the arcades provided women with a cover for *flânery*, since shopping was an acceptable reason for a woman to be alone in public space (see Iskin, 2003). Ferguson's summary of the representation of the *flâneur*, however, again insists on the impossibility of the female stroller, since the activity and purpose of shopping negates the distanced and objective observer. The connection between women and shopping serves to further diminish the possibility of the *flâneuse*, since a woman supposedly 'desires the objects spread before her and acts upon that desire. The *flâneur*, on the other hand, desires the city as a whole, not a particular part of it' (1994, p. 27; see also Wolff, 1994). Iskin (2003), meanwhile, attempts to retain the potential that shopping affords, since to go shopping is to enter into public space and once there to partake in other experiences.

19. In fact, it has been performed in many different homes during its international tour. I saw the piece at Hollybush Road in Newham.

20. This is the case only where there is cultural similarity. I might not understand the homes made by other cultures.

4 Ethics: The Story of the Other

1. Indeed, as G. Thomas Couser notes, parents in fact may 'make' us in more ways than one, given that they 'serve as informal oral biographers', providing the details of our early lives which are beyond our own access or recall (2004, p. 57).

2. 'Verbatim theatre' is related and indebted to a tradition of 'docudrama' or 'theatre of actuality', a form that can be traced to Erwin Piscator's

work from the 1920s (see the useful article by Peter Weiss (1971), which reveals the connection between the forms).

3. Emily Mann's first play, *Annulla Allen: Autobiography of a Survivor* (1974), uses interviews from a woman who had escaped a concentration camp. *Still Life* (1980), incorporating documentary material, explores the impact of the Vietnam War; *Execution of Justice* (1984), about the trial of Dan White, who killed George Mascone and Harvey Milk in 1978 but was found guilty only of voluntary manslaughter, uses a similar process, creating the text from trial transcripts, media reports and interviews. *Greensboro – A Requiem* (1996) focuses on the murder of five anti-Ku Klux Klan protestors, in Greensboro, in 1979 (see Mann, 1997). Anna Deavere Smith's best known performances, *Fires in the Mirror: Crown Heights, Brooklyn, and Other Identities* (1992) and *Twilight: Los Angeles, 1992* (1993), are part of her ongoing series, *On the Road: A Search for American Character*. *Fires in the Mirror* concerned the violence and rioting that erupted following the death of Gavin Cato, a seven-year-old Guyanese-American, and the subsequent killing of Yankel Rosenbaum, a Jewish student from Australia. *Twilight: Lost Angeles* coalesced around the brutal beating of Rodney King and the subsequent acquittal of the involved police officers, an event that sparked rioting in Los Angeles (see Smith, 1994, 1996). Emily Mann directed the premiere of *Twilight: Los Angeles* for the Mark Taper Forum, LA. Eve Ensler's *The Vagina Monologues* (1996) started as an Off-Off-Broadway one-woman show, before becoming a Broadway hit performed by 'celebrity' women. As the title proposes, the piece is based on interviews with women discussing various experiences relating to their vaginas, including desire, pleasure, fear, embarrassment and sexual violence (see Ensler, 2001). Tectonic Theater Project, founded in 1991, has created two 'factual' dramas to date. The first, *Gross Indecency* (1997), a play about Oscar Wilde's trial, incorporated biographical material and employed a docudrama format. Tectonic is best known for *The Laramie Project* (2000), a verbatim drama devised as a response to the brutal, homophobic murder of a young gay man, Matthew Shepard, by two other young male residents of Laramie (see Kaufman *et al.*, 2001).

4. Tricycle Theatre's *Guantanamo: Honour Bound to Defend Freedom* (2004) has become an international success. Out of Joint has staged a number of verbatim dramas recently, including *The Permanent Way* (2003), which explored the relationship between rail privatisation and passenger safety (see Hare, 2003) and *Talking to Terrorists* (2005) which used interviews with 'terrorists' as source material (see Soans, 2005). 7:84's *Private Agenda* (2004) was created from interviews with those working in the public sector, including teachers and nurses while *Tipping Point* (2005), written to coincide with the G8 Summit in Gleneagles, explored local responses to global issues, setting these besides politicians' empty rhetoric. Liverpool Everyman's *Unprotected* (2006) was

created by a team of writers from interviews with sex-workers, their 'clients', the mothers of two prostitutes who had been murdered and various government and social agency workers (see Wilson *et al.*, 2006). Closely related to the verbatim drama form, and sharing a genealogy with docudrama, are 'tribunal plays'. Described by Chris Megson (2004) as 'forensic documentary "replays"', their primary (and in many cases only) source materials are the transcripts of official trials or enquiries. Examples include Tricycle Theatre's *Half the Picture* (1994), a restaging of the Scott Arms-to-Iraq Inquiry, followed by *Nuremberg* (1996), *Srebrenica* (1996) and *The Colour of Justice* (1999), which re-enacted the inquiry into the police response to the death of the young black youth, Stephen Lawrence; and *Justifying War: Scenes from the Hutton Enquiry* (2003).

5. The restorative or interventionary potential of verbatim dramas should not, though, be simply assumed. As Alisa Solomon (2001) notes in relation to *The Laramie Project*, it failed to engage with disturbing facts, including that Matthew Shepard's parents were given overall power in the prosecution, that McKinney was not found guilty of first-degree murder and that McKinney and Henderson were served with a gagging order. Solomon reads *The Laramie Project* as (perhaps unwittingly) contributing to the swell for 'victim rights' and 'vengeance'.

6. Practitioners point to the developments in, and availability of, recording technology as being a crucial catalyst to creating work in this way.

7. David Hare in interview with Richard Boon, Cottesloe Theatre, 27 January 2004; http://www.nationalthatre.org.uk/ [accessed 15 March 2007].

8. It is notable that the cast list for Out of Joint's production *Talking to Terrorists* (2005) informs us that 'A number of names have been withheld or changed at the request of the interviewees'. In Hare's *The Permanent Way* (2003), most 'characters' are also unnamed, with the exception of John Prescott and Lord Cullen.

9. The fact that a play text is often published means that anyone (if they attain the rights) can mount it. When interviewees give their consent to allow their words to be used, do they realise what they are consenting to, in the long term? The play script of *The Laramie Project*, like any other script, is open to any interpretation that companies want to make of it. How does this sit with the much circulated statement by practitioners that they must 'honour' the people they interview? Watching a performance of *The Laramie Project*, produced by Fitchburg State College (Edinburgh Fringe, 2006), was something of a surreal experience. In the 'original', the performers acted not only those they interviewed, but also represented themselves, sharing reflections from their journal entries. When they enacted residents from Laramie, they would also be drawing on the primary experience of having interviewed those people. In the Fitchburg

State College production, the performers have no direct connection with the interviewees. There is also a 'trippling' effect here, as they play the original performers playing those who were interviewed. Perhaps such restagings as this one are in fact *less* ethically problematic in that their distance from any supposed or rhetorical 'real' is, from the outset, much greater.

10. David Hare in interview with Richard Boon, Cottesloe Theatre, 27 January 2004; http://www.nationalthatre.org.uk/ [accessed 15 March 2007].

11. Jill Dolan, concluding her reflections on this same moment, writes that 'perhaps theater can never "say it correct" ' – a position that is close to my own conclusion reached later in this chapter, in relation to Spalding Gray's *Rumstick Road*. For Dolan, the value of *The Laramie Project* is to be found in 'its effort to say it at all, to speak into the public those things that might otherwise never be said' (2005, p. 125).

12. Reminding the reader that there are many different practices and effects, it is worth noting Jill Dolan's proposal that Anna Deavere Smith does *not* attempt to hold a mirror up in order to reflect what is around her, but rather mimics life, retaining the gap between those interviewed and her performance of them. Dolan also insists that though Smith is absent in the performances, she is simultaneously 'centred' in them since it is to Smith that the interviewed spoke (2005, pp. 83–7).

13. It is possible that in some cases participants do share any financial profits that accrue. Quantitative research is required in order to map the variety of contractual practices that govern this type of theatre making, including surveys of ownership of material and the processes by which consent is solicited and given.

14. Verbatim plays tend to be highly topical, and in this they resemble the earlier 'living newspapers'. Their topicality might also suggest a short lifespan.

15. This is not to propose that there were no such processes of negotiation undertaken by the companies already explored. Further research might establish the code of conduct by which each company works or by which each production is made. Different companies may allow their participants more or less say in the construction of the script, thereby allowing them more or less of a voice in the process.

16. According to Savran, an article in the *Village Voice* reported that because of this 'violation of the physician's right to privacy', *Rumstick Road* was deemed unsuitable for consideration for an OBIE award by some of its judges (1988, pp. 94–5).

17. When reading the script it is perhaps too easy to forget that Gray's family is *not* on stage, rather there is an entire cast of performers.

18. Appeals to abstract notions of 'rights' have long been considered problematic. Karl Marx, for example, understood that the belief in 'natural

rights' was grounded on the bourgeois idea of possessive individualism, linked to notions of the free market (Wilson, 1997, p. 6). John Gledhill remarks that the 1948 UN Universal Declaration takes for granted Western conceptions of society and ideas of natural law. The authors of the declaration 'unreflectively assumed that rights should be vested in individuals rather than collectivities' (1997, p. 70). Diane Elam tackles 'rights discourse' using a deconstructionist argument by proposing that it is not subjects that hold rights but rights that construct subjects. The crux of Elam's argument is that the appeal to rights is 'always an appeal to a certain *description* of the human as more human than other descriptions'. Elam, referencing Lyotard, neatly encapsulates the deeply problematic result of natural-rights discourse when she states 'You can have rights, but only if you are human in my way' (1994, pp. 78–9). Whilst appreciating such critiques of 'rights' my Introduction makes it evident that I want to hold onto the possibility of positive social change (even if this cannot be assumed or guaranteed in advance). Such a desire recognises then that much in the world is not right.

19. All excerpts are taken from an unpublished script kindly provided by Kron; the script has recently been published (see Kron, 2006).

Conclusion: These Confessional Times

1. Broadway hits such as *The Vagina Monologues* have been inspirational here.
2. http://www.nytimes.com/2005/02/03/garden/03comp.html?ex=12652596 00&en=aba66c4159 34476b&38;ei=5088&38;partner=rssnyt [accessed 30 August 2005].
3. http://www.caslon.com.au/weblogprofile1.htm [accessed 7 August 2006].
4. Such developments also have an impact on the 'autobiographical subject', representing a significant change in the way life-stories are told. The technological capacities of ICT result in a critical emphasis on 'networks', 'mobilities', 'scapes', 'liquidity' and 'flows', which relates also to the 'self' and 'identity' (Hardey, 2004).
5. There has been much recent critical writing around 'first person' media. Some critics claim a democratisation of television space whilst others perceive confessional technologies as complicit with the production of 'normative identities' (see, for example, Alcoff and Gray, 1993; Corner, 2004; Dovey, 2000; Kilborn, 2003; Livingstone and Lunt, 1994; Shattuc, 1997).
6. Although it is to be noted that a feminist praxis rooted in personal experiences continues to be recognised by so-called third-wave feminists, such as Leslie Heywood and Jennifer Drake, who pay homage to Gloria Anzaldúa and Cherie Moraga by insisting on 'theory in the flesh' and 'lived theory',

which can 'articulate the historically situated experiences of our "generation"', 'good storytelling *and* critical analysis without jargon' (Heywood and Drake, 1997, p. 14).

7. This is the debate staged between Ernst Bloch and Georg Lukács in the 1930s, concerning 'realist' and 'expressionist' aesthetics, and which form best served a (Marxist) political agenda.

8. Thanks to Elaine Aston for drawing my attention to the relationship between the spectator's stories and Baker's secrets.

9. Sofaer has made other work that connects with autobiography, including a performance lecture with his sister, *Disinter/est: Digging Up Our Childhood* (see Sofaer and Sofaer Derevenski, 2002). That performance, with its focus on archaeological practices, shares some of the language and concerns of Pearson and Shanks (2001).

10. Indeed I wrote about this in my thesis *In Search of the Subject: Locating the Shifting Politics of Women's Performance Art* (1999: unpublished).

11. Originally called *Post Porn Modernist* and first performed in 1989, I saw this show in 1995 in Glasgow's CCA, by which time it was called *Post Post Porn Modernist*.

12. Since I saw it at the CCA in 2005, this work has been renamed *Exposed: Experiments in Love, Sex, Death and Art*. In this performance we witness another attempt at reincarnation as Sprinkle breaks from the solo autobiographical form by devising and performing the piece with her lover of three years, artist Elizabeth Stephens. This story is really one of love and commitment in the face of adversity (Sprinkle has been having treatment for breast cancer) and the show embraces a conservative narrative of 'family', making reference to marriage and children. If Sprinkle maintained that in *Post Post Porn Modernist* there may be a little bit of 'you' (the hetero-normative subject) in every porn-star, then here she claims that there may be a little bit of 'you' in every lesbian. In *Post Porn Love* we see another side to Sprinkle's 'self': a self that does not so much challenge as conform.

13. Though I have made much of the 'live' event that is performance, I also want to insist on the effect that other 'versions' of the performance may have. As I sit and watch the recorded version of *Drawing on a Mother's Experience*, for example, I am still engaged in a spectatorial experience and find myself laughing, smiling and groaning, alongside those spectators whose responses are recorded. This is evidently not the same experience as watching the live event in the company of others, including Baker, but it remains an event, with its own potential impact.

Bibliography

7:84 Theatre Company (1995) *Talking Bollocks*. Glasgow.

7:84 Theatre Company (1996) *Talking Bollocks 2*. Glasgow.

7:84 Theatre Company and mct (2000) *Just Pretending*. Glasgow.

7:84 Theatre Company (2005) *Tipping Point*. Glasgow.

Ahmed, S., Castañeda, C., Fortier, A. & Sheller, M., eds. (2003) *Uprootings/Regroundings: Questions of Home and Migration*. Oxford, New York, NY: Berg.

Ahmed, S. (2004) *The Cultural Politics of Emotion*. Edinburgh: Edinburgh University Press.

Alcoff, L. (1991/2) The Problem of Speaking for Others. *Cultural Critique*, 20, 5–32.

Alcoff, L. & Gray, L. (1993) Survivor Discourse: Transgression or Recuperation? *Signs*, 18 (2), 260–90.

Anderson, L. (2001) *Autobiography*. London: Routledge.

Andrejevic, M. (2004) *Reality TV: The Work of Being Watched*. Oxford: Rowman & Littlefield Publishers.

Apel, D. (2002) *Memory Effects: The Holocaust and the Art of Secondary Witnessing*. London: Rutgers University Press.

Ashley, K., Gilmore, L. & Peters, G., eds. (1994) *Autobiography and Postmodernism*. Amherst, MA: University of Massachusetts Press.

Aston, E. (1995) *An Introduction to Feminism & Theatre*. London: Routledge.

Aston, E. (1999) *Feminist Theatre Practice: A Handbook*. London: Routledge.

Aston, E. (2000a) 'Transforming' Women's Lives: Bobby Baker's Performances of 'Daily Life'. *New Theatre Quarterly*, 61, 17–25.

Aston, E. (2000b) Staging Our Selves. In A. Donnell & P. Polkey, eds., *Representing Lives: Women and Auto/Biography*. Basingstoke: Palgrave Macmillan, pp. 119–28.

Aston, E. (2002) Feminist Performance as Archive: Bobby Baker's 'Daily Life' and *Box Story*. *Performance Research*, 7 (4), 78–85.

Aston, E. & Harris, G., eds. (2006) *Feminist Futures? Theatre, Performance, Theory*. Basingstoke: Palgrave Macmillan.

Augé, M. (2000) *Non-places: Introduction to an Anthropology of Super-modernity*. Trans. John Howe. London: Verso.

Auslander, P. (1999) *Liveness: Performance in a Mediatized Culture*. London: Routledge.

Ayers, R. & Butler, D., eds. (1991) *Live Art*. Sunderland: Artists Newsletter Publications.

Bachelard, G. (1994) *The Poetics of Space*. Boston, MA: Beacon Press. Originally published in *La Poétique de l'espace*, 1958. Presses Universitaires de France.

Baglia, J. & Foster, A. (2005) Performing the 'Really' Real: Cultural Representation, and Commodification in *The Laramie Project*. *Journal of Dramatic Theory and Criticism*, Spring, 12–45.

Baier, A. C. (1994) *Moral Prejudices*. Cambridge, MA: Harvard University Press.

Baker, B. (1988) *Drawing on a Mother's Experience*. Glasgow.

Baker, B. (1993) *How to Shop*. London.

Baker, B. (1994) *Kitchen Show*. London.

Baker, B. (2001a) *Box Story*. London.

Baker, B. (2001b) Interview with the author. London.

Bal, M., Crewe, J. & Spitzer, L., eds. (1999) *Acts of Memory: Cultural Recall in the Present*. London: Dartmouth College.

Baldwyn, L. (1996) Blending In: The Immaterial Art of Bobby Baker's Culinary Events. *The Drama Review*, 40 (4), 37–55.

Banes, S. (1998) *Subversive Expectations: Performance Art and Paratheater in New York, 1976–85*. Ann Arbor, MI: University of Michigan Press.

Barrett, M. (2001) Programme Essay, *Box Story*. London: Artsadmin.

Barry, J. (1980) Women, Representation and Performance Art: Northern California. In C. E. Loeffler, ed., *Performance Anthology: Source Book of California Performance Art*. San Francisco, CA: Contemporary Arts Press, pp. 439–62.

Barthes, R. (1977) *Image–Music–Text*. London: Fontana Press.

Barthes, R. (1986) *The Responsibility of Forms: Critical Essays on Music, Art, and Representation*. Trans. Richard Howard. Oxford: Basil Blackwell.

Baumgardner, J. & Richards, A. (2000) *Manifesta: Young Women, Feminism, and the Future*. New York, NY: Farrar, Strauss and Giroux.

BBC R4, *On the Ropes*, 24 July 2001.

Becker, B. (2000) Robbie McCauley: A Journey Toward Movement. *Theater Journal*, 52, 519–42.

Bell, D., Binnie, J., Cream, J. & Valentine, G. (1994) All Hyped Up and Nowhere to Go. *Gender, Place and Culture: A Journal of Feminist Geography*, 1 (1), 31–47.

Bell, E. (2003) 'Orchids in the Arctic': Women's Autobiographical Performances as Mentoring. In L. C. Miller, J. Taylor & M. H. Carver, eds.,

Voices Made Flesh: Performing Women's Autobiography. Madison, WI: University of Wisconsin Press, pp. 301–18.

Benjamin, W. (1968) In H. Arendt, ed., *Illuminations*. New York, NY: Schocken Books.

Benjamin, W. (1999) *The Arcades Project*. Trans. H. Eiland & K. McGlaughlin. Cambridge, MA: Belknap Press of Harvard University Press.

Bennett, J. (2002) Arts, Affect, and the 'Bad Death': Strategies for Communicating the Sense Memory of Loss. *Signs*, 28 (1), 333–51.

Bennett, J. & Kennedy, R., eds. (2003) *World Memory: Personal Trajectories in Global Time*. London: Palgrave Macmillan.

Bennett, S. (1990) *Theatre Audiences: A Theory of Production and Reception*. London: Routledge.

Benstock, S. (1988) *The Private Self: Theory and Practice of Women's Autobiographical Writings*. Chapel Hill, NC: University of North Carolina Press.

Bergland, B. (1994) Postmodernism and the Autobiographical Subject: Reconstructing the 'Other'. In K. Ashley, L. Gilmore & G. Peters, eds., *Autobiography and Postmodernism*. Amherst, MA: University of Massachusetts Press, pp. 130–66.

Bierman, J. (1979) Three Places in Rhode Island. *The Drama Review*, 23 (1), 13–30.

Blumberg, M. (1998). Domestic Place as Contestatory Space: The Kitchen as Catalyst and Crucible. *New Theatre Quarterly*, 55, 195–201.

Blumenthal, L. (1984) On Art and Artists: Linda Montano. *Profile*, 4 (6).

Blythe, A. (2005) . . . On Verbatim Theatre. In R. Soams, *Talking to Terrorists*. London: Oberon Books, pp. 101–3.

Bonney, J., ed. (2000) *Extreme Exposure: An Anthology of Solo Performance Texts from the Twentieth Century*. New York, NY: Theatre Communications Group.

Bordo, S. (1995) *Unbearable Weight: Feminism, Western Culture and the Body*. Berkeley, CA: University of California Press.

Brewer, G. (1996) Talking His Way Back to Life: Spalding Gray and the Embodied Voice. *Contemporary Literature*, 37 (2), 237–57.

Brison, S. J. (1999) Trauma Narratives and the Remaking of the Self. In M. Ball, J. Crewe & L. Spitzer, eds., *Acts of Memory: Cultural Recall in the Present*. London: Dartmouth College, pp. 39–54.

Brodzki, B. & Schenck, C., eds. (1988) *Life/Lines: Theorizing Women's Autobiography*. London: Cornell University Press.

Brooks, P. (2000) *Troubling Confessions: Speaking Guilt in Law & Literature*. Chicago, IL: University of Chicago Press.

Broude, N. & Garrard, M. D., eds. (1994) *The Power of Feminist Art: The American Movement of the 1970s, History and Impact*. New York, NY: Harry N. Abrams.

Bruley, S. (1981) Women Awake, the Experience of Consciousness-Raising. In Feminist Anthology Collective, eds. *No Turning Back: Writings from the*

Women's Liberation Movement 1975–80. London: The Women's Press, pp. 60–6. First published as a pamphlet in 1976.

Butler, J. (1990) *Gender Trouble.* New York, NY: Routledge.

Butler, J. (1992) Contingent Foundations: Feminism and the Questions of 'Postmodernism'. In J. Butler & J. W. Scott, eds., *Feminists Theorize the Political.* London: Routledge, pp. 3–21.

Carlson, M. (1996) Performing the Self. *Modern Drama,* 39, 599–608.

Carr, C. (1999) Shoah Business: Lisa Kron Tells Her Father's Story of the Holocaust. *Village Voice,* April 14–20.

Carter, E., Donald, J. & Squires, J., eds. (1993) *Space and Place: Theories of Identity and Location.* London: Laurence and Wishart.

Caruth, C., ed. (1995) *Trauma: Explorations in Memory.* Baltimore, MD: John Hopkins University Press.

Case, G. A. (2005) Tic(k): A Performance of Time and Memory. In D. Pollock, ed., *Remembering: Oral History Performance.* New York, NY: Palgrave Macmillan, pp. 129–42.

Case, S.-E. (2006) The Screens of Time: Feminist Memories and Hopes. In E. Aston & G. Harris, eds., *Feminist Futures? Theatre, Performance, Theory.* Basingstoke: Palgrave Macmillan, pp. 105–17.

Casey, E. S. (1997) *The Fate of Place: A Philosophical History.* Berkeley, CA: University of California Press.

Champagne, L. (1990) *Out from Under: Texts by Women Performance Artists.* New York, NY: Theatre Communications Group.

Chaudhuri, U., ed. (2001) *Rachel's Brain and Other Storms.* London: Continuum.

Cheeseman, P. (1971) Place and Performance No. 1: Stoke-on-Trent. *Theatre Quarterly,* 1 (1), 66–102.

Chicago, J. & Schapiro, M. (1972) *Womanhouse.* Exhibition catalogue.

Childs, N. & Walwin, J., eds. (1997) *A Split Second of Paradise: New Performance & Live Art.* London: Rivers Oram Press and Artsadmin.

Cixous, H. (1981) The Laugh of the Medusa. In E. Marks & I. de Courtivron, eds., *New French Feminisms.* New York, NY: Schocken Books, pp. 245–64.

Cixous, H. (1986) *The Newly Born Woman.* Trans. B. Wing. Minneapolis, MN: University of Minnesota Press.

Claycomb, R. M. (2003) (Ch)oral History: Documentary Theatre, the Communal Subject and Progressive Politics. *Journal of Dramatic Theory and Criticism,* XVIII (2), 95–121.

Coles, A. (2000) An Ethnographer in the Field: James Clifford Interview. *Site-Specificity: The Ethnographic Turn, de- dis-, ex-,* 4, London: Black Dog Publishing, 52–71.

Colvin, C. (2003) 'Brothers and Sisters, Do Not Be Afraid of Me': Trauma, History and the Therapeutic Imagination in New South Africa. In K. Hodgkin & S. Radstone, eds., *Contested Pasts: The Politics of Memory.* London: Routledge, pp. 153–67.

Cooke, M. (1999) Questioning Autonomy: The Feminist Challenge and the Challenge for Feminism. In R. Kearney & M. Dooley, eds., *Questioning Ethics: Contemporary Debates in Philosophy*. New York, NY: Routledge, pp. 258–82.

Corner, J. (2004) Afterword: Framing the New. In S. Holmes & D. Jermyn, eds., *Understanding Reality Television*. London: Routledge, pp. 290–99.

Couser, G. T. (2004) *Vulnerable Subjects: Ethics and Life Writing*. Ithaca, NY: Cornell University Press.

Cresswell, T. (1996) *In Place/Out of Place: Geography, Ideology and Transgression*. Minneapolis, MN: University of Minnesota Press.

Cresswell, T. (2004) *Place: A Short Introduction*. London: Blackwell.

Cruikshank, M., ed. (1980) *The Lesbian Path*. Monterey, CA: Angel Press.

Curious (2004) *Essences of London: A Portrait of the City Navigated by the Sense of Smell*.

Curious (2004) *On the Scent*. London.

Cvetkovich, A. (2003) *An Archive of Feelings: Trauma, Sexuality, and Lesbian Public Cultures*. Durham, NC: Duke University Press.

Davis, F. (1977) Nostalgia, Identity and the Current Nostalgia Wave. *Journal of Popular Culture*, 11 (2), 414–24.

Debord, G. Theory of the Dérive. Trans. K. Knabb, Bureau of Public Secrets. http://www.bopsecrets.org [accessed 24 December 2005].

de Certeau, M. (1988) *The Practice of Everyday Life*. Berkeley, CA: University of California Press.

deLauretis, T. (1984) *Alice Doesn't: Feminism, Semiotics, Cinema*. London: Macmillan.

de Man, P. (1979) Autobiography as De-facement. *Modern Languages Notes*, 94 (5), 919–30.

Derrida, J. (1999) Hospitality, Justice and Responsibility: A Dialogue with Jacques Derrida. In R. Kearney & M. Dooley, eds., *Questioning Ethics: Contemporary Debates in Philosophy*. London: Routledge, pp. 65–83.

Dolan, J. (1988) *The Feminist Spectator as Critic*. Ann Arbor, MI: University of Michigan Press.

Dolan, J. (2001) Performance, Utopia, and the 'Utopian Performative'. *Theatre Journal*, 53, 455–79.

Dolan, J. (2005) *Utopia in Performance: Finding Hope at the Theater*. Ann Arbor, MI: University of Michigan Press.

Dorling, D. & Fairbairn, D. (1997) *Mapping: Ways of Representing the World*. Harlow: Longman.

Dovey, J. (2000) *FREAKSHOW: First Person Media and Factual Television*. London: Pluto Press.

Dowie, C. (1996) *Why Is John Lennon Wearing a Skirt and Other Stand-Up Theatre Plays*. London: Methuen.

Duncan, J. & Ley, D., eds. (1993) *Place/Culture/Representation*. London: Routledge.

Duncan, N. (1996) Renegotiating Gender and Sexuality in Public and Private Spaces. In N. Duncan, ed., *BodySpace*. London: Routledge, pp. 127–45.

Eakin, P. J. (1998) Relational Selves, Relational Lives: The Story of the Story. In G. T. Couser & J. Fichtelberg, eds., *True Relations: Essays on Autobiography and the Postmodern*. Connecticut: Hofsta University, Greenwood Press, pp. 63–81.

Eakin, P. J. (1999) *How Our Lives Become Stories: Making Selves*. Ithaca, NY: Cornell University Press.

Eisner, R. S. (2005) Cuttings from the Life Narrative of My Older Sister. In D. Pollok, ed., *Remembering: Oral History Performance*. New York, NY: Palgrave Macmillan, pp. 101–28.

Elam, D. (1994) *Feminism and Deconstruction: Ms. En Abyme*. London: Routledge.

Elwes, C. (1985) Floating Femininity: A Look at Performance Art by Women. In S. Kent & J. Morreau, eds., *Women's Images of Men*. London: Writers and Readers Publishing, pp. 164–93.

Eng, D. L. & Kazanjian, D., eds. (2002) *Loss*. Berkeley, CA: University of California Press.

Ensler, E. (2001) *The Vagina Monologues*. London: Virago Press.

Etchells, T. (1999) *Certain Fragments: Contemporary Performance and Forced Entertainment*. London: Routledge.

Felman, S. & Laub, D. (1992) *Testimony: Crises of Witnessing in Literature, Psychoanalysis, and History*. New York, NY: Routledge.

Felski, R. (1989) *Feminist Aesthetics: Feminist Literature and Social Change*. London: Hutchinson Radius.

Ferguson, P. P. (1994) The *Flâneur* on and off the Streets of Paris. In K. Tester, ed., *The Flâneur*. London: Routledge, pp. 22–42.

Ferris, L. (2002) Cooking Up the Self: Bobby Baker and Blondell Cummings 'Do' the Kitchen. In S. Smith & J. Watson, eds., *Interfaces: Women/Autobiography/Image/Performance*. Ann Arbor, MI: University of Michigan Press, pp. 186–210.

Festa, A. (2000) Introduction: Shall We Talk? Linda M. Montano Performs Autobiographical Voices. In L. Montano, *Performance Artists Talking in the Eighties*. London: University of California Press, pp. 1–33.

Findlen, B. (2001) *Listen Up: Voices from the Next Generation*, 2nd edn. Seattle: Seal.

Forced Entertainment (2003) *The Travels*. Exeter.

Forte, J. (1988) Women's Performance Art: Feminism and Postmodernism. *Theatre Journal*, 40 (2), 217–35.

Foucault, M. (1977a) The Political Function of the Intellectual. *Radical Philosophy*, Summer, 12–14.

Foucault, M. (1977b) Nietzsche, Genealogy, History. In D. F. Bouchard, ed., *Language, Counter Memory, Practice*. Oxford: Basil Blackwell, pp. 139–64.

Foucault, M. (1990) *The History of Sexuality, Volume 1, An Introduction.* Trans. Robert Hurley. London: Penguin Books.

Fousekis, N. M. (2005) Experiencing History: A Journey from Oral History to Performance. In D. Pollock, ed., *Remembering: Oral History Performance.* New York, NY: Palgrave Macmillan, pp. 167–86.

Freeman, M. (1993) *Rewriting the Self: History, Memory, Narrative.* London: Routledge.

Freud, S. (1953) Remembering, Repeating and Working-Through. In J. Strachey, ed., *The Standard Edition of the Complete Psychological Works of Sigmund Freud,* Vol. 2. London: Hogarth Press, pp. 145–56.

Freuh, J. (1994) The Body through Women's Eyes. In N. Broude & M. D. Garrard, eds., *The Power of Feminist Art: The American Movement of the 1970s, History and Impact.* New York, NY: Harry N. Abrams, pp. 190–207.

Friel, B. (1981) *Translations.* London: Faber.

Gale, M. B. & Gardner, V., eds. (2004) *Auto/Biography and Identity: Women, Theatre and Performance.* Manchester: Manchester University Press.

Gammel, I., ed. (1999) *Confessional Politics: Women's Sexual Self-Representations in Life Writing and Popular Media.* Carbondale: Southern Illinois University Press.

Gilligan, C. (1982) *In a Different Voice.* Cambridge, MA: Harvard University Press.

Gilmore, L. (1994) *Autobiographics: A Feminist Theory of Women's Self-Representation.* Ithaca, NY: Cornell University Press.

Gilmore, L. (2001) *The Limits of Autobiography: Trauma and Testimony.* Ithaca, NY: Cornell University Press.

Gledhill, J. (1997) Liberalism, Socio-economic Rights and the Politics of Identity: From Moral Economy to Indigenous Rights. In R. A. Wilson, ed., *Human Rights, Culture & Context: Anthropological Perspectives.* London: Pluto Press, pp. 70–110.

Goldberg, R. (1980) Performance – Art for All? *Art Journal,* 40 (1/2), 369–76.

Goldberg, R. (1988) *Performance Art (from Futurism to the Present).* London: Thames and Hudson.

Goldberg, R. (1998) *Performance: Live Art since the 60s.* London: Thames and Hudson.

González, J. (1995) Autotopographies. In G. Brahm Jr & M. Driscoll, eds., *Prosthetic Territories. Politics and Hypertechnologies.* San Francisco, CA: Westview Press, pp. 133–50.

Goodman, L. (1993) *Contemporary Feminist Theatres: To Each Her Own.* London: Routledge.

Grace, S. & Wasserman, J., eds. (2006) *Theatre and AutoBiography: Writing and Performing Lives in Theory and Practice.* Vancouver: Talon Books.

Gray, S. (1978a) Playwright's Notes. *Performing Arts Journal,* III (2), 87–91.

Gray, S. (1978b) Rumstick Road. *Performing Arts Journal,* III (2), 92–115.

Gray, S. (1979) About *Three Places in Rhode Island*. *Tulane Drama Review*, 1, 31–42.

Gray, S. (1985) *Swimming to Cambodia*. New York, NY: Theatre Communications Group.

Gray, S. (1992) *Monster in a Box*. New York, NY: Vintage.

Greene, A. (2000) Interview with Emily Mann. *Journal of Dramatic Theory and Criticism*, Spring, 77–97.

Greenspan, H. (1998) The Power and Limits of the Metaphor of Survivors' Testimony. In C. Schumacher, ed., *Staging the Holocaust: The Shoah in Drama and Performance*. Cambridge: Cambridge University Press, pp. 27–39.

Griffin, G. (2004) Troubling Identities: Claire Dowie's 'Why Is John Lennon Wearing a Skirt?'. In M. B. Gale & V. Gardner, eds., *Auto/Biography and Identity: Women, Theatre and Performance*. Manchester: Manchester University Press, pp. 153–75.

Grilikhes, A. (1997) Taboo Subjects: An Interview with Rachel Rosenthal. In M. Roth, ed., *Rachel Rosenthal*. Baltimore, MD: The John Hopkins University Press.

Grosz, E. (1990) *Jacques Lacan: A Feminist Introduction*. London: Routledge.

Guignon, C. (2004) *On Being Authentic*. London: Routledge.

Guinier, L. & Smith, A. D. (2001) Rethinking Power, Rethinking Theater: A Conversation between Lani Guinier and Anna Deavere Smith. *Theater*, 31 (3), 31–45.

Hall Carpenter Archives Lesbian Oral History Group (1989) *Inventing Ourselves, Lesbian Life Stories*. London: Routledge.

Hall, S. (1991a) The Local and the Global: Globalization and Ethnicity. In A. D. King, ed., *Culture, Globalization and the World-System: Contemporary Conditions for the Representations of Identity*. London: Macmillan, pp. 19–39.

Hall, S. (1991b) Old and New Identities, Old and New Ethnicities. In A. D. King, ed., *Culture, Globalization and the World-System: Contemporary Conditions for the Representation of Identity*. London: Macmillan, pp. 41–68.

Hamera, J. (1991) Loner on Wheels as Gaia: Identity, Rhetoric, and History in the Angry Art of Rachel Rosenthal. *Text and Performance Quarterly*, 11 (1), 34–45.

Hantzis, D. M. (1998) Reflections on 'A Dialogue with Friends: "Performing" the "Other/Self" ' OJA 1995. In S. J. Dailey, ed., *The Future of Performance Studies: Visions and Revisions*. Annandale, VA: National Communication Association, pp. 203–6.

Hardey, M. (2004) Digital Life Stories: Auto/Biography in the Information Age. *Auto/Biography*, 12, 183–200.

Hare, D. (2003) *The Permanent Way*. London: Faber and Faber.

Hare, D. (2005) . . . On Factual Theatre. In R. Soans, *Talking to Terrorists*. London: Oberon Books, pp. 111–13.

Harris, G. (1999) *Staging Femininities: Performance and Performativity.* Manchester: Manchester University Press.

Harvey, J. B. (1997) Deconstructing the Map. In T. Barnes & D. Gregory, eds., *Reading Human Geography: The Poetics and Politics.* London: Arnold, pp. 155–68. Originally published in *Cartographica*, 26, 1–20, 1989.

Hateley, J. (2003) *A: Gender.* Manchester.

Heathfield, A., ed. (2000) *Small Acts: Performance, the Millennium and the Marking of Time.* London: Black Dog Publishing.

Heddon, D. (1999) *In Search of the Subject: Locating the Shifting Politics of Women's Performance Art.* Unpublished thesis.

Heddon, D. (2001) Autobiography of a Lecturer. *Research in Drama Education*, 6 (1), 105–8.

Heddon, D. (2002a) Autotopography: Graffiti, Landscapes & Selves. *Reconstruction: Studies in Contemporary Culture*, 2 (3). Available: http://www.reconstruction.ws/023/heddon.htm.

Heddon, D. (2002b) Performing the Archive: Following in the Footsteps... *Performance Research: A Journal of the Performing Arts*, 7 (4), 64–77.

Heddon, D. (2003) *Glory Box*: Tim Miller's Autobiography of the Future. *New Theatre Quarterly*, 19 (3), 243–56.

Heddon, D. (2004) Performing Lesbians: Constructing the Self, Constructing the Community. In M. Gale & V. Gardner, eds., *Auto/Biography and Identity: Women, Theatre and Performance.* Manchester: Manchester University Press, pp. 217–38.

Heddon, D. (2006a) Personal Performance: The Resistant Confessions of Bobby Baker. In J. Gill, ed., *Modern Confessional Writing: New Critical Essays.* London: Routledge, pp. 137–53.

Heddon, D. (2006b) The Politics of the Personal: Autobiography in Performance. In E. Aston & G. Harris, eds., *Feminist Futures? Theatre, Performance, Theory.* Basingstoke: Palgrave Macmillan, pp. 130–48.

Henderson, M. G. (1998) Speaking in Tongues: Dialogics, Dialectics, and the Black Writer's Literary Tradition. In S. Smith & J. Watson, eds., *Women, Autobiography, Theory: A Reader.* Madison, WI: University of Wisconsin Press, pp. 343–51.

Henke, S. (2000) *Shattered Subjects: Trauma and Testimony in Women's Life Writing.* Basingstoke: Palgrave Macmillan.

Heywood, L. & Drake, J., eds. (1997) *Third Wave Agenda: Being Feminist, Doing Feminism.* Minneapolis, MN: University of Minnesota Press.

Hirsch, M. (1997) *Family Frames: Photography, Narrative and Postmemory.* Cambridge, MA: Harvard University Press.

Hirsch, M. (1999) Projected Memory: Holocaust Photographs in Personal and Public Fantasy. In M. Bal, J. Crewe & L. Spitzer, eds., *Acts of Memory: Cultural Recall in the Present.* London: Dartmouth College, pp. 3–23.

Hirsch, M. (2002) Marked by Memory: Feminist Reflections on Trauma and Transmission. In N. K. Miller & J. Tougaw, eds., *Extremities: Trauma, Testimony and Community.* Urbana, IL: University of Illinois Press, pp. 70–91.

Hirsch, M. & Spitzer, L. (2003) 'We Would Not Have Come Without You': Generations of Nostalgia. In K. Hodgkin & S. Radstone, eds., *Contested Pasts: The Politics of Memory.* London: Routledge, pp. 79–95.

Hodge, S., Smith, P., Persighetti, S., Turner, C. & Weaver, T. (2003) *An Exeter Mis-guide.* Exeter: Wrights & Sites.

hooks, b. (1989) *Talking Back: Thinking Feminist, Thinking Black.* Boston, MA: South End Press.

hooks, b. (1991) *Yearning: Race, Gender and Cultural Politics.* London: Turnaround.

Howell, J. (1979/80) Solo in Soho: The Performer Alone. *Performance Art Journal,* 4 (1) and 4 (2), 152–8.

Howells, A. (2006) *Salon Adrienne.* Glasgow.

Hughes, H. & Román, D., eds. (1998) *O Solo Homo: The New Queer Performance.* New York, NY: Grove Press.

Hutcheon, L. (1989) *The Politics of Postmodernism.* London: Routledge.

Hutchison, Y. (2005) Truth or Bust: Consensualising a Historic Narrative or Provoking through Theatre. The Place of the Personal Narrative in the Truth and Reconciliation Commission. *Contemporary Theatre Review,* 15 (3), 354–62.

Huyssen, A. (1986) *After the Great Divide: Modernism, Mass Culture, Postmodernism.* Bloomington, IN: Indiana University Press.

Huyssen, A. (1995) *Twilight Memories: Marking Time in a Culture of Amnesia.* New York, NY: Routledge.

Huyssen, A. (2003a) *Present Pasts: Urban Palimpsests and the Politics of Memory.* Stanford, CA: Stanford University Press.

Huyssen, A. (2003b) Trauma and Memory: A New Imaginary of Temporality. In J. Bennett & R. Kennedy, eds., *World Memory: Personal Trajectories in Global Time.* London: Palgrave MacMillan, pp. 16–29.

Ima, K. (2004) *The Interlude.* New York City.

Irigaray, L. (1985) *This Sex Which Is Not One.* Trans. Catherine Porter with Carolyn Burke. Ithaca, NY: Cornell University Press.

Iskin, R. (2003) The Pan-European Flâneuse in Fin-de-Siècle Posters: Advertising Modern Women in the City. *Nineteenth-Century Contexts,* 25 (4), 333–56.

Jackson, S. (2005) *Touchable Stories* and the Performance of Infrastructural Memory. In D. Pollock, ed., *Remembering: Oral History Performance.* New York, NY: Palgrave Macmillan, pp. 45–66.

Jelinek, E. C. (1980) *Women's Autobiography: Essays in Criticism.* Bloomington, IN: Indiana University Press.

Jelinek, E. C. (1986) *The Tradition of Women's Autobiography: Essays in Criticism*. Bloomington, IN: Indiana University Press.

Jenson, D., ed. (1991) *'Coming to Writing' and Other Essays*. Cambridge, MA: Harvard University Press.

Jones, T., ed. (1994) *Sharing the Delirium: Second Generation AIDS Plays and Performances*. Portsmouth, NH: Heinemann.

Jordan, J. (2000) In Conversation: Emily Mann. *Theatre Topics*, 10 (1), 1–16.

Jordanova, L. (2000) *History in Practice*. London: Arnold.

Jouve, N. W. (1991) *White Woman Speak with Forked Tongue*. London: Routledge.

Kalb, J. (2000) Documentary Solo Performance: The Politics of the Mirrored Self. *Theater*, 31 (3), 13–29.

Kaprow, A. (1966) *Assemblage, Environments and Happenings*. New York, NY: Harry N. Abrams.

Kaufman, M. *et al*. (2001) *The Laramie Project*. New York, NY: Vintage Books.

Kearney, R. (1999) Narrative and Ethics of Remembrance. In R. Kearney & M. Dooley, eds., *Questioning Ethics: Contemporary Debates in Philosophy*. London: Routledge, pp. 5–11.

Kearney, R. & Dooley, M., eds. (1999) *Questioning Ethics: Contemporary Debates in Philosophy*. London: Routledge.

Kilborn, R. (2003) *Staging the Real: Factual TV Programming in the Age of Big Brother*. Manchester: Manchester University Press.

Kron, L. (2001) *2.5 Minute Ride and 101 Humiliating Stories*. New York, NY: Theatre Communications Group.

Kron, L. *Well* (2006 video recording). New York Library of Performance Arts.

Kron, L. (2004) Interview with the author. New York.

Kron, L. (2006) *Well*. New York, NY: Theatre Communications Group.

Kurasawa, F. (2004) A Message in a Bottle: Bearing Witness as a Mode of Ethico-political Practice. Colloquia Series, Department of Sociology, Yale University. Available: http://research.yale.edu/ccs/papers/kurasawa_witnessing.pdf [accessed 14 July 2005].

Kwon, M. (2004) *One Place after Another: Site-Specific Art and Locational Identity*. Cambridge, MA: MIT Press.

Lacy, S. (1978) Evolution of a Feminist Art. *Heresies*, 2 (2), 78–83.

Ladino, J. (2004) Longing for Wonderland: Nostalgia for Nature in Post-frontier America. *Iowa Journal of Cultural Studies*, 5, 88–109.

Langellier, K. M. (1998) Voiceless Bodies, Bodiless Voices: The Future of Personal Narrative Performance. In S. J. Dailey, ed., *The Future of Performance Studies: Visions and Revisions*. Annandale, VA: National Communication Association, pp. 207–13.

Langer, L. L. (1991) *Holocaust Testimonies: The Ruins of Memory*. New Haven, CT: Yale University Press.

Lanzmann, C. (1995) The Obscenity of Understanding: An Evening with Claude Lanzmann. In C. Caruth, ed., *Trauma: Explorations in Memory*. Baltimore, MD: John Hopkins University Press, pp. 200–20.

Lathem, L. (2005) Bringing Old and Young People Together: An Interview Project. In D. Pollock, ed., *Remembering: Oral History Performance*. New York, NY: Palgrave Macmillan, pp. 67–84.

Lavery, C. (2005a) The Pepys of London E11: Graeme Miller and the Politics of *Linked*. *New Theatre Quarterly*, 21 (2), 148–60.

Lavery, C. (2005b) Walking the Walk, Talking the Talk: Re-imagining the Urban Landscape. Graeme Miller Interviewed by Carl Lavery. *New Theatre Quarterly*, 21 (2), 161–5.

Lefebvre, H. (1991) *The Production of Space*. Oxford: Blackwell.

Lejeune, P. (1989) The Autobiographical Pact. In P. J. Eakin, ed., *On Autobiography*. Minneapolis, MN: University of Minnesota Press, pp. 3–30.

Lester, G. (1997) Journey of a Lifetime: Lisa Kron Talks to Gideon Lester about 2.5 Minute Ride. American Repertory Theatre, 27 Oct. Available: http.www.amrep.org/people/kron1.htm [accessed 22 May 2005].

Leverett, J. (1985) Introduction. In S. Gray, *Swimming to Cambodia*. New York, NY: Theatre Communications Group, pp. ix–xiii.

Lippard, L. (1976) *From the Centre: Feminist Essays on Women's Art*. New York, NY: E.P. Dutton.

Lippard, L. (1980) Sweeping Exchanges: The Contribution of Feminism to the Art of the 1970s. *Art Journal*, 40 (1/2), 362–5.

Lippard, L. (1984) *Get the Message? A Decade of Art for Social Change*. New York, NY: E.P. Dutton.

Lippard, L. (1997) *The Lure of the Local: Senses of Place in a Multicentered Society*. New York, NY: The New Press.

Liverpool Everyman (2006) *Unprotected*. Edinburgh.

Livingstone, S. & Lunt, P. (1994) *Audience Participation and Public Debate*. London: Routledge.

Loeffler, C. E., ed. (1980) *Performance Anthology: Source Book of California Performance Art*. San Francisco, CA: Contemporary Arts Press.

Loomba, A. (1998) *Colonialism/Postcolonialism*. London: Routledge.

Lowenthal, D. (1975) Past Time, Present Place: Landscape and Memory. *Geographical Review*, 65 (1), 1–36.

MacDonald, C. (1995) Assumed Identities: Feminism, Autobiography and Performance Art. In J. Swindells, ed., *The Uses of Autobiography*. London: Taylor & Francis, pp. 187–95.

Madison, D. S. (1998) Performance, Personal Narratives, and the Politics of Possibility. In S. J. Dailey, ed., *The Future of Performance Studies: Visions and Revisions*. Annandale, VA: National Communication Association, pp. 276–86.

Madison, D. S. (2005) My Desire Is for the Poor to Speak Well of Me. In D. Pollock, ed., *Remembering: Oral History Performance*. New York, NY: Palgrave Macmillan, pp. 143–66.

Mann, E. (1997) *Testimonies: Four Plays*. New York, NY: Theatre Communications Group.

Mann, E. & Roessel, D., eds. (2002) *Political Stages: Plays that Shaped a Century*. New York, NY: Applause.

Marcus, L. (1994) *Auto/Biographical Discourses*. Manchester: Manchester University Press.

Margolin, D. (1999) Count the I's, or, the Autobiographical Nature of Everything. *Women and Performance: A Journal of Feminist Theory*, 10–12 (19–10), 23–32.

Marranca, B. (1996) *Ecologies of Theater*. Baltimore, MD: Johns Hopkins University Press.

Martin, B. (1988) Lesbian Identity and Autobiographical Difference[s]. In B. Brodzki & C. Schenck, eds. *Life/Lines: Theorizing Women's Autobiography*. London: Cornell University Press, pp. 77–103.

Martin, C. (1993) Anna Deavere Smith: The Word Becomes You, an Interview by Carol Martin. *The Drama Review*, 37 (4), 45–62.

Massey, D. (1991) Flexible Sexism. *Environment and Planning D: Society and Space*, 9, 31–57.

Massey, D. (1997) A Global Sense of Place. In T. Barnes & D. Gregory, eds. *Reading Human Geography: The Poetics and Politics*. London: Arnold, pp. 315–23. Originally published in *Marxism Today*, 24–9, June 1991.

Massey, D. (2005) *For Space*. London: SAGE Publications.

McCauley, R. (1994) Sally's Rape. In S. Mahone, ed., *Moon Marked and Touched by Sun: Plays by African-American Women*. New York, NY: Theatre Communications Group.

McCauley, R. (1995) *Sally's Rape*, ICA, London.

McCauley, R. (1996) Thoughts on My Career, *The Other Weapon*, and Other Projects. In E. Diamond, ed., *Performance and Cultural Politics*. London: Routledge, pp. 265–82.

McCauley, R. (1997) Mother Worked. In M. Russell, ed., *Out of Character*. New York, NY: Bantam Books, pp. 252–8.

McCauley, R. & Rauch, B. (2001) 'What Happened', A Conversation between Robbie McCauley and Bill Rauch. *Theater*, 31 (3), 109–17.

McDowell, L. (1999) *Gender, Identity and Place: Understanding Feminist Geographies*. Cambridge: Polity Press.

McKay, N. Y. (1998) The Narrative Self: Race, Politics, and Culture in Black American Women's Autobiography. In S. Smith & J. Watson, eds. *Women, Autobiography, Theory: A Reader*. Madison, WI: University of Wisconsin Press, pp. 96–107.

mct (1998) *Fingerlicks*. Glasgow.

mct (1999) *Fingerlicks II*. Glasgow.

Megson, C. (2004) 'Thou Shall Not Be Found Out': Documentary Theatre as Political Intervention at the Tricycle Theatre (1994–2003). Unpublished paper.

Meola, D. (1997). Excerpts from 'Interview with Rachel Rosenthal'. In M. Roth, ed., *Rachel Rosenthal*. Baltimore, MD: John Hopkins University Press, pp. 57–9.

Mercein, J. (2004) *Waiting*. New York City.

Miller, G. (2003) *Linked*. London.

Miller, L. C., Taylor, J. & Carver, M. H., eds. (2003) *Voices Made Flesh: Performing Women's Autobiography*. Madison, WI: University of Wisconsin Press.

Miller, N. K. (2000 (1996)) *Bequest and Betrayal: Memoirs of a Parent's Death*. Bloomington, IN: Indiana University Press.

Miller, N. K. & Tougaw, J., eds. (2002) *Extremities: Trauma, Testimony and Community*. Urbana, IL: University of Illinois Press.

Miller, T. (1991) STRETCH MARKS. *The Drama Review*, 35 (3), 143–70.

Miller, T. (1991/2) California Performance. *Mime Journal*, 2, 123–42.

Miller, T. (1994) My Queer Body. In T. Jones, ed., *Sharing the Delirium: Second Generation AIDS Plays and Performances*. Portsmouth, NH: Heinemann, pp. 309–36.

Miller, T. (1995) *My Queer Body*. Glasgow.

Miller, T. (1997) *Shirts & Skin*. New York, NY: Alyson Book.

Miller, T. (1998) Naked Breath. In H. Hughes & D. Román, eds. *O Solo Homo: The New Queer Performance*. New York, NY: Grove Press, pp. 51–92.

Miller, T. (1999) Memory and Future. *Harvard Gay and Lesbian Review*, VI (2).

Miller, T. (2000) Out of the Box. *Theater*, 31 (3), 89–90.

Miller, T. (2001a) Suck, Spit, Chew, Swallow: A Performative Exploration of Men's Bodies. In P. Lehman, ed., *Masculinity: Bodies, Movies, Cultures*. London: Routledge, pp. 279–99.

Miller, T. (2001b) *Glory Box*. Glasgow.

Miller, T. (2001c) Interview with the author. Glasgow.

Miller, T. (2002) *Body Blows: Six Performances*. Madison, WI: University of Wisconsin Press.

Mock, R., ed. (forthcoming, 2007) *Walking, Writing and Performance: Autobiographical Texts*. Bristol: Intellect.

Montano, L. (2000) *Performance Artists Talking in the Eighties*. London: University of California Press.

Morley, D. (2000) *Home Territories: Media, Mobility and Identity*. London: Routledge.

Mullen, H. (1994) Optic White: Blackness and the Production of Whiteness. *Diacritics*, 24 (2–3), 71–89.

Myslik, W. D. (1996) Renegotiating the Social/Sexual Identities of Places: Gay Communities as Safe Havens or Sites of Resistance. In N. Duncan, ed., *BodySpace*. London: Routledge, pp. 156–69.

National Theatre (2003) *The Permanent Way*. Exeter.

National Theatre of Scotland (2006) *Black Watch*. Edinburgh.

Nead, L. (1992) *The Female Nude: Art, Obscenity and Sexuality*. London: Routledge.

Neuman, S., ed. (1991) *Autobiography and Questions of Gender*. London: Frank Cass.

Newton, A. Z. (1995) *Narrative Ethics*. Cambridge, MA: Harvard University Press.

Nicholson, H. (2005) *Applied Drama: The Gift of Theatre*. Basingstoke: Palgrave Macmillan.

Nymann, A. E. (1999) Sally's Rape: Robbie McCauley's Survival Art. *African American Review*, 33, 577–87.

Oliver, K. (2001) *Witnessing: Beyond Recognition*. Minneapolis, MN: University of Minnesota Press.

Olney, J., ed. (1980) *Autobiography: Essays Theoretical and Critical*. Princeton, NJ: Princeton University Press.

Osment, P., ed. (1989) *Gay Sweatshop: Four Plays and a Company*. London: Methuen.

Paget, D. (1987) 'Verbatim Theatre': Oral History and Documentary Techniques. *New Theatre Quarterly*, III (12), 317–36.

Park-Fuller, L. (2003) A Clean Breast of It. In L. C. Miller, J. Taylor & M. H. Carver, eds. *Voices Made Flesh: Performing Women's Autobiography*. Madison, WI: University of Wisconsin Press, pp. 215–36.

Passerini, L. (2003) Memories between Silence and Oblivion. In K. Hodgkin & S. Radstone, eds. *Contested Pasts: The Politics of Memory*. London: Routledge, pp. 238–54.

Patraka, V. (1992) Binary Terror and Feminist Performance: Reading Both Ways. *Discourse*, 14 (2), 163–85.

Patraka, V. (1996) Robbie McCauley: Obsessing in Public: Interview by Vivian Patraka. In C. Martin, ed., *A Sourcebook of Feminist Theatre and Performance: On and Beyond the Stage*. London: Routledge, pp. 205–38.

Patraka, V. (2000) Introduction to Robbie McCauley. In J. Bonney, ed., *Extreme Exposure: An Anthology of Solo Performance Texts from the Twentieth Century*. New York, NY: Theatre Communications Group, pp. 248–9.

Pearson, M. & Shanks, M. (1997) Performing a Visit: Archaeologies of the Contemporary Past. *Performance Research: On Tourism*, 2, 41–53.

Pearson, M. (2000) Bubbling Tom. In A. Heathfield, ed., *Small Acts: Performance, the Millennium and the Marking of Time*. London: Black Dog Publishing, pp. 172–85.

Pearson, M. (2001) Interview with the author. Cardiff.

Pearson, M. & Shanks, M. (2001) *Theatre/Archaeology*. London: Routledge.

Personal Narratives Group, ed. (1989) *Interpreting Women's Lives: Feminist Theory and Personal Narratives*. Bloomington, IN: Indiana University Press.

Peterson, M. (1997) *Straight White Male: Performance Art Monologues*. Jackson, MS: University Press of Mississippi.

Phelan, P. (1993) *Unmarked: The Politics of Performance*. London: Routledge.

Phelan, P. (2001) Survey. In H. Reckitt, ed., *Art and Feminism*. London: Phaidon Press.

Phillips, P. C. (1995) Maintenance Activity: Creating a Climate for Change. In N. Felshin, ed., *But Is it Art? The Spirit of Art as Activism*. Seattle, WA: Bay Press, pp. 165–94.

Plummer, K. (1995) *Telling Sexual Stories: Power, Change and Social Worlds*. London: Routledge.

Pollock, D., ed. (2005) *Remembering: Oral History Performance*. New York, NY: Palgrave Macmillan.

Pollock, G. (1991) Kitchen Show. In *Kitchen Show: Bobby Baker*, Artsadmin.

Pollock, G. (2003 (1988)) *Vision and Difference: Feminism, Femininity and the Histories of Art*. London: Routledge.

Ponse, B. (1978) *Identities in the Lesbian World: The Social Construction of Self*. London: Greenwood Press.

Probyn, E. (1995) Lesbians in Space. Gender, Sex and the Structure of Missing. *Gender, Place and Culture*, 2 (1), 77–84.

Raven, A. (1997) Womanhouse. In N. Broude & M. D. Garrard, eds. *The Power of Feminist Art: The American Movement of the 1970s, History and Impact*. New York, NY: Harry N. Abrams, pp. 48–64.

Reckitt, H., ed. (2001) *Art and Feminism*. London: Phaidon Press.

Reinelt, J. (1996) Performing Race: Anna Deavere Smith's *Fires in the Mirror*. *Modern Drama*, 39, 609–17.

Reinelt, J. G. & Roach, J. R., eds. (1992) *Critical Theory and Performance*. Ann Arbor, MI: The University of Michigan Press.

Relph, E. (1976) *Place and Placelessness*. London: Pion.

Richards, S. L. (1993) Caught in the Act of Social Definition: *On the Road* with Anna Deavere Smith. In L. Hart & P. Phelan, eds. *Acting Out: Feminist Performances*. Ann Arbor, MI: The University of Michigan Press, pp. 35–53.

Ricoeur, P. (1999a) Memory and Forgetting. In R. Kearney & M. Dooley, eds. *Questioning Ethics: Contemporary Debates in Philosophy*. London: Routledge, pp. 5–11.

Ricoeur, P. (1999b) Imagination, Testimony and Trust: A Dialogue with Paul Ricoeur. In R. Kearney & M. Dooley, eds. *Questioning Ethics: Contemporary Debates in Philosophy.* London: Routledge, pp. 12–17.

Rizzuto, H. (2004) *Ayai, Yai, Yai.* New York City.

Román, D. (1992) Performing All Our Lives: AIDS, Performance, Community. In J. G. Reinelt & J. R. Roach, eds. *Critical Theory and Performance.* Ann Arbor, MI: The University of Michigan Press, pp. 209–21.

Rosenthal, R. (2001) In U. Chaudhuri, ed., *Rachel's Brain and Other Storms.* London: Continuum.

Roth, M. (1980) Autobiography, Theater, Mysticism and Politics: Women's Performance Art in Southern California. In C. E. Loeffler, ed., *Performance Anthology: Source Book of California Performance Art.* San Francisco, CA: Contemporary Arts Press, pp. 463–89.

Roth, M., ed. (1983) *The Amazing Decade: Women and Performance Art in America, 1979–1980.* Los Angeles, CA: Astro Artz.

Roth, M., ed. (1997) *Rachel Rosenthal.* Baltimore, MD: The John Hopkins University Press.

Rouverol, A. J. (2005) Trying to Be Good: Lessons in Oral History and Performance. In D. Pollock, ed., *Remembering: Oral History Performance.* New York, NY: Palgrave Macmillan, pp. 19–44.

Rowbotham, S., Segal, L. & Wainwright, H., eds. (1979) *Beyond the Fragments: Feminism and the Making of Socialism.* London: The Merlin Press.

Rowbotham, S. (1989) *The Past is Before Us: Feminism in Action Since the 1960s.* London: Pandora Press.

Russell, M. (1997) *Out of Character.* New York, NY: Bantam Books.

Sainer, A. (1997) *The New Radical Theatre Notebook.* New York, NY: Applause.

Sandford, M., ed. (1995) *Happenings and Other Acts.* New York, NY: Routledge.

Sangster, J. (1998) Telling Our Stories: Feminist Debates and the Use of Oral History. In R. Perks & A. Thomson, eds. *The Oral History Reader.* London: Routledge, pp. 87–106.

Satin, L., with Jerome, J., eds. (1999) *Performing Autobiography, Women & Performance: A Journal of Feminist Theory,* 10(19), 1–2.

Savran, D. (1988) *Breaking the Rules: The Wooster Group.* New York, NY: Theatre Communications Group.

Sayre, H. M. (1999) True Stories: Spalding Gray and the Authenticities of Performance. In S. Kemal & I. Gaskell, eds. *Performance and Authenticity in the Arts.* Cambridge: Cambridge University Press, pp. 254–71.

Schaffer, K. & Smith, S. (2004) *Human Rights and Narrated Lives: The Ethics of Recognition.* London: Palgrave Macmillan.

Schechner, R. (2002) My Art in Life: Interviewing Spalding Gray. *The Drama Review,* 46, 154–74.

Schneemann, C. (1979) *More than Meat Joy*. New York, NY: New Paltz, Documentext.

Schneider, R. (1997) *The Explicit Body in Performance*. London: Routledge.

Schor, M. (1997) Backlash and Appropriation. In N. Broude & M. D. Garrard, eds. *The Power of Feminist Art: The American Movement of the 1970s, History and Impact*. New York, NY: Harry N. Abrams, pp. 248–63.

Schumacher, C., ed. (1998) *Staging the Holocaust: The Shoah in Drama and Performance*. Cambridge: Cambridge University Press.

Scott, J. W. (1992) Experience. In J. Butler & J. W. Scott, eds. *Feminists Theorize the Political*. London: Routledge, pp. 22–40.

Sedgwick, E. K. (1993) *Tendencies*. Durham, NC: Duke University Press.

Segal, L. (1979) A Local Experience. In S. Rowbotham, L. Segal & H. Wainwright, eds. *Beyond the Fragments: Feminism and the Making of Socialism*. London: Merlin Press, pp. 157–209.

Shank, T. (1979) Mitchell's Death: Linda Montano's Autobiographical Performance. *The Drama Review*, 23 (1), 43–8.

Shank, T. (1982) *American Alternative Theater*. New York, NY: Grove Press.

Shattuc, J. (1997) *The Talking Cure: TV Talk Shows and Women*. London: Routledge.

Shewey, D. (2000) Town in a Mirror: *The Laramie Project* Revisits an American Tragedy. *American Theatre*, May/June, 14–18 and 67–9.

Shields, R. (1994) Fancy Footwork: Walter Benjamin's Notes on *Flânerie*. In K. Tester, ed., *The Flâneur*. London: Routledge, pp. 61–80.

Silk, G. (1998) All by Myself: Piero Manzoni's Autobiographical Use of His Body, Its Parts, and Its Products. In G. T. Couser & J. Fichtelberg, eds. *True Relations: Essays on Autobiography and the Postmodern*. Connecticut: Hofsta University, Greenwood Press, pp. 137–58.

Sinfield, A. (1999) *Out on Stage: Lesbian and Gay Theatre in the Twentieth Century*. New Haven, CT: Yale University Press.

Smith, A. D. (1994) *Twilight Los Angeles, 1992*. New York, NY: Anchor Books, Doubleday.

Smith, A. D. (1996) *Twilight Los Angeles*. Berkeley.

Smith, P. (2004a) *The Crab Walks*. Coryton Cove.

Smith, P. (2004b) *Crab Walks: Six Simple to Use Mythogeographical Maps between Dawlish Warren and Paignton*.

Smith, S. (1991) The Autobiographical Manifesto: Identities, Temporalities, Politics. In S. Neuman, ed., *Autobiography and Questions of Gender*. London: Frank Cass & Co, pp. 186–212.

Smith, S. & Watson, J., eds. (1992) *De/Colonizing the Subject: The Politics of Gender in Women's Autobiography*. Minneapolis, MN: University of Minnesota Press.

Smith, S. (1993) *Subjectivity, Identity and the Body: Women's Autobiographical Practices in the Twentieth Century*. Bloomington, IN: Indiana University Press.

Smith, S. (1998) Autobiographical Manifestos. In S. Smith & J. Watson, eds. *Women, Autobiography, Theory: A Reader*. Madison, WI: University of Wisconsin Press, pp. 433–40. Originally published in Smith, S. (1993b) *Subjectivity, Identity and the Body*. Bloomington, IN: Indiana University Press.

Smith, S. & Watson, J., eds. (1998) *Women, Autobiography, Theory: A Reader*. Madison, WI: University of Wisconsin Press.

Smith, S. (1999) Construing Truth in Lying Mouths: Truthtelling in Women's Autobiography. In M. W. Brownley & A. B. Kimmich, eds. *Women and Autobiography*. Washington, DC: Scholarly Resources, pp. 33–52.

Smith, S. & Watson, J. (2001) *Reading Autobiography: A Guide for Interpreting Life Narratives*. Minneapolis, MN: University of Minnesota Press.

Smith, S. & Watson, J., eds. (2002) *Interfaces: Women/Autobiography/Image/ Performance*. Ann Arbor, MI: University of Michigan Press.

Soans, R. (2005) *Talking to Terrorists*. London: Oberon Books Limited.

Sofaer, J. (1997) *A Biography by Margaret Turner*. London: Outsmart.

Sofaer, J. & Sofaer Derevenski, J. (2002) Disinter/est: Digging Up Our Childhood. *Performance Research*, 7 (1), 45–56.

Solnit, R. (2000) *Wanderlust: A History of Walking*. New York, NY: Viking.

Solnit, R. (2006) *A Field Guide to Getting Lost*. Edinburgh: Canongate Books.

Solomon, A. (2001) Irony and Deeper Significance: Where Are the Plays? *Theater*, 31 (3), 2–11.

Sprinkle, A. (1995) *Post Porn Modernist*. Glasgow.

Sprinkle, A. (2002) *Herstory of Porn: Reel to Real*. Glasgow.

Sprinkle, A. (2005) *Post Porn Love*. Glasgow.

Spry, T. (2003) Illustrated Woman: Autoperformance in 'Skins: A Daughter's (Re)construction of Cancer' and 'Tattoo Stories: A Postscript to 'Skins'. In L. C. Miller, J. Taylor & M. H. Carver, eds. *Voices Made Flesh: Performing Women's Autobiography*. Madison, WI: University of Wisconsin Press, pp. 167–91.

Stanley, J. P. & Wolfe, S. J., eds. (1980) *The Coming Out Stories*. Watertown, MA: Persephone Press.

Stanley, L. (1992) *The Auto/Biographical I: The Theory and Practice of Feminist Auto/Biography*. Manchester: Manchester University Press.

Stanton, D., ed. (1984) *The Female Autograph*. New York, NY: New York Literary Forum.

Steinwand, J. (1997) The Future of Nostalgia in Friedrich Schlegel's Gender Theory: Casting German Aesthetics Beyond Ancient Greece and Modern Europe. In J. Pickering & S. Kehde, eds. *Narratives of Nostalgia, Gender and Nationalism*. London: Macmillan, pp. 9–29.

Stevenson, S. L. (2004) *Well* Review. *Theatre Journal*, 56 (4), 672–4.

Stewart, P. J. & Strathern, A., eds. (2003) *Landscape, Memory and History: Anthropological Perspectives*. London: Pluto Press.

Svich, C. (2003) Moises Kaufman: 'Reconstructing History Through Theatre' – An Interview. *Contemporary Theatre Review*, 13 (3), 67–72.

Tester, K., ed. (1994) *The Flâneur*. London: Routledge.

Theatre Omnibus (2006) *The Laramie Project*. Edinburgh.

Third Angel (2000) Class of '76. In A. Heathfield, ed., *Small Acts: Performance, the Millennium and the Marking of Time*. London: Black Dog Publishing, pp. 45–51.

Third Angel (2003) *Class of '76*. Exeter.

Thompson, D. (1996) Blackface, Rape, and Beyond: Rehearsing Interracial Dialogue in *Sally's Rape*. *Theatre Journal*, 48, 123–39.

Thompson, J. (2005) *Digging Up Stories: Applied Theatre, Performance and War*. Manchester: Manchester University Press.

Tigner, A. L. (2002) The Laramie Project: Western Pastoral. *Modern Drama*, 45 (1), 138–56.

Trezise, S. (2000) *The West Country as a Literary Invention: Putting Fiction in Place*. Exeter: Exeter University Press.

Troyano, A. (2000) *I, Carmelita Tropicana: Performing between Cultures*. Boston, MA: Beacon Press.

Tuan, Y.-F. (1974) Space and Place: A Humanistic Perspective. *Progress in Geography*, 6, 211–52.

Tuan, Y.-F. (1977) *Space and Place: The Perspective of Experience*. Minneapolis, MN: University of Minnesota Press.

Tuan, Y.-F. (2004) Sense of Place: Its Relationship to Self and Time. In T. Mels, ed., *Reanimating Places: A Geography of Rhythms*. England: Ashgate Publishing, pp. 45–55.

Tushingham, D., ed. (1994) *LIVE 1: Food for the Soul*. London: Methuen Drama.

Uyehara, D. (2003) *Maps of City & Body*. New York, NY: Kaya Press.

Valentine, G. (1996) (Re)Negotiating the 'Heterosexual Street': Lesbian Productions of Space. In N. Duncan, ed., *BodySpace*. London: Routledge, pp. 146–55.

Van Alphen, E. (1999) Symptoms of Discursivity: Experience, Memory and Trauma. In M. Ball, J. Crewe & L. Spitzer, eds. *Acts of Memory: Cultural Recall in the Present*. London: Dartmouth College, pp. 24–38.

Wachtel, E. (1993) Spalding Gray: Interview. *Writers & Company*. Toronto: Knopf Canada, pp. 33–48.

Walker, J. (2003) The Traumatic Paradox: Autobiographical Documentary and the Psychology of Memory. In K. Hodgkin & S. Radstone, eds. *Contested Pasts: The Politics of Memory*. London: Routledge, pp. 104–19.

Walker, M. (1998) *Moral Understandings: A Feminist Study in Ethics*. London: Routledge.

Warner, M. (1998) Bobby Baker: The Rebel at the Heart of the Joker. In N. Childs & J. Walwin, eds. *A Split Second of Paradise: New Performance & Live Art*. London: Rivers Oram Press and Artsadmin, pp. 68–87.

Weiss, P. (1971) The Material and the Models: Notes Towards a Definition of Documentary Theatre. *Theatre Quarterly*, 1 (1), 41–3. Originally delivered as a paper in 1968.

Wheeler, W. (1994) Nostalgia Isn't Nasty: The Postmodernising of Parliamentary Democracy. In M. Perryman, ed., *Altered States: Postmodernism, Politics, Culture*. London: Lawrence and Wishard, pp. 94–109.

Whelehan, I. (1995) *Modern Feminist Thought: From the Second Wave to 'Post-feminism'*. Edinburgh: Edinburgh University Press.

Whyte, R. (1993) Robbie McCauley: Speaking History Other-Wise. In L. Hart & P. Phelan, eds. *Acting Out: Feminist Performances*. Ann Arbor, MI: University of Michigan Press, pp. 277–93.

Wilding, F. (1994) The Feminist Art Programs at Fresno and CalArts, 1970–75. In N. Broude & M. D. Garrard, eds. *The Power of Feminist Art: The American Movement of the 1970s, History and Impact*. New York, NY: Harry N. Abrams, pp. 32–47.

Wiley, C. (1998) Teatro Chicano and the Seduction of Nostalgia. *MELUS*, 23 (1), 99–115.

Wilkie, F. (2002) Mapping the Terrain: A Survey of Site-Specific Performance in Britain. *New Theatre Quarterly*, 70, 140–60.

Williams, D. (1998) Frontwords. *Performance Research: On Place*, 3 (2), v–viii.

Wilson, E., Fay, J., Green, T. & Nunnery, L. (2006) *Unprotected*. London: Josef Weinberger.

Wilson, N. (2001) Interview with the author. London.

Wilson, R. A., ed. (1997) *Human Rights, Culture & Context: Anthropological Perspectives*. London: Pluto Press.

Winter, J. (2001) The Memory Boom in Contemporary Historical Studies. *Raritan*, 21 (1), 52–66.

Winterson, J. (1985) *Oranges Are Not the Only Fruit*. London: Pandora Press.

Withers, J. (1997) Feminist Performance Art: Performing, Discovering, Transforming Ourselves. In N. Broude & M. D Garrard, eds. *The Power of Feminist Art: The American Movement of the 1970s, History and Impact*. New York, NY: Harry N. Abrams, pp. 158–73.

Wolff, J. (1994) The Artist and the *Flâneur*: Rodin, Rilke and Gwen John in Paris. In K. Tester, ed., *The Flâneur*. London: Routledge, pp. 111–37.

Wolverton, T. (2002) *Insurgent Muse: Life and Art at the Woman's Building*. San Francisco, CA: City Lights Books.

Woodstock, L. (2001) Hide and Seek: The Paradox of Documenting a Suicide. *Text and Performance Quarterly*, 21 (4), 247–60.

Young, H. (2003) Touching History: Suzan-Lori Parks, Robbie McCauley and the Black Body. *Text and Performance Quarterly*, 23 (2), 134–53.

Young, J. (1994) *The Texture of Memory: Holocaust Memorials and Meaning*. Massachusetts: Yale University Press.

Zagreda, E. (2004) *Corn Bread and Feta Cheese: Growing Up Fat and Albanian.* New York City.

Zimmerman, B. (1985) The Politics of Transliteration: Lesbian Personal Narratives. In E. B. Freedman, B. C. Gap, S. L. Johnson & K. M. Weston, eds. *The Lesbian Issue – Essays from Signs.* Chicago, IL: University of Chicago Press, pp. 251–70.

Index